The Delights of Good
Italian Cooking

Appetisers, Sauces for Meat and Pasta Dishes, Baked and Stuffed Pasta, Soups, Meat and Game, Fish and Shellfish, Omelettes, Salads and Vegetable Dishes, Desserts and Confectionery, as well as a rich selection of quickly-prepared, care-free, appetising One-Plate Meals

280 TRIED AND TESTED RECIPES,
WITH ILLUSTRATIONS AND ANNOTATIONS,
NUMEROUS VARIATIONS AND SERVING SUGGESTIONS

EDITED BY PAOLO PIAZZESI

BONECHI

THE PHOTOGRAPHS *complementing this book were taken expressly by Dario Grimoldi at the restaurant "Mario" in Fiesole (Florence). Marco Scheggi and Maura Borracelli collaborated with the cooking and display of the dishes. The other illustrations, including those of Italian landscapes and monuments, derive from the publisher's archives.*

ALL THE RECIPES *have been tried out by Marco Scheggi and Maura Borracelli. Among them are a few of their own creation or development (M. Scheggi: pp. 24 (at the top), 51, 77, 119; M. Borracelli: pp. 29, 41, 42 (at the top), 76 (at the bottom), 89, 162 (at the top) and 190 (at the top).*

Editorial origination by Casa Editrice Bonechi
Design and production by Paolo Piazzesi
Photographs by Dario Grimoldi
Translated by Stephanie Johnson

E-mail:bonechi@bonechi.it
Internet:www.bonechi.it - www.edit.it

Printed in Italy by Centro Stampa Editoriale Bonechi

ISBN 978-88-476-2111-4

A 10 9 8 7 6 5 4 3 2 1

Preface

AS WELL AS SATISFYING YOUR URGE TO TRY *your hand in the kitchen, this book aims to collect together, for your appreciation, the best of Italian cooking as it has traditionally been passed down to us, with a breath of innovation. The intention is to highlight the inexhaustible reserve of gastronomic know-how, creative resourcefulness, culinary rigour and elegance - even in aesthetic terms - intrinsic in this cuisine, making it accessible for all. Cookery which is rich but practicable, varied but simple, age-old but in step with the times and which can count on dishes capable of brilliantly satisfying both the needs of the family board and the demands posed by a special occasion, without undue anguish.*

Consequently, we have here something more than just a selection of recipes. We have a rich and colourful illustrated atlas which will stimulate good taste through the images contained, while promptly guiding you. It is an efficacious, reliable handbook to enable you to get by among pots and pans in style. But it is also the map of a wonderful journey through Italy and her treasures, amongst which her food is certainly not the most negligible, along with the ingredients which go into it (which can, thank goodness, easily be found everywhere today from olive oil to basil, from tagliatelle *to* prosciutto*, from Parmesan to mozzarella cheeses). It is not by chance that our inimitable cuisine has asserted itself in restaurants the world over as an international school of reference, taking its place (long overdue) besides other culinary traditions, slaves to their inborn artificiality, often out of all proportion to the quite banal, outmoded results. Italian cookery manages to harmoniously combine the opposing, distant of cultures butter and oil into a superior alimentary civilisation, drawing the best from both and exalting their partnership. This comes about chiefly because the fundamental principle of our cookery is to* make the most of what we have, *i.e. the ingredients themselves, combined with imagination and flair, with the aid of but a few condiments and cooking periods which are, for the most part, brief. If our recipes have nothing artificial about their goodness and appeal (not even as regards their elegance), it is because they are not borne out of the desire of cooks in stately homes to stupefy, but from the appetite and imagination of peasants, shepherds and fishermen. This standard of substantial simplicity is not even shattered by great dishes which come to us directly from sumptuous Renaissance banquets or from rich, aristocratic dining tables. From a dietary point of view, the benefit is evident. But what a boon it for the palate, freed from turbid, pretentious sauces, and for the eye, too (which, especially in Italy, claims its share), gratified by the true, vivid colours of the dishes, unobscured by dripping fat. Our dishes are prepared in a wink (almost all of them), are digested without any problems and can be tasted on the palate... but also through the heart. Because our cuisine - and this is ineluctable everywhere - is, above all, cheer: enormous, irresistible, contagious cheer.*

The genuineness of Italian food is the guarantee of its vitality. For this reason, it is very up-to-date and so it will remain in respect of the fluctuations in taste and change in alimentary demand.

It is for this reason that you will not only find dishes of ancient national or regional tradition in orthodox versions, but a faithful portrait of Italian cookery as it is today, following the introduction of new ingredients and new methods of preparation. Beside classical recipes, there are new ones, up-dated ones and variations, all indications of eternal youth. This aspect makes our book (conceived along these lines) all the more widely enjoyable. Whether you wish to compose a classical traditional menu from start to finish, consisting of various dishes, suitable for a wintry Sunday willingly passed at home, indulging in the pleasures of good food; or whether you are studying the formula for a refined buffet meal, perhaps under the light of the moon; or even whether you are searching for the intelligent recipe which, on its own, or with a few simple complements, resolves your problem of devotedly putting meals together for family and friends without slaving away for hours in the kitchen. We must not forget that, under a spring sun, our cuisine does indeed offer many solutions, alternatives and possibilities - just think of the incredible array of fresh or dried pasta, stuffed or baked. Even during the week, at one time, a normal family lunch used to consist of at least three courses (Mother was, of course, around at home); the first course, a main and side dish, finishing up with fruit. That used to be the custom, now more and more infrequent even on feast days, or when guests pop in, on more or less official occasions. Cooking is no longer a necessity (I am talking about serious cooking, not heating up frozen foods in the microwave) because - fortunately - the conservation industry and food distribution patterns allow us, without great effort, to resolve the problem of how to keep body and soul together just the same. It occurs ever more frequently that good, simple, tasty, pleasant food is prepared

principally for the inestimable pleasure of doing so, without the frills, but presented with flair. As well as to Chiara and Vieri, this book is dedicated to those who like to cook for themselves, for their dear ones and for their friends, to those who consider it nice and civil to gather around a dinner table where home-made foods of quality are served personally and where they can enjoy the company as well as the food.

A few suggestions to round off. The appetiser, customary in any dinner which respects itself, should be followed, in true Italian tradition, by a generous pasta dish or soup, an abundant meat or fish course with relative side plate, then cheese, sweet, fruit, coffee and liqueur. But, as we have just said, the tendency today is to eat less, preferring quality to quantity. In deference to habit, the portions of ingredients in the recipes in the relative sections are calculated as if for the classical antipasto. *But, seeing as they are light, tasteful dishes, if anyone should decide to bolster them up somewhat and eliminate the first course, all that has to be done is to proportionately increase the amounts (according to common sense).*

Furthermore, an entire chapter has been dedicated to those who, rather than a dinner made up of the usual succession of courses, prefer a more or less substantial, often original and always tantalising one-plate meal, backed up by a fresh salad and crowned with a generous dessert. Our portions are calculated for serving as one-course meals. If they are reduced proportionately, the respective recipes can readily be inserted into a traditionally-structured menu (after all, these derive from traditional dishes, though touched up under the light of contemporary habits).

Notes and Suggestions to Reader

- Metric measurements are given first, followed by imperial and finally those for American readers. I strongly recommend sticking to the same group of measurements throughout the recipe.
- Salt and pepper are not mentioned in the list of ingredients, as their use goes without saying. The correct moment for seasoning the particular dish is given, with the dosage indicated in a deliberately generical way.
- For the sake of brevity, sometimes the expressions "very hot", "hot" "medium" and "slow" are used to indicate the temperature of the oven, according to the following table:
  - **Very hot oven = 200°C/400°F/Gas Mark 6**
  - **Hot oven = 180°C / 350°F / Gas Mark 4**
  - **Medium oven = 170°C/325°F/Gas Mark 3**
  - **Slow oven = 160°C / 300°F / Gas Mark 2**
- Mention is made of various Italian cheeses. If you cannot find the "genuine article", here is a basic description to help you decide on worthy substitutes: *Parmesan cheese* is the hard, dry cheese known world-wide as a complement to many dishes and needing no introduction here; *Pecorino* is a hard or semi-hard sheep's milk cheese and is available at varying stages of ripening; Made from ewe's milk, *Ricotta* is soft and fresh, looking rather like cottage cheese; *Provolone* is a mild or sharp hard cheese which is usually smoked. The herb oregano is frequently used in Mediterranean cooking. It may be substituted with less pungent marjoram. Wild fennel may be replaced by the leafy tops of bulb fennel or else use sweet cicely. Where mention is made of oil, whether in cooking or for dressing, *extra vergine* olive oil is referred to. Other vegetable and seed oils (provided they are of good quality) may be used for frying alone. When butter is cited, the unsalted variety is always intended. 30g (1oz) of fresh brewer's yeast can be substituted with half a packet of active dried yeast.
- Quantities in the recipes are usually calculated for four servings (unless otherwise specified at the head of the list of ingredients).

Pisa

Rome

Sicily

Pompei

Venice

Assisi

Starters

Sauces

Pasta, Soup and Rice Dishes

Meat and Game

Special Dishes

Fish and Shellfish

Omelettes

Salads and Vegetable Dishes

Desserts, Cakes and Pastries

Sorrento

The Amalfi coast

Spello

Florence

Starters and Sauces

Acciughe al limone

ANCHOVIES WITH LEMON

- 400G / 14OZ ANCHOVIES
- JUICE OF 2 LEMONS
- 1 HOT RED PEPPER
- PEPPERCORNS
- PARSLEY (OPTIONAL)
- OLIVE OIL

PREPARATION TIME: 1/4 HOUR, PLUS MACERATION IN LEMON JUICE

SQUEEZE THE LEMONS to extract the juice. Wash the anchovies under running water, then bone and dry the fillets. Lay them without overlapping on a serving dish. Sprinkle over lots of lemon juice and olive oil. Add the pepper, the hot red pepper in pieces and the chopped parsley, if liked. Leave to macerate, preferably in the refrigerator, for about an hour or, better still, two hours before serving. In any case, the anchovies will not be ready until they have become an even pinkish-white colour.

Anguilla marinata

MARINATED EELS

- 1KG / 2 1/4LB EELS (PREFERABLY SMALL ONES)
- 250ML / 8 FL OZ / 1 CUP RED WINE VINEGAR
- 3 CLOVES OF GARLIC
- 1 WHITE-SKINNED ONION
- 1 SMALL COFFEE CUP OF FLOUR
- BAY LEAVES
- PEPPERCORNS
- OLIVE OIL

PREPARATION TIME: 40 MINUTES

BUY THE EELS ALREADY GUTTED and skinned (except if they are small ones, then leave them with their skins on). Cut the fish into chunks, coat with flour and fry in 4 tablespoons of oil, allowing them to turn nicely golden. Drain the eels and turn into a bowl. Cover with small pieces of garlic and onion rings, some bay leaves and peppercorns and drown the whole lot in red wine vinegar. The longer it is all left to marinate, the better it will be. So it is a good idea to get the dish ready at least a day before announcing its eminent arrival to your eager table mates.

Aspic di crostacei

SHRIMPS IN ASPIC

- 1L / 2PT / 4 CUPS ASPIC JELLY (PREFERABLY MADE WITH FISH STOCK)
- 1 EGG
- 400G / 14OZ SHRIMP TAILS
- 150G / 5OZ STUFFED OLIVES
- 400G / 14OZ RUSSIAN SALAD (SEE BELOW)

PREPARATION TIME: FROM 4 TO 5 HOURS, INCLUDING TIME FOR THE FINAL SETTING

MAKE UP THE ASPIC JELLY and keep it warm in a water bath. Boil the shrimps for ten minutes and shell them. Hard boil the egg and slice it. Pour a little of the aspic into a mould and allow to set in the refrigerator. Lay some egg slices on top and cover with a layer of Russian salad. Arrange the shrimps all around to form a crown. Pour some more aspic into the mould and allow to set in the refrigerator. Spoon over another layer of Russian salad down the centre and arrange the olives along the sides. Cover with still more aspic and allow to set. Stand some shrimps upright around the mould to form a border, fill the centre with the remaining Russian salad, cover with the aspic left and return to the refrigerator for a few hours. Turn out onto a serving dish after holding the mould briefly under hot water. Garnish as you please.

RUSSIAN SALAD to serve four: a quarter of a cauliflower, 150g (5oz) green beans, 3 small carrots, 2 potatoes, 150g (5oz) shelled garden peas and a courgette (zucchini). Beetroot is not an indispensable ingredient. Wash the vegetables and steam them until they are cooked but still crisp (times vary according to each vegetable). Peel the potatoes, dice all the vegetables and mix them together in a bowl. Season with salt, pepper and a little oil emulsified with a drop of vinegar and a pinch of mustard. You may finish off with a few drained capers, a filleted anchovy, sliced gherkins, little mushrooms in oil and a hint of tarragon. Finally, cover the whole lot with the requisite mayonnaise (see page 145). But not with the above recipe.

Avocado in bella vista

AVOCADO PEAR SALAD

- 8 BUNCHES OF TENDER, MIXED SALAD LEAVES (FRESH MIXED CHICORY AND LAMB'S LETTUCE)
- 2 FRESH AVOCADO PEARS
- 150G / 5OZ PALM HEARTS
- 1 LEMON
- BALSAMIC VINEGAR
- OLIVE OIL

PREPARATION TIME: 1/4 HOUR

WASH THE MIXED SALAD leaves with great care, shake them dry and arrange bunches of them in the centre of a serving dish.

Halve the avocado pears and remove the stone. Slice the flesh and sprinkle with lemon juice to prevent it from blackening.

Starting in the centre, arrange the avocado slices around the salad leaves like the spokes in a wheel. Make a border of slices of avocado pear alternated with slices of palm heart.

Finish up by putting a palm heart to crown the salad leaves in the centre of the plate. Dress sparingly with a vinaigrette sauce made from olive oil, salt and drops of *aceto balsamico*, the pure, narurally sweet vinegar from the North of Italy.

Carciofini sott'olio

ARTICHOKES PRESERVED IN OIL

- 12 GLOBE ARTICHOKES (20 IF THEY ARE VERY SMALL)
- 1/2 L / 1PT / 2 CUPS WHITE WINE
- 60ML / 2 FL OZ / 1/4 CUP WINE VINEGAR
- 2 LEMONS
- 12 BAY LEAVES
- 2-3 CLOVES
- A PINCH OF OREGANO
- A SPRIG OF PARSLEY
- PEPPERCORNS
- OLIVE OIL

PREPARATION TIME: 1 HOUR, PLUS TIME FOR DRAINING AND MARINATING THE ARTICHOKES

THIS APPETISER is not made for instant use, but should be prepared at least a week before actually needed.

Trim the artichokes, remove all their stalks and cut them into wedges if they are rather large. Place in a saucepan and pour in enough water to cover, acidulated with lemon juice to prevent them from blackening. Now add the wine, vinegar, peppercorns and cloves and cook for twenty minutes.

Remove from the pan and place them upside-down on a tea cloth to dry. The longer they are left to drain the better, even if it takes a whole day - if moisture is trapped between the leaves, the flavours in the oil will not be able to penetrate the artichokes. Put them in one or more glass jars with tightly-fitting caps and cover with oil, distributing bay leaves, oregano and chopped parsley equally among them. Store, well-closed, in a dark place and wait expectantly....

Cecìna

CHICKPEA LOAF

- 400G / 14OZ CHICKPEA (GARBANZO) FLOUR
- OLIVE OIL

PREPARATION TIME: 3/4 HOUR

THIS RECIPE is called *Panissa* or porridge in Liguria, in Livorno it is just *Torta* (or cake), whilst the name of Cecìna (with the accent on the "i") is used in Versilia.

It does not belong to the bread group of *focaccias* and *schiacciatas* because, customarily, it used to be eaten as a sandwich filling (humble it may be, but it is delicious, thanks to the intense flavour of the chickpeas enhanced with oil - just try it!).

The age-old *cecìna*, if cut into wedges and laid out on a nice tray, today rises to the occasion and becomes an original, succulent antipasto.

Serve with an anchovy spread or with a bowl of high-quality olive oil in which sage, rosemary and bay leaves have been heated with a finely-chopped clove of garlic. How about teaming it up with little dried mushrooms, first soaked and then sautéed in butter! Indeed, why not make all three sauces to serve in separate bowls?

POUR ABOUT TWO LITRES (4 pints or 8 cups) of luke-warm water into a bowl and gradually sprinkle in the chickpea (garbanzo) flour, continuously stirring so that no lumps form. Add barely a tumbler of oil and 2 or 3 pinches of salt.

Leave the porridge (which must be quite runny) to one side for half-an-hour. Then pour the mixture into a wide, shallow, oiled oven dish and bake in a hot, or rather, very hot oven. When the crust is nice and golden, the *cecìna* is ready.

Crocchette

CROQUETTES

FOR THE BÉCHAMEL:
- 80G / 3OZ / 6 TBSP BUTTER
- 100G / 1/4LB / 2/3 CUP WHITE FLOUR
- 125ML / 4 FL OZ / 1/2 CUP MILK
- GRATED NUTMEG

- 1 CHICKEN BREAST
- HALF AN ONION, HALF A CARROT AND HALF A STICK OF CELERY
- A SPRIG OF PARSLEY
- 300G / 11OZ SPINACH
- 320G / 13OZ / 2 CUPS PLUS 2 TBSP WHITE FLOUR
- GRATED PARMESAN CHEESE
- BREWER'S YEAST
- 3 EGGS (1 SEPARATED) PLUS 1 EGG YOLK
- DRY BREADCRUMBS

PREPARATION TIME: 1 1/2 HOURS, PLUS RESTING TIME

PUT THE CHICKEN BREAST to boil with the aromatic vegetables, parsley and salt. Blanch the spinach and drain. Make the béchamel sauce (see page 52). Bone the chicken breast and chop it up. Add half the béchamel, a little Parmesan, one egg yolk, salt and pepper. Mix the chopped spinach into the remaining béchamel with one egg yolk, Parmesan, salt and pepper. Dilute the brewer's yeast in warm water, knead it into 220g (1/2lb / 1 1/2 cups) white flour, with one egg white and salt. Put aside for an hour. Make little balls with the chicken mixture, coat them in flour and egg-and-crumb them. Fry them, keep them warm in the oven and season with salt. Proceed in the same way with the spinach croquettes, making them into a cylindrical shape. Then drain and season them with salt and add them to the others. Last of all, roll the dough into bread sticks and cut into short lengths; fry, drain and season with salt before placing all the croquettes on a serving dish together with lemon wedges. This is a "nibble" to serve before dinner and munch on while conversing.

Crostini ai fegatini

CHICKEN LIVERS ON TOAST

- 300G / 11OZ CHICKEN LIVERS
- 1 ONION
- 50G / 2OZ / 1/4 CUP CAPERS
- 60ML / 2 FL OZ / 4 TBSP WHITE WINE
- SLICES OF WHITE BREAD
- 2 TBSP STOCK
- OLIVE OIL

PREPARATION TIME: 3/4 HOUR

IN ORDER TO CLEAN the livers properly, you will need to remove all traces of green bile, then rinse them under running water.

Chop the onion up finely and colour gently in a pan with 2-3 tablespoons of oil. Add the livers and fry them. Season with salt and pepper, pour over the wine and allow it to evaporate. After cooking half-an-hour over medium heat, add the drained capers.

Remove from the heat, chop everything up finely and return to the pan to absorb the cooking juices. Slice some white bread, divide into halves or quarters, depending on the size of the loaf, and toast it. Moisten with just a little stock and spread some of the mixture over. These *crostini* are good whether hot or cold.

Crostini ai funghi

MUSHROOMS ON TOAST

- 300G / 11OZ FRESH *BOLETUS EDULIS* OR CULTIVATED MUSHROOMS
- 2 CLOVES OF GARLIC, PARSLEY
- 90ML / 3 FL OZ / 6 TBSP STOCK
- A SMALL LOAF OF WHITE BREAD
- OLIVE OIL

PREPARATION TIME: 20 MINUTES

MUSHROOMS are cleaned by scraping off the lumps of earth with the back of a knife and wiping off other traces of dirt with a damp cloth. Chop them up and place with the garlic and 4 tablespoons of oil in a saucepan to cook for a good quarter-hour. Season with salt and pepper and moisten with a little stock. Continue cooking until all the stock has been added and the sauce is somewhat reduced. Add the chopped parsley at the end. Spread the mixture over slices of white bread which have been fried briefly in butter.

Crostini di fagiana

HEN PHEASANT ON TOAST

- 400G / 14OZ FLESH OF A HEN PHEASANT (COMPLETE WITH THE LIVER)
- HALF AN ONION
- 50G / 2OZ CAPERS
- BAY LEAVES
- A LITTLE STOCK
- 60ML / 2 FL OZ / 4 TBSP RED WINE
- SLICES OF WHITE BREAD
- OLIVE OIL

PREPARATION TIME: 1/2 HOUR

SWEAT THE VERY FINELY-CHOPPED onion in a flameproof casserole with 4 tablespoons of oil.

Sauté the pheasant meat (the hen is much more delicate than the cock, though some people find the flavour of the latter rather more defined) together with the liver, cut up with a couple of bay leaves. Douse with the wine, allowing it to evaporate gently.

Remove the meat from the casserole and chop it up finely with the capers. Return to the pan and cook over low heat, adding 2 tablespoons of stock, salt and pepper.

When the sauce is cooked, spread it over slices of stale white bread.

Crostini di milza

SPLEEN CANAPÉS

- 300G / 11OZ CALF'S SPLEEN
- 1 ONION
- 80G / 3OZ / 6 TBSP BUTTER
- 125ML/ 4 FL OZ / 1/2 CUP RED WINE
- 2 ANCHOVY FILLETS
- TOMATO CONCENTRATE (PASTE)
- SLICES OF WHITE BREAD

PREPARATION TIME: 3/4 HOUR

SKIN THE SPLEEN by scraping the flesh off with the back of a large knife blade. Wash the anchovies, bone and fillet them.

Finely chop the onion and fry until golden in melted butter. Add the spleen, a scant tablespoon of tomato concentrate (paste) and season with salt and pepper.

Simmer gently for about half-an-hour, then add the wine and the filleted anchovies.

Reduce the mixture for a further 10 minutes, stirring carefully. Slice the bread and spread the mixture over.

Quite delicious!

Crostini di polenta

CORNMEAL SLICES

- 300G / 11OZ CHICKEN LIVERS
- 300G / 11OZ CORNMEAL
- 50G / 2OZ / 4 TBSP CAPERS
- HALF A CARROT
- HALF AN ONION
- HALF A STICK OF CELERY
- KNOB OF BUTTER
- PINCH OF PAPRIKA
- DRY WHITE (OR RED) WINE
- OLIVE OIL

PREPARATION TIME: 3/4 HOUR

SAUTÉ THE FINELY-CHOPPED aromatic vegetables in 3 tablespoons of oil. When they have coloured, add the chicken livers, the broken-up capers, the paprika, salt and pepper. Pour over the wine and allow to evaporate slowly for half-an-hour. Cut the polenta into rectangular slices and fry in olive oil or, if you prefer (the outcome is frankly even better), in lard. Remove the livers from the heat, cut them up finely and return to the pan briefly with the butter, stirring. Spread over the hot polenta.

THESE CROSTINI ARE ALSO delicious with sausages (see below), wild boar meat, hare, venison and other game. The procedure does not change, but cooking times must be adjusted. Of course, some people add a little tomato paste together with the wine.

Crostini di salsiccia

SAUSAGE CANAPÉS

- 4 FRESH SAUSAGES
- 150G / 5OZ *STRACCHINO* (WHITE, SOFT, MILD CHEESE)
- SLICES OF WHITE BREAD

PREPARATION TIME: 20 MINUTES

SKIN THE SAUSAGES and, with a fork, work them into the *stracchino* cheese (with a pinch of salt) in a bowl, until you have a very soft, smooth mixture. Spread it onto fairly thick slices of white bread or else onto fried slices of polenta corn meal. Bake in a medium oven for a quarter-hour.

Crostini agrodolci

SWEET AND SOUR CANAPÉS

- 50G / 2OZ / 4 TBSP CAPERS
- 30G / 1OZ / 3 TBSP SULTANAS (WHITE RAISINS)
- 1 TSP WHITE FLOUR
- 1 TBSP PINE-NUTS
- 50G / 2OZ / 1/4 CUP SUPERFINE GRANULATED SUGAR
- 1 THICK SLICE OF PROSCIUTTO, COMPLETE WITH ITS FAT
- SLICES FROM A SMALL LOAF OF WHITE BREAD
- A PIECE OF CANDIED CITRON
- 2 TBSP VINEGAR

PREPARATION TIME: 20 MINUTES

PUT THE FLOUR IN A SAUCEPAN OVER THE HEAT and mix in two tablespoons of superfine sugar, until it turns brown. Pour in 60ml (2 fl oz /4 tablespoons) of water together with the vinegar and bring to the boil until all lumps have been smoothed out. Meanwhile, roughly chop the capers, pine-nuts and candied citron, wash and dry the sultanas and dice the prosciutto.

Throw everything into the casserole and boil for about ten minutes. When the mixture is cooked, spread it onto slices of bread which have been toasted in the oven.

PELLEGRINO ARTUSI, Italy's most respected cookery expert, used to go mad for these original sweet-and-sour canapés. He recommended tasting the mixture while cooking because only the palate can be trusted to judge the balance between sweet and savoury. He also advised adjusting the quantities of vinegar personally "because not all qualities have the same strength".

Crostini fritti al formaggio

FRIED CHEESE SANDWICHES

- 8 SLICES EMMENTHAL, GRUYÈRE OR TILSITER CHEESE
- WHITE BREAD
- ANCHOVY PASTE
- 1 TSP CAPERS
- 1 EGG
- 8 TBSP WHITE FLOUR
- DRY BREADCRUMBS

PREPARATION TIME: 20 MINUTES

CUT THE CHEESE and slices of bread into little squares (do not make them too small, however).

Make up little sandwiches, by filling two slices of cheese with a slice of bread, a pinch of anchovy paste, a caper and a pinch of pepper.

Coat the cheese sanwiches in flour, dip into the beaten egg and then into the dry breadcrumbs.

Fry the "sandwiches" over moderate heat in oil or butter, allowing them to turn evenly golden all over.

Fette col cavolo nero

KALE WITH TOAST

- 10 LEAVES OF DARK GREEN CABBAGE OR KALE
- 4 CLOVES OF GARLIC
- UNSALTED WHITE BREAD
- OLIVE OIL

PREPARATION TIME: 1 1/4 HOURS

WASH AND TRIM THE CABBAGE or kale leaves, stripping them of the midribs, then put them in a saucepan of cold water and bring to the boil for about an hour. Turn off the heat and leave the vegetable to cool in the saucepan until luke-warm.

Drain the leaves and reserve the cooking liquor. Squeeze the water out gently and shred finely. Meanwhile, cut 4 or 5 medium-thick slices of white bread, divide them in half and toast them, then rub with the cloves of garlic and sprinkle with a scant tablespoon of the cabbage liquor. Heap the cabbage onto the toast and season with pepper and plenty of first-quality olive oil.

Fettunta

GARLIC TOAST

- SLICES OF UNSALTED WHITE BREAD
- GARLIC CLOVES
- OLIVE OIL

PREPARATION TIME: 1/4 HOUR

THE BREAD, which must be white and preferably rather stale, must be absolutely unsalted and sliced reasonably thickly. Toast on both sides over the fire or on top of the stove to colour the bread on both sides without blackening it. Rub with the garlic immediately, arrange on a plate, dress with plenty of olive oil and season with salt. Serve at once.

VARIATIONS ARE PRACTICALLY infinite, some of them obviously extravagant with aromatic flakes of truffle, some are more modest with slices of pecorino cheese and some rubbed with a very ripe cut tomato. However, if the bread is not very good and, most of all, if the oil is not pure nectar from olives at their first pressing, then it is not your scrumptious *fettunta*. To be relished with a glass of Chianti

Insalata di polpo

BOILED OCTOPUS SALAD

- 1KG / 2¼LB OCTOPUS
- 5 RIPE OR TINNED TOMATOES, CUBED (OPTIONAL)
- 100G / 4OZ / ½ CUP + 2 TBSP BLACK OLIVES
- 100G / 4OZ / ½ CUP + 2 TBSP GREEN OLIVES
- 100G / 4OZ CELERY
- 300G / 11OZ RADISHES
- JUICE OF 2 LEMONS
- A SPRIG OF PARSLEY
- 1 SWEET PEPPER
- 1 CLOVE OF GARLIC
- 4 TBSP WHITE WINE VINEGAR
- OLIVE OIL

PREPARATION TIME: 3 HOURS, INCLUDING THE MARINATION OF THE VEGETABLES AND OCTOPUS

AFTER TRIMMING AND WASHING the octopus, plunge it into a saucepan with plenty of cold, lightly-salted water. Bring to the boil, then cover the pan immediately and lower the flame, simmering gently for a good one-and-a-half hours.

When cooked, leave the octopus to cool in the liquor (otherwise it will go tough and rubbery).

Meanwhile, wash and trim the the vegetables and herb, chop it all up roughly and marinate in the olive oil, lemon juice and vinegar.

When the octopus has cooled completely, take it out of the saucepan, drain thoroughly, cut to pieces and add to the marinade. Mix well and leave to rest in the refrigerator for half-an-hour before serving on a plate garnished with slices of lemon.

Insalata di trippa

TRIPE SALAD

- 600G / $1^1/4$LB TRIPE
- 2 CELERY HEARTS
- 4 RIPE TOMATOES (OPTIONAL)
- 100G / 4OZ EMMENTHAL
- LETTUCE LEAVES
- 1 LARGE HEAD OF RED CHICORY
- 1 CUCUMBER
- 100G / 4OZ / $^1/2$ CUP + 2 TBSP BLACK AND GREEN OLIVES
- BASIL
- 2 TSP CAPERS
- OLIVE OIL

PREPARATION TIME: 45 MINUTES

CLEAN THE TRIPE thoroughly and boil for a good hour in a large saucepan filled with boiling, lightly-salted water. Drain and cool under a stream of running cold water. Dry well with a tea cloth and shred finely.

Wash, peel and trim all the vegetables, cutting them up finely. Dice the cheese, stone the olives, drain the capers and add it all to the tripe in a soup tureen.

Season with salt, white pepper and olive oil. You may also use vinegar, if you wish (but be careful not to misuse it!).

This salad is excellent consumed at once or after a lengthy spell in the refrigerator.

Nidi di patate

POTATO NESTS

- 4-5 FAIR-SIZED POTATOES
- 2 EGGS
- 50G / 2OZ / $^1/4$ CUP BUTTER
- NUTMEG (OPTIONAL)
- GRATED PARMESAN CHEESE
- 4-5 SOUP LADLES / 1-$1^1/4$ CUPS MEAT AND MUSHROOM SAUCE (SEE PAGE 35)

PREPARATION TIME: $^3/4$ HOUR

BOIL, PEEL AND MASH the potatoes. Put them in a bowl and mix in the beaten eggs, salt, pepper, 35g (1oz or $2^1/2$ tbsp) of butter and some grated Parmesan (you may also add a little grated nutmeg, if you like). Take a ball of the mixture the size of a mandarin and shape it into a nest, with a hollow in the centre. Line the nests up on a buttered baking tray and bake for a quarter-hour in a medium oven. Remove the tray, fill the nests with the sauce, dust with Parmesan and return to the oven for a few minutes.

AN EXCELLENT DISH, particularly to start a lunch on a winter's day. It could be served instead of pasta, with some of the nests filled with Bolognese meat sauce, for example, and others with a four-cheese sauce (Gorgonzola, taleggio, fontina and Gruyère) with a few cubes of bacon.

Olive e salvia fritta

FRIED OLIVES AND SAGE FRITTERS

- 20 LARGE GREEN OLIVES
- 40 LARGE, UNBLEMISHED SAGE LEAVES
- 8 ANCHOVIES
- HALF A BALL OF MOZZARELLA
- A SPRIG OF PARSLEY
- 1 EGG
- 150G / 5OZ / 1 CUP WHITE FLOUR
- OIL FOR FRYING

PREPARATION TIME: 1/2 HOUR

RINSE THE ANCHOVIES, gut them, discard the head and bones and fillet them. Stone the olives with the relevant stoner and put a piece of anchovy, a cube of mozzarella and a parsley leaf into the cavity. Wash the sage leaves and put them to dry on a tea cloth.

Make the batter by beating the eggs in a bowl, sprinkling in half of the flour and whisking it all in. Dilute with a little water if necessary.

Coat the olives in flour, dip them into the batter and fry them. Drain the oil off and keep them hot in a heated oven which has been switched off.

Enclose a piece of anchovy between two sage leaves, coat with flour and dip into the batter. Fry the tiny, oblong-shaped "sandwiches" (as illustrated in the photograph below). Drain them, add to the olives and season sparingly with salt. Serve them with an apéritif before a meal, or else as an overture to a fish lunch.

Olive nere al forno

BAKED BLACK OLIVES

- SALTED BLACK OLIVES (A LARGE HANDFUL FOR EACH SERVING)
- 60ML / 2 FL OZ / 4 TBSP WHITE WINE

PREPARATION TIME: 1/2 HOUR

PLACE THE OLIVES in a shallow oven dish and sprinkle copiously with wine (it is a Sicilian recipe, so it would be better coupled with a mellow wine from the South of Italy). Let the olives wilt gradually in a slow oven, removing them a little before they dry up completely.

This is an excellent, simple and tasty "nibble".

Ostriche a sorpresa

OYSTER SURPRISE

- 1KG / 2 1/4LB OYSTERS
- 2 LEMONS
- 1 SMALL JAR OF CAVIARE
- 4 SLICES OF SMOKED SALMON
- A SPRIG OF PARSLEY

PREPARATION TIME: 20 MINUTES

OPEN THE OYSTER shells with the relevant tool and wash them in cold salted water.

Dress them with a few drops of lemon juice and a grinding of pepper. Place a teaspoon of caviare next to the mollusc and on top strips of salmon in the shape of a diamond.

Garnish with a parsley leaf, close the shells up and arrange the oysters like the spokes of a wheel on a serving dish, spacing them out with lemon wedges.

At this point, pop the cork on a bottle of champagne, or pour a good *prosecco* into a carafe (if not better, it is, at least, no worse) and serve with a vaguely belle époque air…

A VERY DELICATE, scenographic appetiser. It may well be aphrodisiac as some would hold, but it is certainly delicious, if freshly prepared.

At one time a mortgage would have been necessary to afford this dish, but, just as with salmon and (to a lesser extent) caviare, mass distribution methods and modern farming techniques have luckily brought these delectable molluscs more within our reach.

Of course, oysters can be eaten scalded and dressed in various sauces, or breaded and fried, or even wrapped in bacon (in Great Britain, this delicate combination is poetically called Angels on Horseback).

But how good they are raw, with a little pepper and lemon….

Panzanella

BREAD AND TOMATO SALAD

- 400G / 14OZ WHITE BREAD
- 3 LARGE RIPE TOMATOES
- 3 SMALL, FRESH ONIONS
- LOTS OF FRESH BASIL
- VINEGAR
- OLIVE OIL

PREPARATION TIME: 1/2 HOUR, PLUS CHILLING TIME

SLICE THE BREAD and put to soak in cold water (enough to dampen it but not to submerge it completely) for a quarter-hour. Squeeze free of water and crumble it into a soup terrine. Add the coarsely-chopped tomatoes, the sliced onion and the basil. Season with salt and stir.

Place the bowl in the refrigerator and serve cool, not icy, finishing off with a few drops of olive oil and vinegar. Some like their *panzanella* with a finely-sliced clove of garlic.

THERE ARE MANY possible variations; all the rage is the inclusion of cucumber, but some cooks also use olives and cheese (pecorino or Greek feta); or else very tender lettuce leaves, radish roses and snow white celery hearts; otherwise you could add sliced hard-boiled egg and pieces of tuna in oil. Use unsalted, stale bread and genuine oil.

Pomodori ripieni di riso

RICE-STUFFED TOMATOES

- 4 FAIRLY RIPE TOMATOES
- 200G / 7OZ / 1 CUP PAR-BOILED RICE
- 100G / 4OZ MOZZARELLA CHEESE
- 50G / 2OZ / 1/4 CUP CAPERS
- A PINCH OF OREGANO
- A FEW BASIL LEAVES
- DRY BREADCRUMBS
- OLIVE OIL

PREPARATION TIME: 3/4 HOUR

COOK THE RICE in boiling salted water and drain when the rice grains are cooked but still firm, leaving them fairly moist. Wash the tomatoes and slice them in half horizontally, scooping out the insides and eliminating the seeds. Chop up the top half.

Dice the mozzarella into a bowl and add the rice (by now quite cold), the chopped tomato, the capers, a drop of oil, salt, pepper and origano. Mix all the ingredients thoroughly and distribute the filling among the tomato shells, piling it up into domes which you will then dust with dry breadcrumbs. Place them in a well-oiled oven dish and bake in a hot oven for about twenty minutes.

This is a summer hors d'oeuvre, so it is better eaten cold.

Salmone marinato

MARINATED SALMON

- A SLICE OF FRESH SALMON OF ABOUT 600G / 1 1/4LB
- 2 LEMONS, SQUEEZED
- 125ML/ 4 FL OZ / 1/2 CUP WHITE WINE
- 1 ORANGE, SQUEEZED
- A BUNCH OF FINES HERBES (PARSLEY, CHERVIL, CHIVES AND TARRAGON)
- 120G / 5OZ / 1/2 CUP PLUS 2 TBSP GRANULATED SUGAR
- 120G / 4OZ *GROS SEL*
- OLIVE OIL

PREPARATION TIME: 20 MINUTES, PLUS MARINATING TIME

FIRST CLEAN AND TRIM the salmon (its substitution with salmon trout is grudgingly conceded if true salmon is not available), carefully eliminating the spine.

Then mix the citrus juices with the wine, add the fines herbes, the *gros sel*, the sugar and a tablespoon of oil, liquidise and pour into an oven dish.

Arrange the salmon in the dish, cover with a tea cloth and put in the refrigerator for at least 24 hours. Then drain and place on a serving dish.

To calculate the weight of salt and sugar accurately, remember that each must be equal to 20% of the fish weight.

Scampi in coppa

GOBLET OF SCAMPI

- 600-700G / $1^1/_4$ - $1^1/_2$LB SCAMPI TAILS
- A SMALL ONION
- HALF A CARROT
- HALF A STICK OF CELERY
- A SPRIG OF PARSLEY
- PEPPERCORNS
- 8-10 FRESH LETTUCE LEAVES
- 125ML/ 4 FL OZ / $^1/_2$ CUP MAYONNAISE (SEE PAGE 145)
- JUICE OF HALF A LEMON
- TOMATO KETCHUP
- 30ML / 1 FL OZ / 2 TBSP EAU DE VIE (VODKA OR MARC)
- 4 RADISHES
- OLIVE OIL

PREPARATION TIME: $^3/_4$ HOUR, PLUS TIME FOR CHILLING

CLEAN THE VEGETABLES and parsley and cut to pieces. Boil for a quarter-hour in lightly-salted water with some peppercorns and a drop of oil. Add the scampi and boil them. Drain, shell and allow to cool. In the meantime, blend the mayonnaise (it should be frothy and with a more generous quantity of mustard than usual) in a bowl with a couple of teaspoons of ketchup, the lemon juice and the spirits. Add the scampi and mix well, then transfer to individual glass goblets (unless you have crystal ones!), artistically lined with lettuce leaves.

Place in the refrigerator until the moment of serving (a couple of hours at least), garnishing each with a nich, fresh, rosy-skinned radish, with bright green leaves....

Sformato di melanzane

AUBERGINE OR EGGPLANT PUDDING

- 4 AUBERGINES (EGGPLANTS)
- 3 EGGS
- 50G / 2OZ GRATED CACIOCAVALLO CHEESE
- BASIL AND MINT LEAVES
- 2 TOMATOES, FRESH OR TINNED
- 1 ONION
- 2 TBSP DRY BREADCRUMBS
- OLIVE OIL

PREPARATION TIME: $^3/_4$ HOUR

WASH THE AUBERGINES and grill whole for half-an-hour. Spoon all the flesh out of the skins, discarding the seeds.

In a bowl, mix the beaten eggs, the grated cheese, the chopped herbs, the tomatoes cut into pieces, the finely-chopped onion and salt.

Turn half the mixture into an oiled-and-crumbed baking dish and bake in a hot oven for barely 15 minutes.

An Italian *sformato* is like a soufflé but fewer eggs are necessary and it is as undemanding as a pudding.

Uova ripiene con crostini

STUFFED HARD-BOILED EGGS ON CANAPÉS

- 4 SLICES OF BREAD
- 5 EGGS
- A HANDFUL OF CAPERS
- 1 SOUP LADLE / 4 TBSP HOME-MADE TOMATO SAUCE (SEE PAGE 33)
- 1 TBSP ANCHOVY PASTE
- A FEW DROPS OF VINEGAR (OPTIONAL)
- 30G / 1OZ / 2 TBSP BUTTER
- A SPRIG OF PARSLEY
- MAYONNAISE (SEE PAGE 145)

PREPARATION TIME: 30 MINUTES

HARD BOIL THE EGGS, allowing ten minutes from the moment the water starts boiling. Leave to cool, and shell them. Work the anchovy paste slowly into a knob of melted butter in a small saucepan, then cool until luke warm. Remove the crust from the slices of bread and cut them in half.

Brown on both sides in the remaining butter and dry on kitchen paper, sprinkling each slice with a drop of vinegar - if you wish. Spread the bread with the prepared anchovy paste (only use two thirds, no more) and pour over the tomato sauce.

Slice a hard-boiled egg very thinly in an egg-slicer and lay one-and-a-half slices in the centre of each slice of fried bread, placing a caper in the centre. Cut the other eggs in half, scoop out the yolks, crushing them in with the rest of the anchovy paste mixture, and adding finely-chopped parsley and a little tomato sauce.

Stuff the egg halves with the mixture and garnish with a caper. Each serving should consist of two egg halves and two slices of fried bread.

Place them on individual hors d'oeuvre plates, decorating with a curl of mayonnaise and a sprig of parsley, to add some bright colour.

If the recipe is tasty with ordinary white bread, you can imagine how good it is with other types of bread, such as *focaccia* (a flat loaf made with oil), Tyrolese wholemeal bread and so on.

This *antipasto* could be complemented with the traditional slices of *salame* sausage, prosciutto, olives, pickles and vegetables preserved in oil.

Acciugata

ANCHOVY SAUCE

- 100G / 4OZ ANCHOVIES
- OLIVE OIL

PREPARATION TIME: 10 MINUTES

RINSE THE ANCHOVIES in running water. Remove the heads, placing the fillets in plenty of olive oil in a small saucepan. While they are heating up over a slow flame, crush them gently and methodically with a fork until they break up and are absorbed completely into the oil.

A LITTLE ANCHOVY SAUCE on fried escalopes and chicory (or on a slice of grilled or broiled ox heart)... and you will really appreciate the flavour. There are some who add chopped capers, garlic and parsley to this simple, age-old sauce (excellent for serving with pasta, too). This gives rise to a kind of inverted *salsa verde*, which, at certain latitudes could pass off as a rather elaborate *bagna cauda* hot dip ...

Do as you please: I, myself, prefer it without any other frills. Take note that it can be made with anchovy paste, but then it loses out on fragrance (and on its enjoyment, too; in my perverted way, I like seeing the very fine ventral bones of the anchovies glistening in the sauce...).

Pesto alla genovese

GENOESE BASIL AND GARLIC SAUCE

CHOP THE GARLIC FINELY. Rinse and dry the basil, tearing up the leaves in your fingers. Put both the ingredients in a mortar with the salt (which helps the basil to retain its bright green colour) and pound away methodically, adding the cheese a little at a time.

With the pestle, blend in a tablespoon of oil (of as good a quality as possible) to the pulp. Then take up a wooden spoon and gingerly stir in one tablespoon of oil three or four times.

Leave your *pesto* to rest some time before use. Remember that, covered in oil, it keeps perfectly for a long time in little jars with screw-top caps. In this way all its fragrance can be enjoyed even out of season.

Ideal for dressing pasta or boiled potatoes.

- AN ABUNDANT HANDFUL OF BASIL LEAVES
- 3 CLOVES OF GARLIC
- PINCH OF SALT
- 3-4 TBSP GRATED PARMESAN CHEESE
- OLIVE OIL

PREPARATION TIME: 20 MINUTES

THE BASIL SHOULD BE of the Genoese variety, small-leafed with an intense aroma. But the result is inviting even with other qualities. Indeed, I like it so much that I would accept even frozen basil without batting an eyelid. Just as with *pesto*, conserving fresh basil leaves is not complicated; just layer them in air-tight glass jars with a pinch of salt and cover them with oil. They should be hand-picked before flowering, otherwise the aroma is less pronounced. Indeed, to go by general belief, they should have no contact at all with any metal, let alone a knife blade.

So it is that *pesto* should only be pounded in a stone mortar with a wooden pestle. But, if you do not wish to spend the time and effort, by all means defy tradition and use a food processor, adding, however, only one tablespoon of oil while the herb is being ground.

The rest is added little by little in a bowl, stirring to blend with a wooden spoon. Finally, the pine-nuts, wrongly held to be canonical and indispensable.

As far as I know, they are a mere digression, and I believe an unsuitable one at that, but if they appeal to some ....

Pommarola

HOME-MADE TOMATO SAUCE

WASH AND TRIM THE TOMATOES (without skinning them). Cut to pieces and place in a saucepan with the coarsely-chopped aromatic vegetables, the parsley and the whole garlic clove. It is not necessary to add water; indeed it is counter-productive.

Begin cooking over a low flame, but make sure that it proceeds evenly over very moderate heat, skimming the surface to remove the water in excess. After a good hour, take the sauce off the heat and sieve,taking care that as much skin as possible is left behind. Return it to the saucepan and cook for about a half-hour over a very moderate flame, adding the hot red pepper, a pinch of *gros sel* and a trickle of oil.

When cooked, add the fresh basil, turn off the heat and allow the sauce to rest as long as possible.

AMONG THE MANY VARIETIES of tomato which exist, the ones traditionally held to be most suitable for a good *pommarola* are the famous (though rather exaggeratedly so) San Marzano strain (the most used by far), the "Ventura" and the "Napoli", each one smooth-skinned and pulpy. But surprising results can also be obtained from segmented varieties with less compact flesh but which are richer in juice and with a decidedly more velvety flavour. In fact, I prefer the latter to the former.

- 2KG / 4 1/2LB RIPE TOMATOES
- 2 ONIONS
- 1 CARROT
- 2 STICKS OF CELERY
- 1 CLOVE OF GARLIC
- 1 HOT RED PEPPER
- A SPRIG OF PARSLEY
- A SPRIG OF BASIL (IN SEASON)
- OLIVE OIL

PREPARATION TIME: 2 HOURS

Ragù alla bolognese

BOLOGNESE MEAT SAUCE

- 300G / 11OZ MINCED (GROUND) BEEF
- 100G / $^1/_4$LB STREAKY BACON, UNSMOKED
- 50G / 2OZ / 4 TBSP BUTTER
- 1 ONION
- 1 STICK OF CELERY
- 1 CARROT
- 2 CLOVES
- 125ML/ 4 FL OZ / $^1/_2$ CUP LEAN MEAT STOCK
- 1 TSP TOMATO CONCENTRATE (PASTE)
- BLACK PEPPERCORNS

PREPARATION TIME: 3 HOURS

PUT THE MEAT in a saucepan to sauté in the butter, together with the very finely-chopped bacon, the vegetables (also chopped) and the cloves. When the meat has turned a nice brown colour, add the stock, a little at a time and reduce over a moderate flame. Now add the tomato concentrate, salt and pepper and cover completely with water (or, if you prefer, with some very light, unsalted vegetable stock). Turn the flame down to the minimum and cook very slowly (herein lies the secret), adding more water (or stock) if called for, but without exaggerating; the ragù must be moist but not liquid. The more it cooks (without burning, naturally), the better it will be. So arm yourself with patience, and you will savour a fine plate of *tagliatelle*, generously dressed with your exquisite meat sauce...

IN BOLOGNESE CULINARY TRADITION, milk was used instead of water to mitigate the decidedly spicy flavour of this superb sauce (but it is preferable to stick to the recipe, perhaps using just one clove). If you like, half-an-hour before cooking is terminated, you may add chicken giblets or diced air-cured ham, as the great Artusi suggests. (He also suggests skimming the *ragù* of fat before adding it to the pasta.)

Sugo casalingo

Meat and Mushroom Sauce

Leave the mushrooms to steep for a half-hour. Put the chopped vegetables and herbs to sweat in a flameproof casserole with 4 tablespoons of oil. Sauté the meat. When nicely browned, douse with the wine, adding the drained, dried and finely-chopped mushrooms.

Allow to evaporate. Add the tomato, season with salt to taste and peppercorns. Bring to the boil and put on the lid, leaving to cook a couple of hours over very low heat. This flavoursome sauce is the ideal dressing for any type of pasta, whether fresh or dried, made of durum wheat or not, short (as in the photograph) or long, as well as polenta.

- 250g / 9oz minced (ground) beef
- 100g / 1/4lb / 1/2 cup tomato pulp
- 1 tbsp dried mushrooms (or fresh ones, in season)
- 1 onion
- 1 stick of celery
- 1 carrot
- A sprig of sage
- A sprig of rosemary
- 60ml / 2 fl oz / 4 tbsp red wine
- Olive oil
- Black peppercorns

Preparation time: 2 1/2 hours

A garden overlooking the sea, with pines, palms and flowers – an ideal setting to savour specialities of Italian cuisine

Pasta, Soup and Rice Dishes

Acquacotta

TOMATO AND BREAD SOUP

- 2 ONIONS
- 4 SLICES OF WHITE BREAD
- 4 EGGS
- 300G / 11OZ / 1 1/2 CUPS FRESH, RIPE OR TINNED (CANNED) TOMATOES
- BASIL
- 1/2 L / 1PT / 2 CUPS STOCK
- RIPENED PECORINO CHEESE, GRATED
- AN HEART OF CELERY
- OLIVE OIL

PREPARATION TIME: 1 1/2 HOURS

PUT THE FINELY-SLICED onions to sweat very slowly in a saucepan with 5-6 tablespoons of oil. When they are very soft, on the point of breaking up, add the roughly-chopped tomatoes and celery, basil, salt and pepper.

Cook for a good hour, every now and then adding a soup ladle (4 tablespoons) of stock. Lay a slice of toast on the bottom of each soup bowl and pour in the boiling soup.

Break an egg into the middle and leave just long enough for it to poach. Dust with plenty of very coarsely-grated pecorino cheese.

This rich peasant soup originated in the Maremma district of Tuscany

"First-rate", is all that can be said.

Agnolotti piemontesi

SPINACH-STUFFED RAVIOLI

- 400G / 14OZ FRESHLY-MADE PASTA
- 300G / 11OZ MINCED (GROUND) BEEF
- 1 ONION, 1 CLOVE OF GARLIC
- 400G / 14OZ SWISS CHARD OR SPINACH
- 1 LEAN SAUSAGE, 1 EGG
- 60ML / 2 FL OZ / 4 TBSP WHITE WINE
- 140ML / 9 TBSP / $\frac{1}{2}$ CUP + 2 TBSP VEGETABLE STOCK
- 8 TBSP GRATED PARMESAN
- 80G / 3OZ / $\frac{1}{4}$ CUP + 2 TBSP BUTTER

PREPARATION TIME: 2 HOURS, PLUS TIME FOR THE DOUGH TO REST

MAKE UP THE PASTA, following the instructions for lasagne (see page 52), and divide in half. Wash the Swiss chard (which I prefer to spinach in this case, even though the latter is more frequently used) and blanch in a little salted water. Chop up the garlic and onion and sauté in a saucepan with 30g (1oz / 2 tbsp) of melted butter. Add the minced (ground) meat and sear it. Pour the wine over and allow to evaporate, then add the stock, salt and pepper. Put the lid on and cook at length over a very low flame. After about half-an-hour, take the lid off, crumble in the skinned sausage and allow the flavours to blend for another quarter-hour, until the liquid has reduced completely. Transfer the mixture to a bowl and mix in the chopped Swiss chard, the beaten egg and 2-3 tablespoons of cheese. Allow to rest for ten minutes.

On a floured pastry board, roll out half the pasta dough and place nut-sized spoonfuls of the filling at regular intervals of $1\frac{1}{2}$ inches, then cover with the other half of the dough, pushing down well so that it sticks. With a knife or a pastry wheel, cut out $1\frac{1}{2}$ inch squares (if the stuffing has been spaced properly it will not be a difficult task), pressing down on the edges to seal them well. Cook a few at a time in plenty of salted water and remove with the aid of a slotted spoon. Dress with lots of butter (or how about some sage-flavoured butter?) and lashings of grated cheese.

Anolini in brodo

STUFFED PASTA TRIANGLES IN BROTH

- 400G / 14OZ EGG PASTA
- 300G / 11OZ BRAISED BEEF (*STRACOTTO*) WITH ITS SAUCE (SEE PAGE 131)
- 1 EGG
- GRATED PARMESAN CHEESE
- BEEF AND CHICKEN STOCK (SEE PAGE 63)

PREPARATION TIME: 1 $\frac{1}{2}$ HOURS, PLUS RESTING TIME FOR THE DOUGH

MAKE UP THE PASTA, following the instructions for lasagne (see page 52). Chop up the braised beef and heat it gently in its sauce in a small saucepan until it has all been absorbed. Mix the meat with the egg and 3-4 tablespoons of grated cheese in a bowl, binding the mixture well. Divide the stuffing into nut-sized pieces and line them up, evenly-spaced, on the rolled-out pasta sheet (each "nut" will be in the centre of a 2-inch, even-sided triangle).

Cut the pasta with a knife or pastry wheel, then close up the *anolini* by folding the edges over on themselves and pressing down with your fingers so that they remain closed. Boil them in a light broth of chicken and beef, as the housewives in Parma and Piacenza do. Serve with lashings of grated Parmesan cheese.

Bavette al granchio

Thin Noodles with Crab Meat

- 350g / $^3/_4$lb bavette (thin noodles)
- 600g / 1$^1/_4$lb crab meat
- 2 cloves of garlic
- A sprig of parsley
- 60ml / 2 fl oz / 4 tbsp white wine
- Olive oil

Preparation time: $^1/_2$ hour

If you buy rather small crabs, you can leave them whole, pincers and the lot. In this way you save yourselves the bother of cracking them and you will consequently obtain a nice decorative effect.

Sweat the garlic and parsley, all chopped up together, in a capacious frying pan with 5 tablespoons of oil. Add the crabs and moisten with the wine, allowing it to evaporate over a high flame.

Season with a pinch of salt and cook slowly for about twenty minutes.

Meanwhile, cook the *bavette* (or other ribbon pasta such as spaghetti) and drain *al dente*. Stir into the crab sauce in the frying pan. Serve with the whole crabs in full display; each diner can then decide whether to face the trouble of cracking them to extract the flesh or not. This first course is delicious, mostly due to the musky flavour of the crabs, which clearly must be very fresh.

The word "cheese" must not even be whispered.

Bavette alla rucola

NOODLES WITH ROCKET SALAD

- 400G / 14OZ EMMER BAVETTE (OR WHOLE WHEAT NOODLES)
- 4 FRESH, RIPE TOMATOES
- 2 BUNCHES ROCKET SALAD (RUCOLA - *ERUCA SATIVA*)
- OLIVE OIL

PREPARATION TIME: 20 MINUTES

BOIL THE NOODLES in plenty of salted water. Pour 6 tablespoons of olive oil into a saucepan (without putting it on the heat), together with the diced tomato, the rocket salad (washed and chopped), salt and pepper.

Drain the pasta *al dente*, toss it into the saucepan and heat it through quickly in the sauce over a fierce flame, but without letting it fry. Grated Parmesan may be handed round at the table.

Bavette fredde all'aceto

Cold Noodles in Vinegar

- 400g / 14oz emmer bavette (or whole wheat noodles)
- 100g / 4oz carrots
- 100g / 4oz celery
- 100g / 4oz courgettes (zucchini)
- 50g / 2oz red chicory
- A sprig of basil
- Cider vinegar
- Pecorino cheese
- Olive oil

Preparation time: 20 minutes

Clean and trim the vegetables, chopping them up roughly (discard the white pulp of the courgettes or zucchini) and soak in cold water. Boil the noodles in salted water. After 4 minutes, add the drained vegetables, with the exception of the chicory. After another 4 to 5 minutes, drain them *al dente*, first plunging the colander of pasta into iced water to cool it down completely. Dry the pasta and vegetables thoroughly and dress with oil and vinegar, adding the chicory, slivers of pecorino, salt and pepper. Stir and serve, garnished with basil.

Bucatini all'amatriciana

Bucatini with Tomato and Bacon Sauce

- 400g / 14oz bucatini or spaghetti
- 60g / 2oz streaky bacon or unsmoked slab bacon
- 1 small onion
- 500g / 1lb 2oz / $2^1/2$ cups ripe or tinned (canned) tomatoes
- Grated sharp Roman pecorino cheese
- Olive oil

Preparation time: 20 minutes

Clean the onion, chop it up and sauté in a saucepan with the diced bacon and 4 tablespoons of oil. As soon as it colours, add the rinsed, seeded and roughly-chopped tomatoes. Season with salt and pepper and turn up the flame for a few minutes, so that the tomatoes absorb the flavours without turning into a mush. Boil the *bucatini*, drain and dress with the sauce. Dredge with pecorino cheese.

"All'amatriciana" means that the sauce originated in Amatrice in the province of Rieti. If you like a strong touch, add a couple of cloves of garlic and some hot red pepper to the sautéed bacon and onion.

Cannelloni ripieni

STUFFED PASTA TUBES

MAKE UP SOME FRESH PASTA dough, following the instructions for lasagne on page 52, adjusting the quantities as needed. Roll it out and cut into rectangles of 3x4 inches (alternatively, use ready-cut, dried egg pasta rectangles). Wash the spinach and scald in a very little salted water.

- 500G / 1LB 2OZ EGG PASTA DOUGH
- 200G / 7OZ MINCED (GROUND) BEEF
- 400G / 14OZ FRESH SPINACH
- 1 EGG
- 50G / 2OZ / 4 TBSP BUTTER
- 140ML / 5 FL OZ / 1/2 CUP + 2 TBSP BÉCHAMEL SAUCE (SEE PAGE 52)
- 1 CLOVE OF GARLIC
- GRATED PARMESAN CHEESE
- NUTMEG
- 1 SOUP LADLE / 4 TBSP HOME-MADE TOMATO SAUCE
- OLIVE OIL

PREPARATION TIME: 1 1/4 HOURS, PLUS RESTING TIME FOR THE DOUGH

Brown the minced meat in a little olive oil, along with the garlic (later removed). In a bowl, mix the meat into the finely chopped spinach, half the warmed béchamel and the beaten egg. Also add a grating of nutmeg, the Parmesan cheese and some salt and pepper. Boil the pasta rectangles in plenty of salted water for 2 or 3 minutes.

Take them out of the water with the aid of a slotted spoon and place them on a damp tea cloth. Put a dose of the filling in the centre of each one and roll them up closely. Place in a buttered oven dish, dot with butter and cover with home-made tomato sauce. Bake in a medium oven for twenty minutes and serve them hot and golden.

A variation which is practically vegetarian: instead of the meat filling, crumble in 100g (4oz) ricotta cheese along with the spinach. Dice a ball of mozzarella and a thick slice of mortadella sausage and add to the stuffing. In this case, eliminate the Parmesan and the nutmeg.

Crema di ceci e gamberi

Cream of Chickpea (Garbanzos) and Shrimps

- 1kg / 2 1/4lb chickpeas (garbanzos)
- 2 small cod or other white fish
- 200g / 7oz shrimp tails
- A sprig of parsley
- 1 spring onion (or leek)

Preparation time: 2 1/4 hours, plus soaking time

All the fish must be scaled and gutted, with their heads, tails and fins removed. It is a very good idea to delegate this task to the fishmonger.

Boil the previously soaked chickpeas (garbanzos) for a couple of hours over low heat, together with the spring onion, the fish and a pinch of salt. A quarter-hour before turning off the heat, steam the shrimp tails for 5 minutes.

When the chickpeas are cooked, drain them and purée in a *mouli légumes*, removing the spring onion and the fish. Add enough of the cooking liquor to make a smooth cream which you will pour into the soup bowls. Shell the shrimps and arrange them on the top.

Trickle a little oil over and garnish with a leaf of fresh parsley, dusting with freshly-ground white pepper.

Crema di porri e patate

CREAM OF LEEK AND POTATO

- 500G / 1LB 2OZ POTATOES
- 2 LEEKS
- 1L / 2PT / 4 CUPS CHICKEN (OR VEGETABLE) STOCK
- 1/4L / 1/2 PT / 1 CUP BOILING MILK
- 100G / 4OZ / 1/2 CUP BUTTER
- 1/2L / 1PT / 2 CUPS SINGLE (HEAVY) CREAM
- A SPRIG OF CHERVIL
- 4 SLICES OF WHITE BREAD

PREPARATION TIME: 1/2 HOUR

PEEL THE POTATOES, cut into chunks and fry in half the butter with the finely-sliced leeks. Add the stock and cook gently for 6-7 minutes. Meanwhile, heat the milk in a small saucepan.

Crush the potatoes, sieve them and return to the stock with salt and white pepper, adding the boiling milk and then the single cream.

Heat slowly in a water bath, without it ever reaching boiling point, until the soup is smooth and of a pouring consistency.

Serve with slices of butter-fried bread and a dusting of chopped chervil (or fresh parsley, if you prefer).

You may liquidise the soup for a really smooth consistency.

Farfalle ai 4 formaggi

FARFALLE WITH A SAUCE OF FOUR CHEESES

- 350G / 3/4LB FARFALLE (BUTTERFLY SHAPED NOODLES)
- 50G / 2OZ GORGONZOLA (BLUE-VEINED, SHARP CHEESE)
- 50G / 2OZ TALEGGIO (DRY, SALTY, CURD CHEESE)
- 50G / 2OZ FONTINA
- 80G / 3OZ PARMESAN
- KNOB OF BUTTER

PREPARATION TIME: 25 MINUTES

Remove the rind from the cheeses and cut them into pieces. Put them in a frying pan with the butter and allow them to melt very slowly without allowing them to change colour or stick to the pan. Add half of the Parmesan towards the end. In the meantime, boil the pasta, drain while *al dente* and turn into an oven dish with the melted cheese. Dredge with the remaining Parmesan, a pinch of white pepper and bake in a hot oven for 7-8 minutes until an appetising crust forms on the top.

Fonduta valdostana

FONDUE FROM THE VAL D'AOSTA

CUT THE FONTINA INTO pieces and place in a heat-resistant earthenware pot. Cover with the milk and leave in a cool place (even in the refrigerator) for at least a couple of hours. If you wish to leave the cheese to macerate for longer in the milk, by all means do so, but be careful not to exaggerate. My advice is to prolong it no further than just overnight.

Drain off the milk, add the butter and some freshly-ground pepper to the pot and cook very slowly in a water bath. Be careful that the water that the pot stands in never reaches boiling point.

When the fats have melted, continue stirring slowly and constantly with a wooden spoon until the mixture is thick and creamy - about a quarter-hour.

Remove from the heat, add the egg yolks, stir and return to the water bath for a few more minutes, stirring continuously and carefully.

Pour the fondue into individual soup bowls and serve, accompanied with slices of good, fresh bread, if you like.

Another, less orthodox way of serving it (but perhaps more convivial and "civilised") consists in keeping the fondue hot in a container over a spirit stove placed in the centre of the table - just like a fondue Bourguignonne - and dipping pieces of toasted or butter-fried bread into the cheese (this is the solution in the illustration opposite).

In this circumstance, the fondue becomes a generous and delicate whole meal if backed up with a salad of boiled vegetables or a nice fresh vegetable dip, but remember to be generous with quantities.

- 500G / 1LB 2OZ FONTINA (SWEET, SEMI-SOFT CHEESE)
- 350ML / 3/4PT / 1 1/3 CUPS MILK
- 60G / 2OZ / 4 TBSP BUTTER
- 2 EGG YOLKS

PREPARATION TIME: 40 MINUTES, PLUS TIME FOR THE CHEESE TO MACERATE IN THE MILK

PERHAPS IT IS NOT A VERY ORTHODOX choice to put the *fondue valdôtaine* among first-course rice and pasta dishes…

But try starting off a luncheon by serving it smooth and candid, the surface dotted with tiny slivers of the extremely precious white truffle. Just see if anyone dares to protest!

You can follow it up with a nice steak tartar and enjoy heaven on earth.

Some supplement the fondue with plain boiled rice, but that leaves me rather indifferent. Should you prefer a more "sporting" presentation, spread it on slices of lightly toasted bread (but do not forget the Sybaritic complement of slivers of truffle).

Fusilli alla pizzaiola

FUSILLI WITH A CHEESE AND TOMATO SAUCE

- 350G / 3/4LB FUSILLI (SPIRAL-SHAPED NOODLES)
- 3-4 SOUP LADLES / 3/4-1 CUP HOME-MADE TOMATO SAUCE
- 12 BLACK OLIVES, STONED
- 2 ANCHOVIES (OPTIONAL)
- A HANDFUL OF SALTED CAPERS
- A TWIG OF OREGANO
- 1 MOZZARELLA

PREPARATION TIME: 20 MINUTES

BOIL THE *FUSILLI* until four-fifths cooked, i.e. just before the *al dente* stage, and drain. Turn into an oven dish and pour over the tomato sauce, adding the olives, the rinsed and dried capers (the salted rather than the pickled ones are better suited for this recipe), the anchovies, rinsed, filleted and cut up (if you like them), and finally the diced mozzarella.

Stir well a couple of times and bake in a hot oven for 7-8 minutes until a crust forms on the surface.

Take the dish out, dust with oregano and serve, aromatic and stringy.

Garmugia lucchese

BEEF AND SPRING VEGETABLE SOUP

- 2 SPRING ONIONS
- 2 CLOVES OF GARLIC
- 2 GLOBE ARTICHOKES
- 150G / 5OZ GREEN PEAS, SHELLED
- 100G / 4OZ FRESH BROAD BEANS
- 8 ASPARAGUS
- 150G / 5OZ RUMPSTEAK
- 1L / 2PT / 4 CUPS VEGETABLE STOCK
- 2 SLICES OF WHITE BREAD, TOASTED
- A SPRIG OF PARSLEY
- OLIVE OIL

PREPARATION TIME: 1 HOUR

SLICE THE GARLIC and onions very finely and sauté with the chopped parsley stalks in a saucepan with 5 tablespoons of oil. Over a moderate flame, brown the cubed meat. Meanwhile, wash and trim the vegetables, cutting the green asparagus tips into chunks and the artichokes into wedges. Add the vegetables to the sautéed onion, season with salt and pepper and allow the flavours to blend, then add the stock, cover with the lid and cook for about three quarters-of-an-hour. Pour the *garmugia* over crouton cubes in the soup bowls. We advise those who cannot do without cheese to use Parmesan or, better still, pecorino.

Gnocchi alla romana

SEMOLINA DUMPLINGS WITH BUTTER AND CHEESE

- 250G / 9OZ / 2 1/2 CUPS SEMOLINA
- 1L / 2PT / 4 CUPS MILK
- 2 EGGS
- 3 TBSP BUTTER
- GRATED PARMESAN
- DRY BREADCRUMBS
- NUTMEG (OPTIONAL)

PREPARATION TIME: 1 HOUR

BRING THE MILK to boil in a saucepan with half a litre (1 pint or 2 cups) of water and a pinch of salt. When the surface starts to bubble, sprinkle in the semolina, stirring continuously so that no lumps form and cook for ten minutes.

Turn off the heat and leave to cool somewhat, then add the eggs and a liberal handful of Parmesan, stirring all the time.

Turn the semolina out onto a chopping board and spread it out to a half-inch thickness with a knife blade. Use an upturned glass tumbler to cut out a few rounds.

Butter an oven dish, arrange a layer of semolina discs, dredge with grated cheese, a sprinkling of dry breadcrumbs and (if you like) a little grating of nutmeg.

Dot with butter. Continue layering the semolina discs until they have all been used up.

Bake in the oven for a good quarter-hour until there is a golden crust and then serve the *gnocchi* nice and hot (though they are also good eaten cold; indeed, some prefer them so).

Gnocchi

Potato Dumplings

- 800g / $1^3/4$lb potatoes
- 300g / 11oz / 2 cups white flour
- 150g / 5oz / $^1/2$ cup + 1 tbsp fresh cream cheese (e. g. crescenza etc.)
- 50g / 2oz / 4 tbsp butter
- 250ml / 8 fl oz / $1^1/4$ cups single (heavy) cream
- grated Parmesan

Preparation time: 1 hour

If too much flour goes into the dough, the dumplings will be hard; if you put too much potato, they will disintegrate in the saucepan. The doses in this recipe are indicative, seeing that the balance depends on the "flouriness" of the potatoes, their absorbency capacity and the quality of the flour used. Let me tempt you: drop a few slivers of black truffle into the cheese sauce while it is melting. If you decide on a more traditional dressing, there is nothing better than a tomato sauce. Fish the *gnocchi* out with a slotted spoon and turn them into a soup tureen. As each layer of dumplings is formed, mask with some sauce and some cheese. Alternatively, flavour with a *pesto* sauce and some Parmesan cheese and pop into a hot oven for a few minutes. The culinary expert, Pellegrino Artusi, advises cooking them in milk and serving them without draining and with no other condiment than a pinch of salt and some Parmesan "if you want them to be still more delicate". I wonder if the variation proposed by the distinguished doyen of Italian cuisine meets the appreciation of modern palates! Otherwise, to remain more in sympathy with the times, dress your *gnocchi* in sage-flavoured butter.

Cook the potatoes, peel and press them through a sieve while still hot (or you could use a *mouli légumes*). With your hands, mix in the flour and a pinch of salt. Continue working the dough at length and then allow it to rest a quarter-hour. Roll it into long fingers which you will then divide into cylinders about an inch long.

Dust lightly with flour and, with your thumb, press them gently, one by one, onto the back of a grater. Cook in plenty of salted boiling water. They are cooked when they float to the surface. Remove with a slotted spoon.

In the meantime, melt the cheese with the butter and cream. When the sauce has reached the desired coating consistency, heat the *gnocchi* briefly in it and serve, liberally dusted with Parmesan.

Gramigna del Creatini

Pasta with Spinach and Chickpeas (Garbanzos)

- 300g / 11oz gramigna (short, curved pasta tubes)
- 100g / 1/4lb leaf spinach
- 150g / 5oz / 3 cups boiled chick peas (garbanzos)
- 80g / 3oz salty unsmoked bacon
- 1 clove of garlic
- olive oil

Preparation time: 12 minutes, plus chickpea (garbanzo) boiling time

Wash and pick over the spinach. Cook for 5 minutes in a saucepan with a litre (2 pints or 4 cups) of boiling water, to be put aside for later.

Boil the pasta while, in a large frying pan, you sauté the shredded bacon in 2 tablespoons of oil.

After a minute, add the chickpeas (garbanzos), the drained and roughly-chopped spinach and the cooking liquor. Cook for 3 minutes over a fierce heat.

As soon as the pasta is cooked *al dente*, drain and sauté in the frying pan with the spinach, blending it all thoroughly.

Transfer to a serving dish and serve very hot, trickling over a little olive oil.

Lasagne

BAKED LASAGNE

FOR THE PASTA DOUGH:
- 400G / 14OZ / 2 2/3 CUPS WHITE FLOUR
- 4 EGGS

FOR THE BÉCHAMEL:
- 50G / 2OZ / 1/3 CUP WHITE FLOUR
- 50G / 2OZ / 4 TBSP BUTTER
- GRATED NUTMEG
- 1/2L / 1PT / 2 CUPS MILK
- 100G / 4OZ / 1/2 CUP BUTTER
- BOLOGNESE RAGÙ MEAT SAUCE (SEE PAGE 34)
- GRATED PARMESAN CHEESE

PREPARATION TIME: 1 HOUR, PLUS TIME FOR THE PASTA DOUGH TO REST

FIRST OF ALL, the pasta. Break the eggs into the hollow at the top of the flour heaped up on a board and knead the dough, shaping it into a ball which you will leave to rest under a tea cloth for an hour. Roll out the dough into a thin sheet and cut into large rectangles. For the béchamel sauce, put two saucepans on the hob: one with the milk over a high flame, the other with the butter over a low flame. When the butter has melted, add the flour a little at a time, stirring carefully so that no lumps form, but do not allow it to colour. Blend in the hot milk little by little, stirring the whole time, and add a pinch each of salt and nutmeg, allowing the sauce to thicken for another ten minutes. Cook the lasagne in boiling water - a few rectangles at a time so that they do not stick to each other - for 5-6 minutes. Fish them out with a slotted spoon and spread over a damp tea cloth without overlapping them. Butter an oven dish, cover the bottom with the ragù and the béchamel and make a layer of lasagne. Cover with ragù, béchamel and Parmesan cheese and dot with butter. Then make another layer of lasagne and continue until all the ingredients are used up, bearing in mind that the top layer must be of béchamel sauce. Bake the pie in a medium oven for about twenty minutes.

IF YOU WANT REALLY GOOD lasagne, there must be no water in the dough. If you like the green type, add a handful of cooked and puréed spinach, working the dough at lenght so that the purée combines perfectly into the pasta without any residues. Remember to flour the dough lightly just before rolling it out. Should you wish for a lighter dish, use tomato sauce instead of the meat sauce, diced mozzarella instead of the béchamel and add a basil leaf to aromatise it. Or why not try a "Mediterranean" version of this dish as made in the region of Campania, with rounds of sausage, crumbled ricotta cheese and slices of hard-boiled egg. In Liguria, on the other hand, the meat sauce is, of course, substituted with *pesto*, which, in conjunction with the béchamel, develops a soft, round flavour… not bad at all! It goes without saying that, as happens with many other traditional dishes which are rather complicated to prepare, it is rather too rich in calories. Rather than just a first course, a plate of lasagne is today considered more a substantial whole meal which can be teamed with boiled vegetables. Not to be forgotten is a cheerful young red wine.

Linguine mare e monti

LINGUINE WITH MUSHROOMS AND TUNA FISH

- 350G / 3/4LB LINGUINE (RIBBON NOODLES)
- 1 CLOVE OF GARLIC, A SPRIG OF PARSLEY, OLIVE OIL
- 35G / 1 1/2OZ DRIED MUSHROOMS
- 600G / 1 1/4LB / 3 CUPS TINNED (CANNED) OR PURÉED TOMATOES
- 150G / 5OZ TUNA FISH IN OIL

PREPARATION TIME: 1/2 HOUR, PLUS THE SOAKING TIME FOR THE MUSHROOMS

SOAK THE MUSHROOMS in cold water for half-an-hour. Sauté the garlic in a saucepan with 4 tablespoons of oil, removing it when it starts to colour.

At this point, add the drained and dried mushrooms with the tomatoes in their liquid, cover and reduce slowly for a good twenty minutes.

Now add the tuna fish, drained of its oil with the flesh broken up. Adjust for salt and simmer a few more minutes. Meanwhile, boil the pasta and drain it at the *al dente* stage. Pour over lots of sauce, dust with pepper and chopped parsley, and rush the dish to the table.

Maccheroni della Norma

MACARONI WITH AUBERGINES (EGGPLANTS) AND RICOTTA

- 400G / 14OZ MACARONI
- 400G / 14OZ / 2 CUPS RIPE OR TINNED (CANNED) TOMATOES
- 100G / 4OZ / 1/2 CUP DRIED RICOTTA CHEESE
- 2 AUBERGINES (EGGPLANTS)
- 1 CLOVE OF GARLIC, BASIL
- OLIVE OIL

PREPARATION TIME: 1/2 HOUR

WASH AND DRY the aubergines (eggplants), dice them and sauté with 6 tablespoons of oil and the garlic in a frying pan. Remove from the fire and turn into an oven dish. Put the roughly-chopped tomatoes in the frying pan and cook for ten minutes. Add to the aubergines. Boil the macaroni to the *al dente* stage, drain and toss into the oven dish. Add salt, pepper, crumbled ricotta and chopped basil. Stir and serve boiling hot.

Minestra maritata

MIXED MEAT AND VEGETABLE SOUP

FOR THE STOCK
- HALF A BOWLING FOWL
- 350-400G / 12-14OZ RUMP-STEAK
- 1 DRY SAUSAGE
- 1 RASHER OF STREAKY OR UN-SMOKED BACON, ABOUT 80G / 3OZ
- 80G / 3OZ PROSCIUTTO WITH ITS FAT
- 80G / 3OZ PORK RIND (PIGSKIN)
- 1 ONION
- 1 CARROT
- 1 STALK OF CELERY

- HALF A HEAD OF CABBAGE
- HALF A HEAD OF CHICORY
- HALF A HEAD OF ENDIVE
- 2 STALKS OF CARDOON OR BLACK SALSIFY
- 2 CLOVES OF GARLIC
- OLIVE OIL

PREPARATION TIME: 5 HOURS

THE PORK RIND must be scalded and scraped. Singe and rinse the bowling fowl. Place all the meats in plenty of cold, salted water with the onion, carrot and celery. Cover the saucepan and simmer over gentle heat for two-and-a-half hours or more. The pieces of pork must be removed some time before that, as soon as they are cooked, and kept warm. Once everything is ready, strain the stock and keep hot.

Drain, cool and mash the vegetables with a fork. Sauté them briefly in a flameproof casserole dish where you have browned the cloves of garlic in 4 tablespoons of oil, removing them once coloured.

Cube the pork meat and add to the vegetables in the casserole, together with the hot stock. Stir, put on the lid and simmer the soup for a couple of hours.

Allow to cool a little before serving.

THIS IS A VERY LONG and complex recipe, but then it is rather special. Traditionally served on Neapolitan tables at Easter, it is the epitome of a complete, succulent meal. Indeed, after consuming the delicious soup (you may add croutons of toasted bread to it, if you like), a plate of boiled meat and chicken cannot be sniffed at, especially if complemented with a nice piquant green parsley sauce.

A young red wine will round it off nicely.

Minestrone

VEGETABLE SOUP

- 200G / 7OZ FRESH WHITE BEANS (100G / 1/4LB IF DRIED)
- 2 RED-SKINNED ONIONS
- 2 CARROTS, 2 STALKS OF CEL-ERY, 2 POTATOES
- 3 COURGETTES (ZUCCHINI)
- A BUNCH OF SWISS CHARD
- 1/4 OF A SAVOY CABBAGE
- 2L / 4PT / 8 CUPS VEGETABLE STOCK
- 200G / 7OZ / 1 CUP RICE (OPTIONAL)
- OLIVE OIL

PREPARATION TIME: A COUPLE OF HOURS

CLEAN AND TRIM the vegetables, dice them (the onions, though are sliced) and sauté over medium heat in 6 tablespoons of oil in a large saucepan, stirring frequently. Cover the pan and lower the flame so that the vegetables cook in their own juice as long as possible.

When the liquor has reduced, add enough stock (or boiling water) to cover the vegetables abundantly. Season with salt and pepper and continue cooking for a good hour, keeping the lid on.

THE MINESTRONE IS READY, but if you want more than just vegetables, throw in some rice or small pasta tubes, add boiling water, put the lid on again and cook for a further 15-20 minutes. Minestrone is excellent the day after, too, perhaps served cold and dressed with a trickle of oil. In this case, however, it is best to avoid rice and the like unless you urgently need something for sticking up unauthorised posters. Of course, goes the saying "each to his own" and there are indeed infinite variations, depending on the season and your taste. There is the custom in Tuscany, for example, of flavouring the oil used for sautéing with a twig of rosemary which is removed before the vegetables are added. Among the latter are welcomed a couple of tomatoes, a bunch of endive or a nice, white leek, along with an aromatic bunch of parsley.

The Neapolitan version contemplates a mirepoix of bacon, garlic and half a carrot, as well as the onion. Double the quantities of tomato (which is added before the other vegetables) and add peas, chicory, aubergine (eggplant) and sweet peppers (towards the end, though, as they cook quickly). In fact, it is a rule of thumb that, if the variety of vegetables used is increased (and consequently the relative cooking times), then they should be added a few at a time, first the "hard" ones, such as potatoes and white beans, then the "medium" ones like courgettes (zucchini), peas, cabbage and chicory, finishing up with the "tender" ones. A few basil leaves lend a final, crowning touch.

In Rome, too, chicory (much loved here) has pride of place among the essential ingredients. Three or four ripe tomatoes are mixed into the chopped onion, lard

or bacon, garlic, celery and parsley to make a thick sauce in which to stew the roughly-chopped vegetables, subsequently adding a little warm water. The inclusion of pasta is customary. In Emilia-Romagna, the original sauté is made up of lard or ham fat, garlic and parsley, while the choice of vegetables coincides with the basic recipe, with the addition of a little tomato purée. As you can see, all tastes are catered for. Trust your nose to lead you into choosing the composition of the initial mirepoix from among seasonable fare. You will never go wrong!

Pan lavato col cavolfiore

CAULIFLOWER AND BREAD PUDDING

- 1.5KG / $3^1/4$LB CAULIFLOWER
- 400G / 14OZ STALE BREAD, SLICED
- GRATED PARMESAN
- FRESHLY-GROUND PEPPER
- OLIVE OIL

PREPARATION TIME: $^3/4$ HOUR

DISCARD THE OUTER LEAVES and the central core of the cauliflower and boil the sprigs and tenderer leaves for half-an-hour. Drain off the cooking water and keep to one side.

Toast the slices of bread, lay them in a deep dish and sprinkle over a little of the liquor. Alternate them with layers of boiled cauliflower sprigs and leaves. Each layer will be seasoned with salt, pepper, olive oil and Parmesan cheese. Whether you use vinegar or not is up to you.

Serve at once, after trickling a little high-quality olive oil over the dish.

Pansoti in salsa di noci

PANSOTI WITH WALNUT SAUCE

FOR THE PASTA:
- 400G / 14OZ / $2^2/3$ CUPS WHITE FLOUR
- 4 EGGS

THE FILLING:
- 300G / 11OZ FRESH YOUNG BORAGE LEAVES
- 300G / 11OZ SWISS CHARD
- 150G / 5OZ RICOTTA CHEESE
- 50G / 2OZ / $^1/4$ CUP PARMESAN CHEESE
- 2 EGGS

THE SAUCE:
- 500G / 1LB 2OZ WALNUTS
- HALF A CLOVE OF GARLIC
- BREADCRUMB, SOAKED IN MILK
- 60ML / 2 FL OZ / 4 TBSP OLIVE OIL

PREPARATION TIME: $^3/4$ HOUR

Break the eggs into the hollow made at the top end of the flour mounded up on a pastry board. Add a pinch of salt and knead thoroughly, sprinkling over 2 tablespoons of water, a little at a time. While the dough is resting, clean and trim the herbs, dry them and cook in a very little salted water. Drain, squeeze out the liquor and chop. Put the beaten eggs, the sieved ricotta, salt and pepper together in a bowl. Mix well and add the Parmesan. Roll out the pasta not too thickly and cut out some $2^1/2$in. squares, which you will then fold in half to form a triangle. In the middle of each, place a spoonful of stuffing and close up the *pansoti* by folding the three tips over on themselves and pressing down on the sides with your fingers. Now the sauce. Shell the walnuts, skin the kernels and chop them up. Mix into the well-squeezed breadcrumb, the garlic and a pinch of salt, adding the oil a little at a time, until you have a nice, smooth sauce of a pouring consistency. Cook the *pansoti* in plenty of boiling water, fishing them out with a slotted spoon as they float to the surface after 6-8 minutes. Turn them into a soup tureen with the sauce, stir well and serve nice and hot.

PANSOTI COME FROM THE LIGURIA region. Thanks to their herby filling (see the recipe for olive-press soup on page 85 for the properties and benefits of borage), they are excellent and very digestible.

Pappa al pomodoro

TOMATO BREAD SOUP

- 400G / 14OZ STALE, WHITE BREAD
- 3 RIPE TOMATOES
- 3/4L / $1^1/_2$PT / 3 CUPS VEGETABLE STOCK
- 4 LARGE BASIL LEAVES, PLUS A FEW SMALL ONES AS A GARNISH
- 1 CLOVE OF GARLIC
- OLIVE OIL

PREPARATION TIME: $^3/_4$ HOUR

SAUTÉ THE CRUSHED CLOVE OF GARLIC in 4 tablespoons of olive oil in a saucepan, then toss in the roughly-chopped tomatoes, allowing the flavours to blend for about ten minutes.

Add the basil and stock and finally chunks of bread (let's get this straight: not crumbs of bread, but not in too large pieces, either!).

Stir briskly, cover with the lid and cook until the quantity of liquid has halved and the bread has become mushy. Allow to rest for about ten minutes and serve in soup bowls, trickling a little olive oil into each one and garnishing with a small basil leaf.

Pappardelle sul cinghiale

Pappardelle with Wild Boar Sauce

- 400g / 14oz pappardelle (see page 52)
- Wild boar sauce (see page 97)

Preparation time: 15 minutes

When you prepare a first-rate wild boar stew, make sure that there is plenty of sauce so that you can also make a pasta dish. Sieve 2-3 soup ladles (8-12 tablespoons) of sauce, thus reducing the pieces of vegetable to a purée, and place in frying pan with a few chunks of the meat, allowing it all to blend well and reduce. Drain the *pappardelle* at the *al dente* stage, season carefully with salt and serve very hot, dusting with Parmesan cheese.

Passato di verdure

Cream of Vegetable Soup

- 3 potatoes
- Half a cauliflower
- A few celery leaves
- 2 courgettes (zucchini)
- 1 leek
- 1 onion
- 1/2l / 1pt / 2 cups vegetable stock
- 200g / 7oz pasta (rigatoni, ditali, etc.)
- Grated Parmesan cheese
- Olive oil

Preparation time: 1 1/4 hours

Clean, trim and wash the vegetables. Cut them into pieces and sweat with a pinch of salt in 3-4 tablespoons of oil in a saucepan over a slow flame. Stir three or four times, put on the lid and allow the vegetables to cook in their own juice for about 40 minutes (adding a little vegetable stock, if necessary).

Purée the vegetables in a *mouli légumes* and return to the saucepan. Dilute the soup with some more vegetable stock until the desired consistency is reached.

Bring the pan back to the boil and throw in the pasta. Cook it for ten minutes to the *al dente* stage. Turn the cream of vegetable soup into the individual soup bowls and add a drop of raw olive oil, if you like, and lashings of Parmesan cheese.

Pasta con le sarde

PASTA WITH SARDINES

- 350G / 3/4LB RIGATONI OR SEDANI (PASTA STRAWS)
- 350G / 3/4LB SARDINES
- 4 ANCHOVIES
- 1 ONION
- A HANDFUL PINE-NUTS AND ONE OF SULTANAS (WHITE RAISINS)
- A PINCH OF POWDERED SAFFRON
- 4 ANCHOVIES
- A BUNCH OF WILD FENNEL LEAVES
- 1 HOT RED PEPPER
- 1 CLOVE OF GARLIC
- DRY BREADCRUMBS
- OLIVE OIL

PREPARATION TIME: 40 MINUTES

PUT THE SULTANAS TO SOAK in water. Fillet the anchovies, discarding the heads and tails. Do the same with half of the sardines, but open out the rest without filleting them. Chop the onion and sauté in 5 tablespoons of oil, dissolving in it the anchovy and sardine fillets, cut to pieces. Add the sultanas (squeezed of the soaking water), pine-nuts, salt, a few wild fennel leaves, the saffron and hot red pepper and allow the flavours to blend, without letting the sauce get too dry. Bring some fennel leaves to boil in water with a few grains of *gros sel*. Toss in the pasta and cook to the *al dente* stage. Sauté the other sardines with 3-4 tablespoons of oil, the garlic and a little wild fennel. Colour the fish on both sides. Drain the pasta and turn into an oven dish. Pour the sauce over the whole sardines, then scatter with breadcrumbs and bake in a hot oven for 10 minutes.

WILD FENNEL, which is an essential component of this typical Sicilian recipe, can also be found in the dried form. If it should be impossible to track down, substitute it with dill (see page 176), though the outcome is not the same.

My only advice to aficionados of Italian cuisine who do not live in countries bordering on the Mediterranean is to co-opt an acquaintance, or else to pick a nice bunch of wild fennel or sweet cicely yourselves, should the occasion of a trip to Italy arise.

Pasta e fagioli

BEANS AND PASTA

- 700-800G / $1^1/_2$- $^3/_4$LB CANNELLINI BEANS (300-400G / 11-14OZ IF DRIED)
- 200G / 7OZ RIGATONI (SHORT, FLUTED NOODLES)
- 2 CLOVES OF GARLIC
- A RASHER OF UNSMOKED, FATTY BACON
- 1 SPRIG OF SAGE
- 1 SPRIG OF ROSEMARY
- 1 HOT RED PEPPER
- OLIVE OIL

PREPARATION TIME: 2 HOURS

COOK THE BEANS over gentle heat for 45 minutes or an hour at the most (an hour-and-a-half if they are dried, after soaking in water, together with the herbs and garlic, for a couple of hours). In either case, do not add salt which tends to harden the skins. Purée by putting through a vegetable mill, carefully eliminating the husks. Put the garlic, rosemary, sage and cubed bacon to sauté briefly in a saucepan with 4 tablespoons of oil. Pour on the bean purée. Season lightly with salt and the red hot pepper to taste. Stir to blend the flavours and bring slowly to the boil. Throw the pasta into the purée and cook until firm, diluting with a little of the bean cooking water, but only if necessary - the soup must be thick and rather solid. It is excellent hot, but is absolutely delicious if heated up with the addition of a drop of first-rate olive oil.

IF YOU PREFER, leave a few beans whole and add them to the saucepan with the purée. Some cooks hold that a carrot is not out of place in the mirepoix (but then cut out the bacon), or that the soup loses nothing if you add a little tomato, even tomato concentrate (paste).

Pastina in brodo

Pasta Cooked in Broth

For the broth:
- 300g / 11oz beef rump-steak
- A quarter of a boiling fowl
- Half an ox tongue
- Ox knuckle bone
- 1 onion
- 1 carrot
- 1 stick of celery
- A small bunch of parsley

- 250g / 9oz egg pasta in small shapes
- Grated Parmesan

Preparation time: 2 1/2 hours

Put the meat, together with the vegetables and a little salt, in 4 litres (8 pints) of cold water. Bring to the boil and simmer over moderate heat for a couple of hours, skimming off the scum and excess fat. Remove the of pieces meat and strain the broth through a fine-meshed strainer. Pour a quantity into a small saucepan, diluting with a little warm water should it be too thick, and bring back to the boil. Throw in the type of pasta that you prefer. Once cooked, turn into a soup tureen or individual soup bowls, serving a bowl of grated Parmesan cheese separately.

It is a known fact that, to extract all the flavour into the broth, the meat must be put into cold water which is then brought to the boil. Hot water, on the contrary, would seal in the juices. So, when we want a good plate of boiled meat, the water is heated first of all. If you like your broth less greasy, use a portion of roasting chicken instead of a boiling fowl. Should you want it to be very light, do not use the steak. The meat which has been used to make broth (skin the tongue at once, while it is hot) can be made into rissoles, breaded and fried.

Penne strascicate

PENNE SAUTÉED IN SAUCE

- 350G / 3/4LB PENNE (SHORT, PASTA TUBES)
- 2-3 SOUP LADLES / 8-12 TBSP MEAT SAUCE (SEE PAGE 34)
- GRATED PARMESAN

PREPARATION TIME: 20 MINUTES

BOIL THE PASTA to just before the *al dente* stage. Transfer to a large flameproof casserole dish with the very hot (though not boiling) sauce. Stir with a wooden spoon over fierce heat, dusting with grated Parmesan cheese. Therein lies the secret: finish cooking the pasta in the sauce (which must, of course, be delicious, otherwise…). Serve immediately.

Pennette alla corsara

PENNETTE WITH OCTOPUS SAUCE

- 350G / 3/4 LB PENNE (SHORT, PASTA TUBES)
- "POLPO IN GALERA" SAUCE (SEE RECIPE ON PAGE 165)
- PARSLEY, FINELY-CHOPPED

PREPARATION TIME: 15 MINUTES

IT IS INDISPENSABLE to have the relevant sauce already at hand in order to prepare this delicious pasta dish, and seeing as it is obtained by making up the recipe for Octopus Stewed in Tomato Sauce, it goes without saying that the pasta dish should be teamed up with that stupendous plate of seafood. Boil the *pennette* to the *al dente* stage and turn briefly but thoroughly in a large quantity of the sauce in the pan. Serve dusted with finely-chopped parsley and decorate with a few rosy tentacles for scenographic effect .

Pici all'aglione

GARLICKY PASTA

FOR THE PASTA:
- 500G / 1LB 2OZ / $3^1/3$ CUPS UNBLEACHED STRONG PLAIN FLOUR
- A PINCH OF SALT
- 125ML / 4 FL OZ / $^1/2$ CUP WATER

FOR THE SAUCE:
- 1KG / $2^1/4$LB RIPE TOMATOES OR PURÉED TOMATOES
- 1 ONION
- 1 CARROT
- 1 STICK OF CELERY
- 4-5 CLOVES OF GARLIC
- OLIVE OIL
- RIPENED PECORINO CHEESE

PREPARATION TIME: $2^1/2$ HOURS

PICI, ORIGINALLY from the district near Siena, between Montalcino, Chiusi and Monte Amiata, is also fabulous served with traditional meat sauce (of beef or lamb), with a mushroom sauce, *all'amatriciana* (with bacon and onions), or with fresh water fish such as pike.

Bear in mind that this pasta does not keep, neither can you dry it. So when you make it, eat it all up… and relish it!

TO MAKE THE PASTA, pour the water into the hollow at the top of a mound of flour. Add salt and knead the dough until springy and firm. Roll out into an inch-thick sheet and cut into strips half-an-inch wide which you will place on a floured board, lengthening and whittling them down with your fingers. Boil the *pici* in plenty of salted water and sprinkle liberally with the garlic sauce and some grated semi-hard pecorino cheese (from Siena or Rome). *Aglione*, which is a stupendous dressing though not really suitable if you are part of an intense social whirl, is typical of the Siena district (Radicofani and thereabouts, to be precise). It is made by embellishing a thick *pommarola* sauce (see page 33) with various large, crushed cloves of garlic, and cooking it for a long time, at least a couple of hours.

Pizzoccheri

BUCKWHEAT NOODLES

FOR THE PASTA:
- 300G / 11OZ / 2 1/3 CUPS BUCKWHEAT FLOUR
- 120G / 4OZ / 1 SCANT CUP WHITE FLOUR
- 4 EGGS
- 125ML / 4 FL OZ / 1/2 CUP MILK

- 120G / 4OZ SAVOY CABBAGE
- 250G / 9OZ POTATOES
- 120G / 4OZ / 1/2 CUP + 1 TBSP BUTTER
- 150G / 5OZ BITTO CHEESE (SEE NOTE BELOW)
- 1 CLOVE OF GARLIC
- A TWIG OF SAGE
- GRATED PARMESAN CHEESE

PREPARATION TIME: 1 HOUR

MIX THE TWO TYPES of flour with the eggs and milk and knead the dough briskly. Leave to rest for about ten minutes and roll out into a sheet an eighth-of-an-inch thick (so not too thin) and cut into ribbons a quarter-inch wide.

Peel the potatoes, cut up and boil with the shredded cabbage in salted water. Five minutes before the vegetable are cooked, add the pasta so that they finish cooking together. Meanwhile, melt the butter in a skillet and add the sage and garlic. Drain the pasta and sauté it in the herby butter.

Serve in soup bowls, alternating a layer of *pizzoccheri* with one of the sliced *bitto* cheese. Dust with grated Parmesan cheese.

THESE NICE, brown ribbons of pasta are a speciality from the Valtellina Valley in the North. *Bitto* is a semi-cooked, hard, delicately-flavoured cheese from the area of Sondrio. It may be replaced with another compact, lightly-salted cheese, such as Asiago, Edam or a fresh, mild provolone (the important thing is that it must not be too seasoned or sharp).

Ribollita

Bread Soup

To serve 6 people

- 2 onions
- 2 bunches of spinach
- 3 bunches of Swiss chard
- 400g / 14oz dried beans
- half a Savoy cabbage
- tomato concentrate (paste) or 150g / 5oz / 3/4 cup tinned tomatoes
- 1 bunch of Tuscan 'black' cabbage or kale
- 1 leek
- 300g / 11oz stale, unsalted, white bread
- olive oil

Preparation time: 3 hours to make the soup and 24 hours resting time for the réchauffé

The recipe reveals genuine peasant origins. Here we have the skilled recycling of the previous day's vegetable soup, with the addition of white, unsalted bread. So it is that, thanks to the further boiling, the simple and genuine flavours of the soup combine even better into a round, delicate balance, constituting a dish of considerable gastronomic standing. As is the case with any preparation of humble origin, it goes without saying that every town, nay, every family boasts their own recipe, which may mean substantial variations to the list of ingredients. For example, some people may eclectically appreciate the addition of potatoes, tomatoes, celery and carrots. In any case, it is a delicious dish, which, in its refined simplicity, expresses the best in Tuscan cuisine. But it must be done properly, with time and effort dedicated to it, mistrusting all short cuts which produce uneatable and (alas!) very common imitations.

Bring the beans to the boil in a saucepan of cold water. Let them simmer for a long time. Once cooked, purée them in a *mouli légumes*, though not without saving a couple of spoonfuls whole. Pour the purée back into the cooking liquor. Wash and trim the vegetables, chopping them up coarsely. In a saucepan containing 7-8 tablespoons of oil, sweat a finely-chopped onion, adding just a little of the diluted concentrate (or, if you prefer, a tin of well-drained tomatoes). Add the other vegetables, season with salt and pepper, cover and simmer for 6-7 minutes. Then pour in the bean purée with its liquor.

After a good hour of slow cooking, add the whole beans and the bread, sliced not too thinly. Cook very slowly for a further quarter-hour, then turn off the heat and allow the soup to rest until it is just warm. At this point, it can even be eaten, but then it is just a soup, however delicious, and not the real *ribollita*. In order for the metamorphosis to occur, it must be brought to the boil again a day later and left until just warm. Serve with a trickle of very pure olive oil from the first pressing.

This is the true, genuine, inimitable *ribollita*, with bread as soft as a whisper and the vegetables which melt in your mouth. Some interpret the réchauffé with a spell in a hot oven (certain restaurants do it to cut corners). It is an expedient permitted only if you are in a great hurry... .

Riso col cavolo

RICE WITH CABBAGE

- 350G / 3/4LB / 1 1/2 CUPS RICE
- 1/2L / 1PT / 2 CUPS STOCK
- OLIVE OIL

FOR A MORE REFINED VERSION:

- HALF A SAVOY CABBAGE
- 80G /3OZ UNSMOKED BACON
- 1 CLOVE OF GARLIC

FOR A MORE RUSTIC VERSION:

- 8-10 LEAVES OF TUSCAN 'BLACK' CABBAGE OR KALE
- 300G / 11OZ TRIPE
- ONION, CARROT AND CELERY

PREPARATION TIME: 1 HOUR

SAUTÉ THE CUBED BACON and the garlic in a saucepan with 3 tablespoons of oil. Add the cabbage or kale (washed, dried and cut up). Allow the flavours to blend and pour in the stock. Simmer gently for twenty minutes. Add the rice and cook to the *al dente* stage. This dish must be served hot and not too liquid. A version in a more countrified style (in the illustration below) uses a mirepoix of aromatic vegetables (but no bacon), some tripe (the dark part would be better) and leaves of Tuscan 'black' cabbage or kale, washed and cut up. Flavour the tripe in the mirepoix, add the cabbage and just a little stock and cook slowly for a quarter-hour. Add the rice (and a little stock, if necessary) and finish cooking.

Riso con le quaglie

RICE WITH QUAILS

- 350G / 3/4LB / 1 1/2 CUPS RICE
- 4 QUAILS
- 4 RASHERS (SLICES) OF STREAKY, UNSMOKED BACON
- 80G /3OZ / 1/4 CUP + 2 TB-SP BUTTER
- 125ML/ 4 FL OZ / 1/2 CUP WHITE WINE
- 1L / 2PT / 4 CUPS VEGETABLE STOCK
- 1 ONION
- PARMESAN CHEESE

PREPARATION TIME: 3/4 HOUR

SAUTÉ THE CHOPPED ONION in half the butter. Then add the rice, toasting it nicely. Cook the rice in the stock as for a risotto. While it is cooking, prepare the quails (as you know, these fine fowl can be obtained oven-ready in stores). Wrap a rasher of bacon around each bird, secure with a wooden toothpick, season the stomach cavity with salt and pepper (if liked, you may also add a leaf of sage). Brown in a flameproof casserole dish with the remaining butter, turning them over from time to time to cook evenly and basting with the wine, which you will allow to evaporate. After about a quarter-hour, they will be ready.

Lay them on the rice spread over a serving dish, masking it all liberally with the cooking juices.

THIS GENEROUS, DECORATIVE rice dish could be accompanied by a nice mixed salad and a cellar-cooled rosé wine. In this way you have a light, but substantial supper dish which will not subdue the lively, witty talk at table.

Risotto ai carciofi

ARTICHOKE RISOTTO

- 350G / 3/4LB / 1 1/2 CUPS ITALIAN ARBORIO RICE
- 6 FRESH GLOBE ARTICHOKES (NOT TOO LARGE)
- 1 WHITE-SKINNED ONION
- 40G / 1 1/2OZ / 3 TBSP BUTTER
- BARELY 1L / 2PT / 4 CUPS VEGETABLE STOCK
- 60ML / 2 FL OZ / 4 TBSP DRY WHITE WINE
- PARSLEY
- GRATED PARMESAN CHEESE
- OLIVE OIL

PREPARATION TIME: 1 HOUR

KEEP THE STOCK over a weak flame so that it is not cold when the moment comes for its addition (the reason is obvious: if you add cold stock to warm rice, it takes too long to heat up and the rice becomes soggy and overcooked). Prepare the artichokes, washing, trimming and cutting them into thin wedges which you will put in acidulated water so that they do not blacken.

Chop the onion finely and sauté in half the butter and 4 tablespoons of oil in a saucepan. Then add the drained and dried artichokes and brown them, pouring on the wine. When it has evaporated, add the rice and toast it over a high flame until it turns brown and translucent.

At this point, lower the flame and finish cooking the risotto, pouring in the warm stock little by little. When almost cooked, whip in the remaining butter and the Parmesan to finish your risotto off to a T. Serve it hot, dredging with very fresh chopped parsley.

Risotto al radicchio trevigiano

Risotto of Red Chicory

- 350g / 3/4lb / 1 1/2 cups Italian rice (pregerably Carnaroli)
- 600g / 1 1/4lb *radicchio trevigiano* or red chicory
- 60g / 2oz / 4 tbsp butter
- grated Parmesan cheese
- 1/2l / 1pt / 2 cups vegetable stock
- 60ml / 2 fl oz / 4 tbsp white wine

Preparation time: 1/2 hour

Melt two thirds of the butter in a saucepan and add the rinsed and finely-shredded red chicory. Sweat it very slowly and add the rice, toasting it until it becomes brown and translucent.

Pour in the wine and allow to evaporate over a high flame. Then add the stock, a little at a time in the usual way for risotto, stirring frequently, and cook for a good quarter-hour.

At the end of cooking, the rice should be dry with separate grains, firm but soft to the tooth.

As soon as your risotto is removed from the heat, whip in the cold butter and Parmesan.

Stir with care and serve.

Risotto con la zucca

Pumpkin (Squash) Risotto

- 300g / 11oz pumpkin (squash)
- 350g / 3/4lb / 1 1/2 cups Italian rice
- 80g / 3oz / 1/4 cup + 2 tbsp butter
- 1 white-skinned onion
- 1l / 2pt / 4 cups vegetable stock
- Grated Parmesan cheese

Preparation time: 1/2 hour

Peel the pumpkin and cut into pieces. Place in a saucepan to soften with a knob of butter and a glass of water. After half-an-hour, remove from the heat and purée. Put the finely-chopped onion to sauté with a large knob of butter in another saucepan. Add the rice and allow to "toast", stirring it into the sautéed onion over a high flame, until the grains are browned and translucent.

Now add the pumpkin (squash), season with salt (no skimping here or the risotto will be too sweet) and pepper and lower the flame. Stir in the stock little by little, in the usual way for risotto. Shortly before the end of cooking time, whip in a knob of butter and the Parmesan. Serve hot.

Rombetti sull'anatra

Pasta with Duck Sauce

- 400g / 14oz fresh pasta *rombetti* or lozenges (see page 52)
- Half a duck
- Onion, carrot and celery
- 400g / 14oz ripe tomatoes
- 125ml/ 4 fl oz / 1/2 cup red wine
- A sprig of parsley
- Grated Parmesan
- Olive oil

Preparation time: 2 hours, plus pasta resting time

Prepare the pasta by following the directions for lasagne on page 52. Cut into 2-inch lozenges. Wash and singe the duck and joint it. Chop up the aromatic vegetables and sauté in 4 tablespoons of oil in a saucepan. Add the duck and brown for ten minutes, basting with the wine and allowing it to evaporate. Add the tomatoes and cook gently for an hour. At the end, add the bird's liver and heart, as well, and allow to reduce for a further ten minutes. Boil the rombetti, adding them to the boiling water a few at a time and removing them with a slotted spoon. Place them in a soup tureen, covering them with sauce as you go.

Dust with grated Parmesan and the parsley and serve.

At the end you will find yourself with a nice stewed duck for a main course. Instead of duck, some regions use goose, bigger and with perhaps more delicate flesh, though also rather fattier. Some people suggest putting the pasta with the sauce into a buttered oven dish and baking it in a hot oven, but is the extra effort worth it?

Spaghetti aglio e olio

Spaghetti with Garlic and Olive Oil

- 350g / 3/4lb spaghetti
- 3 cloves of garlic
- A large sprig of parsley
- A couple of hot red peppers
- Olive oil

Preparation time: 10-15 minutes

While the spaghetti are boiling in plenty of salted water, fry the cut-up cloves of garlic very gently in 6 tablespoons of good quality olive oil (there is no skimping on this ingredient) in a skillet. As soon as the garlic begins to colour, add half of the chopped parsley and the hot red peppers. Raise the flame and sauté the spaghetti (drained *al dente*) together with half a soup ladle (2 tablespoons) of their cooking water. When the latter has reduced, dust with the rest of the fresh parsley and hurry it to the table.

Spaghetti alla carbonara

Spaghetti with Bacon and Eggs

- 350g / 3/4lb spaghetti
- 70g / 3oz joint of unsmoked bacon
- 2 egg yolks
- Grated pecorino cheese or ripe, sharp provolone

Preparation time: 12 minutes

The spaghetti must be cooked as usual. In the meantime, dice the bacon and fry in a skillet with a few drops of water (yes, water it must be, as pork products dislike oil). Beat the egg yolks with the grated cheese (the sharper it is, the more fun it is) in a soup tureen, dusting with freshly-ground black pepper. Drain the spaghetti well, toss into the tureen, add the bacon and stir everything (as in the illustration). You may dredge with some more cheese to taste at the moment of serving.

Spaghetti delicati

SPAGHETTI WITH RICOTTA, SPINACH AND WALNUTS

- 350G / 3/4LB WHOLEMEAL SPAGHETTI
- 100G / 4OZ / 1/2 CUP RICOTTA CHEESE
- 100G / 4OZ SPINACH
- 40G / 1 1/2OZ / 1/3 CUP WALNUT KERNELS
- OLIVE OIL, GARLIC

PREPARATION TIME: 20 MINUTES

Wash and trim the spinach, blanch in boiling water and chop. Sauté in a frying pan with 5 tablespoons of oil. Bring some salted water to the boil in the meantime and throw in the spaghetti. Add the walnut kernels and the ricotta to the frying pan, allowing the flavours to blend gradually. Drain the pasta when it reaches the *al dente* stage, add to the ricotta mixture in the pan and continue cooking, shaking the pan, for 2 minutes.

Stracci di Papa Sisto

POPE SIXTUS' PASTA

- 300G / 11OZ FRESH EGG PASTA DOUGH (SEE PAGE 52)
- 3 SAUSAGES
- 200G / 7OZ / 1 CUP TINNED (CANNED) TOMATOES
- HOT RED PEPPER

PREPARATION TIME: 20 MINUTES

SAUTÉ THE SAUSAGES SLOWLY but persistently in a frying pan until they disintegrate. Then add the tomatoes, salt, pepper and hot red pepper, reducing the liquid for a good ten minutes.

Throw the pasta into salted boiling water (refer to the recipe for lasagne to make up the pasta dough, cut into irregular lozenge shapes).

Drain rather *al dente*, sauté in the sauce in the frying pan for a few minutes and serve without delay.

An easy recipe for informal suppers.

Strozzapreti al burro e salvia

DUMPLINGS IN SAGE BUTTER

- 300G / 11OZ RICOTTA CHEESE
- 400G / 14OZ SPINACH
- 1 WHOLE EGG AND 1 YOLK
- 30G / 1OZ / 2 TBSP WHITE FLOUR
- NUTMEG (OPTIONAL)
- GRATED PARMESAN CHEESE
- 50G / 2OZ / 4 TBSP BUTTER
- A SPRIG OF SAGE

PREPARATION TIME: 25 MINUTES

WASH THE SPINACH and boil in very little water. Squeeze the water out, chop finely and transfer to a bowl. With your fingers, mix in the ricotta, the whole egg and the yolk, a handful of Parmesan, the flour, very little salt, white pepper and a pinch of grated nutmeg (if to your liking).

When the mixture is evenly blended, roll into little nut-sized balls which you will coat with flour (just like in the picture opposite) and then drop them, one by one, into a saucepan of salted boiling water.

After a few minutes, fish them out with a slotted spoon as they float to the surface. Put them into a soup tureen.

Melt the butter in a small saucepan and pour in the *strozzapreti*. Dust liberally with Parmesan and scatter with whole sage leaves.

Tagliatelle tartufo e noci

TRUFFLE AND WALNUT TAGLIATELLE

- 400G / 14OZ EGG PASTA DOUGH (OR READY-MADE TAGLIATELLE)
- 150G / 5OZ MASCARPONE (FRESH FULL-FAT CREAM CHEESE)
- 1 EGG YOLK
- A DOZEN WALNUT KERNELS
- GRATED PARMESAN CHEESE
- 1 WHITE TRUFFLE WEIGHING AT LEAST 40G / 1 1/2 OZ

PREPARATION TIME: ABOUT 15 MINUTES, PLUS THE TIME NEEDED TO MAKE AND REST THE DOUGH

CLEAN THE TRUFFLE and scrape it with a toothbrush and a damp cloth, as is the custom. To make the tagliatelle, proceed as for lasagne (see page 52). Leave the dough to rest for some time and cut the dough into quarter-inch ribbons. Otherwise, buy the pasta ready-made (but that removes half the fun). Beat the egg yolk in a bowl and add the cream cheese, blending it in with a wooden spoon. Season with a pinch of salt and one of freshly-ground pepper. Cook the tagliatelle (it will take 2-3 minutes), drain and pour on with the sauce. Break up the walnuts, dredge with Parmesan and stir well.

AND WHAT ABOUT THE TRUFFLE? you will say. Take the tureen with the pasta to the table, serve and leave each guest to help himself to truffle, using the special instrument to grate estimable flakes onto his own plate.

To console the thriftier hostess, let me add that this dish is excellent even without the truffle, but you only live once, and truffle adds that special touch to distinguish your cooking... .

Timballi di tagliatelle

TIMBALES OF TAGLIATELLE

THE TIMBALES:
- 4 SQUARE SHEETS OF FRESH OR FROZEN PASTRY
- 80G / 3OZ / 1/4 CUP + 2 TBSP BUTTER
- 100G / 1/4LB PRAWN TAILS, SHELLED
- 100G / 1/4LB TAGLIATELLINE (NARROW RIBBONS OF PASTA)
- 200G / 7OZ ASPARAGUS TIPS
- SINGLE (HEAVY) CREAM
- 1 SPRING ONION

THE SAUCE:
- 100G / 1/4LB ASPARAGUS
- 40G / 1 1/2OZ / 3 TBSP BUTTER
- 30G / 1OZ / 2 TBSP WHITE FLOUR
- 1/2 / 1PT / 2 CUPS STOCK (PREFERABLY OF FISH)

PREPARATION TIME: 1/2 HOUR

BLANCH THE ASPARAGUS TIPS. Melt a knob of butter in a frying pan and sauté the prawn tails (half of them whole and half of them chopped up) and the spring onion, sliced finely. Cook the pasta to the *al dente* stage, drain and toss in 2 tablespoons of cream, heated in the frying pan. Briefly scald the pastry sheets and lay them out on a damp tea towel. Butter four oven moulds, one per person, and line them with the pastry. Fill up with the tagliatelle, the prawns and the asparagus. Fold the edges of the pastry over towards the centre and bake in the oven at 220°C (425°F, Gas Mark 7) for about ten minutes. Get the sauce ready in the meantime. Purée the boiled asparagus and cook in the frying pan for a few minutes with the butter and flour, until the sauce has reached the correct thickness. Spread the sauce out on each dinner plate and place a timbale in the centre. Your admiring guests will just refrain with difficulty from enquiring which restaurant prepared such a delicacy.

Timballo delle crete senesi

Spinach and Cheese Timbale in Tomato Sauce

- 2 egg whites
- 4 slices of toast
- 8 Swiss chard leaves
- 150g / 5oz raveggiolo (soft Tuscan cheese)
- 300g / 11oz / 1 1/4 cups ricotta cheese
- fresh tomato sauce

Preparation time: 40 minutes

After sieving the ricotta and the raveggiolo, fold in the whisked egg whites and put the mixture into the refrigerator to rest a while.

Wash and trim the Swiss chard leaves and blanch for 2-3 minutes. Drain, allow to cool and dry them well. Butter 4 individual moulds, line them with the Swiss chard leaves and fill them up with the cheese mixture. Bake in a water bath in the oven at 200°C (400°F, Gas Mark 6) for a quarter-hour.

Serve the small timbales hot, dredging them with fresh tomato sauce, accompanied by slices of toasted bread.

Wrapped up in green fern leaves, the delicate raveggiolo, typical of Tuscany and Umbria, is a cheese made from ewe's milk (though today it is also made from cow's milk). White and uncured, it has a soft, moist consistency and must be eaten as soon as it is made. Substitute it with other similar cheese, but that is not really the same. A glass of good white Trebbiano wine brings out the velvety taste of these timbales.

Tortelli di patate

POTATO PASTA RINGS

FOR THE PASTA:
- 500G / 1LB 2OZ / 3 1/2 CUPS WHITE FLOUR
- 5 EGGS

FOR THE FILLING:
- 600G / 1 1/4LB POTATOES
- 100G / 4OZ / 1/2 CUP PARMESAN CHEESE
- NUTMEG
- 3 CLOVES OF GARLIC
- A LARGE SPRIG OF PARSLEY

PREPARATION TIME: 2 HOURS

A PEASANT VARIATION: add a little minced (ground) meat and a crumbled sausage to the filling and dredge the *tortelli* with meat sauce and cheese. Which version is better?

BOIL THE POTATOES, peel and mash them in a bowl with 2 cloves of garlic and some parsley chopped up together, the salt and cheese.

Mix it all thoroughly with your fingers, then add a little oil in which the other clove of garlic has been sautéed with a little parsley and continue mixing. The longer the filling is left to rest, the better it will be.

Now deal with the pasta. Break the eggs into the flour, heaped up on a pastry board. Knead it all until springy and firm and roll it out.

Cut into strips 1-1 1/2 inches wide, on which you will place large spoonfuls of the filling at 1-1 1/2 inch intervals.

Cover each strip with another one and cut out the *tortelli* with a pastry wheel, making sure that the edges are well-sealed.

Boil them in plenty of boiling salted water, drain and dress them with butter, sage and Parmesan cheese.

Tortellini

Stuffed Pasta Rings

- 400g / 14oz fresh egg pasta dough
- A slice of prosciutto
- 1 pork loin chop
- 1 veal cutlet from the best end
- 1 slice of mortadella
- Half a chicken breast
- 1 tsp ox bone marrow
- 125ml/ 4 fl oz / $^{1}/_{2}$ cup stock
- Generous knob of butter
- 1 egg yolk
- Grated Parmesan cheese
- Nutmeg

Preparation time: 2 hours, plus resting time for the pasta dough

I know, a lot of effort and patience is needed, but it is worth it. The *tortellini* must be small, smaller still if you want to serve them in broth. They will keep for a week or more if you put them in a dry place between two tea cloths. Indeed, they are not usually prepared for eating immediately, but after a day or more (if they make it till then …).

Prepare the pasta as you would for lasagne (see page 52), with the addition of an egg yolk because the pasta dough must be stiff and firm. Wipe and trim all the raw meat of gristle and fat, mincing (grinding) it up very finely. Melt the butter in a saucepan and brown the meat. Add the chopped prosciutto, the mortadella in pieces and the softened bone marrow (if you do not have any, substitute with a small piece of a stock cube). Allow the flavours to blend for ten minutes, dousing with a little stock. Remove from the heat and reduce to a very fine paste in a food processor. Transfer the meat to a bowl and mix in the egg yolk, 3-4 tablespoons of Parmesan, salt, pepper and a pinch of grated nutmeg. Mix well and leave aside for a while. Meanwhile, make the pasta rings. Roll out the dough, cut out a number of rounds of not more than $1^{1}/_{2}$ inches in diameter with the aid of a liqueur glass. Knead the trimmings to make other rounds. Put a nail-sized pellet of filling in the centre of a round then, holding it between the thumb and the middle finger of both hands, fold the dough over on itself, making sure that one edge overlaps the other at the top. Press down to seal and, with your index fingers, fold the top edge over to close. Then bend the lateral ends towards the centre, rolling the *tortellino* around your little finger. You will soon get the hang of it. As they are good anyhow you present them, the choice is yours. Cook them in broth, dress them in butter, in a sauce (but do not ruin them by smothering in cream). If you accept my advice, boil them in plenty of barely-salted water to the *al dente* stage, turn into an oven dish, pour over some tomato or meat sauce, béchamel and Parmesan and bake in a slow oven for 15 minutes.

Trenette al pesto

Trenette with Pesto

- 350g / $^{3}/_{4}$lb trenette (long, narrow noodles)
- 1 potato
- Pesto sauce (see page 32)
- Grated Parmesan cheese

Preparation time: 20 minutes

Peel the potato and cut into $^{1}/_{4}$in-thick slices. Put it into a saucepan with enough cold water to cook the pasta in, and bring to the boil. Add salt and toss in the pasta. Drain while *al dente*, dress with the *pesto* (diluted with a little of the pasta cooking water), together with the potato slices. Dredge with Parmesan and serve. The typical *trenette* of Liguria, which should, by tradition, be dark and made of unrefined semolina, are flat, ribbon-like noodles. They can be replaced by *linguine*.

Trofie coi broccoli

TROFIE DUMPLINGS WITH BROCCOLI

- 400G / 14OZ SMALL DRY GNOCCHI (FLOUR DUMPLINGS)
- 300G / 11OZ BROCCOLI (*CIME DI RAPA* OR TURNIP TOPS)
- 2 CLOVES OF GARLIC
- OLIVE OIL

PREPARATION TIME: 20 MINUTES

TROFIE ARE SMALL FLOUR dumplings originally from the district around Recco, a resort on the coast near Genoa. They go splendidly with *pesto* sauce or with the delicious sauces of Ligurian tradition called *tocchi*. They are replaceable with other types of dumplings (they must be of flour, though, not potato) or else, in deference to tradition, with *orecchiette*, classic pasta from Apulia, or even with spiral-shaped *fusilli*.

WASH THE GREENS and blanch in a saucepan full of salted water for 5 minutes. Remove them (but reserve their cooking water), drain and sauté them in 6 tablespoons of good quality olive oil in a frying pan, together with the crushed cloves of garlic (some cooks add an anchovy fillet, too). In the meanwhile, cook the pasta in the vegetable water and drain at the *al dente* stage. Toss them into the frying pan and sauté with the green vegetables, removing the garlic and dusting with freshly-ground pepper. You can also add a handful of grated cheese, if you like. Parmesan or pecorino? The choice is up to you.

Vermicelli alla puttanesca

VERMICELLI IN A PIQUANT SAUCE

- 350G / $^3/_4$LB VERMICELLI OR SPAGHETTI
- 400G / 14OZ FRESH RIPE TOMATOES OR TINNED (CANNED) ONES
- 3 ANCHOVIES
- 2 TBSP CAPERS, DRAINED
- BLACK OLIVES, STONED
- 2 CLOVES OF GARLIC
- 1 HOT RED PEPPER
- OLIVE OIL

PREPARATION TIME: 20 MINUTES

IF YOU PREFER FRESH to tinned tomatoes, remember that you must blanch, peel and seed them. Sauté the garlic and hot red pepper very gently in 4-5 tablespoons of oil in a frying pan. Before the garlic changes colour, add the roughly-chopped tomatoes, the whole olives and the capers. Cook over fierce heat for 5 minutes, stirring. Reduce over a moderate flame for another 10 minutes and remove from the heat. At this point, add the washed, filleted and broken-up anchovies, allowing them to be absorbed into the sauce. In the meanwhile, boil the vermicelli. Drain them while still very much *al dente* and turn into the pan with the sauce. Return them to a high heat, sauté them and serve very hot.

SOME COOKS FRY half an onion instead of the garlic, but I am of the opinion that something is lost. The fragrance of the latter is more suited to this rough, sun-drenched sauce.

I shall say little about the unwonted name referring to the oldest profession: some say that it came from wenches in the brothels of bygone times who would whip up a quick sauce with what was at hand between one client and the next.

And in no house in the South of Italy (whether legitimate or otherwise) could there be a lack of garlic, capers, hot red pepper, olives and tomatoes.

The story, if true, gives a saucier flavour to the dish, which, in any case, seems to me worthy enough, whatever its origin.

Ziti in bianco al gratin

BAKED MACARONI IN A WHITE SAUCE

- 400G / 1LB 2OZ *ZITI* (MACARONI)
- 350ML / 3/4PT / $1^1/_3$ CUPS MILK
- 100G / 4OZ / $^1/_2$ CUP BUTTER
- 1 SCANT TBSP WHITE FLOUR
- DRY BREADCRUMBS
- NUTMEG
- GRATED PARMESAN CHEESE

PREPARATION TIME: 25 MINUTES

MELT A THIRD OF THE BUTTER in a small saucepan, add a scant tablespoon of flour and cook slowly for 2 minutes, stirring with the wooden spoon, without allowing it to colour. Now add the milk, little by little, making a smooth, velvety white sauce, which you will season with salt, a little pepper and grated nutmeg.

Cook the pasta to the *al dente* stage (break them into smaller pieces, if you prefer), drain, dress with butter and Parmesan and then the white sauce. Turn into a buttered oven dish, sprinkle with dry breadcrumbs and bake in a medium oven for about ten minutes.

Zuppa del Tarlati

Chicken Soup

Make the stock by cooking the chicken, the vegetables and the parsley in 2 litres (4 pints or 8 cups) of lightly salted water for a good hour. Bone the chicken. Sauté the chopped onion, garlic and carrot in a saucepan, then brown the jointed chicken, add the broth and boil for a quarter-hour. Take the pan off the fire and blend in the cream, the egg yolk beaten up with a couple of tablespoons of Parmesan, a little nutmeg and salt and put aside for a few minutes. Serve the slightly cooled soup in soup bowls into which you have previously put a few croutons.

For the stock:
- A quarter of a chicken
- 1 onion
- 1 carrot
- 1 stick of celery
- 1 small tomato
- 1 sprig of parsley

For the soup:
- Half an onion
- 1 clove of garlic
- Half a carrot
- 60ml / 2 fl oz / 4 tbsp white wine
- 1 egg yolk
- Grated Parmesan
- Single cream
- 2 slices of white bread
- Nutmeg
- Olive oil

Preparation time: 1 1/2 hours

This is an ancient recipe which originated from Arezzo in Tuscany. The name Tarlati referred to a bishop and city lord who lived in the fourteenth century and who was a distinguished art-lover as well as a gourmet. The dish is as delicate as it is nutritious, not at all complicated.

Zuppa di farro

Emmer (Wheat Berry) Soup

- 200g / 7oz / 1 1/4 cups emmer (wheat berry)
- 200g / 7oz borlotti beans
- A sprig of rosemary
- A few sage leaves
- A clove of garlic
- Half an onion
- Olive oil

Preparation time: about 1 1/4 hours, plus soaking time

Soak the borlotti beans in water overnight.

When you drain them, be sure to keep about one-and-a-half litres (3 pints or 6 cups) of their water.

Place the beans in fresh cold water, cover with the lid and cook for a good half-hour over very low heat. Meanwhile, chop up the onion, garlic and herbs finely and sweat in 6 tablespoons of olive oil in a saucepan.

Now add the emmer (wheat berry) and allow to toast very

well in the mirepoix. Then pour in the water which you put aside and simmer gently for a good hour. Half-way through cooking, add three quarters of the beans, mashing the rest to add at the end to give volume to the soup.

Leave it a few minutes to rest and serve with a sprinkling of freshly-ground pepper and a trickle of good quality olive oil.

If you like, you can serve each person with a large slice of white toast, rubbed over with garlic, and watch them attack this delicious soup with zeal.

Zuppa di vongole

Clam Soup

- 1.3kg / $2^3/4$lb baby clams
- 400g / 14oz / 2 cups tinned (canned) tomatoes
- 2 cloves of garlic
- Parsley, chopped
- Hot red pepper
- 60ml / 2 fl oz / 4 tbsp white wine
- White bread, sliced
- Olive oil

Preparation time: 20 minutes, plus clam-purging time

Wash the clams and place them in fresh water to purge themselves, changing it frequently. Gently sauté the finely-chopped garlic and parsley in a flameproof casserole dish with 6 tablespoons of oil. Hastily pour the wine over and, when it has evaporated, add the tomatoes, the hot red pepper and salt and allow the flavours to blend for about ten minutes.

Then add the clams and cook briskly for 5 minutes until the shells have opened (discard any which have not done so).

Toast the slices of bread, one per portion, rub with garlic and place them in the individual soup bowls. Lay a sizeable portion of steaming clams on each piece of toast, dousing it all liberally with the very flavoursome cooking liquor.

Relish the soup with a nice glass of white wine.

Some cooks place an overturned saucer on the bottom of the container where the clams are being cleaned out, so that the sand collects under it and does not get drawn back into circulation. Believe it or not, it really works! This recipe obviously goes for any marine mollusc, mussels and Venus clams included, although the latter are very difficult to find nice and fresh, because they live in the mud on the sea bed near ports and the mouths of rivers, in sluggish water.

Zuppa "alla lombarda"

Bean Soup

- 1kg / $2^1/4$lb fresh white beans, unshelled weight
- White bread, sliced
- 3 cloves of garlic
- Sage leaves
- Peppercorns
- Olive oil

Preparation time: $2^1/4$ hours

The beans, hulled and rinsed, are to be put into a saucepan of cold, salted water, where they will cook very slowly for a couple of hours with the lid on, together with the garlic, sage, pepper and a couple of tablespoons of olive oil. Toast a slice of bread per head, place on the bottom of individual soup bowls, cover liberally with the beans and fill up with their boiling liquor. A light sprinkling of freshly-ground pepper, a trickle of good quality oil and you are in heaven or thereabouts....

Rather than a proper bean soup, this is a ready, genial way to relish beans in soup. Despite reference to Lombardy in the name of the soup, the recipe is in fact Tuscan, though probably it has very far Lombard origins. But that is the way it is: honour to the land of Italy's present-day famed cook, Gualtiero Marchesi, for giving rise to such a delicacy, but honour also to the people in the adopted land of last century's culinary expert Pellegrino Artusi who managed to pass it down to us.

Zuppa frantoiana

OLIVE-PRESS SOUP

SOAK THE BEANS overnight, drain and boil them in a saucepan with 2 litres (4 pints or 8 cups) of water, a twig of sage and 3 cloves of garlic for about one-and-a-half hours.

Half-an-hour before the end of cooking, put the oil in a flameproof casserole and sweat the diced bacon and the finely-sliced rings of onion very gently in it.

Meanwhile, clean and trim the vegetables, cut them to small pieces and add to the bacon and onion, together with a little chopped parsley. Stir, cover and cook for about twenty minutes.

When the beans are cooked, sieve them and add to the other vegetables in the casserole, stir well, add a pinch of ground hot red pepper and the salt.

Bring back to the boil and cook for another 40 minutes with the lid on the pan.

Lay 4 slices of toasted bread rubbed with garlic in a tureen and cover with the soup.

Then, cover the first layer with another layer of bread which is also drenched with the soup and continue like this until all the ingredients are used up.

Leave to rest for 5 minutes and serve, after sprinkling liberally with extra-virgin olive oil. Grated cheese, considered optional by some, is not advisable in my opinion.

- 2 RASHERS (SLICES) OF STREAKY, UNSMOKED BACON
- 3 CLOVES OF GARLIC
- 12 TBSP / 3/4CUP VERY PURE EXTRA-VIRGIN OLIVE OIL
- 12 SLICES OF UNSALTED WHITE BREAD
- 100G / 3 1/2 OZ YOUNG BORAGE LEAVES
- 100G / 3 1/2OZ POTATOES
- 150G / 5OZ DRY BEANS
- 200G / 7OZ SAVOY CABBAGE
- 200G / 7OZ ONION
- 200G / 7OZ COURGETTES (ZUCCHINI)
- GROUND HOT RED PEPPER
- A SPRIG OF PARSLEY, A TWIG OF SAGE, A HANDFUL OF THYME
- 1 STICK OF CELERY
- 1 CARROT

PREPARATION TIME: 2 1/4 HOURS, PLUS SOAKING TIME

BORAGE (*Borrago officinalis*) is a herbaceous plant with lovely little blue flowers which grows spontaneously in meadows, but it is often cultivated in a corner of the vegetable garden as it has an excellent flavour and is the main ingredient for a delicious omelette.

With the leaves being evenly covered in hairs, they can only be eaten cooked.

The splendour of Spring in the Tuscan Maremma

Meat and Game

Agnello al forno

BAKED LAMB

- 1KG / 2 1/4LB LAMB ON THE BONE (PREFERABLY FROM THE LEG)
- 1 CARROT
- 1 ONION
- 2 CLOVES OF GARLIC
- A TWIG OF ROSEMARY
- 125ML/ 4 FL OZ / 1/2 CUP RED WINE
- 1/2L / 1PT / 2 CUPS LIGHT VEGETABLE STOCK
- OIL

PREPARATION TIME: 2 HOURS 20 MINUTES

WASH AND TRIM the vegetables and cut to pieces. Put them in a large, well-oiled roasting pan, together with the whole garlic cloves and the rosemary. Lay the leg of lamb on top and season with salt and freshly-ground pepper.

Sear the meat on all sides over a gentle flame, then transfer the pan to the oven at 200°C (400°F, Gas Mark 6), dousing with the wine.

When the wine has reduced somewhat, pour over a few spoonfuls of stock and continue cooking, repeating the operation from time to time so that the meat does not dry up. After a couple of hours, the lamb should be evenly-covered by a nice, brown crust. Remove it from the pan and briefly reduce the juices in the pan.

Pour the gravy over the leg of lamb and serve nice and hot, with a garnish of fresh peas dressed in olive oil or new potatoes au gratin.

Agnello alla verza

LAMB CUTLETS IN CABBAGE LEAVES

- 800G / 1 3/4LB SADDLE OF LAMB
- PORK NET (CAUL FAT)
- 10 LARGE LEAVES OF SAVOY CABBAGE
- 30G / 1OZ / 2 TBSP WHITE FLOUR
- 45G / 1 1/2OZ / 3 TBSP BUTTER
- 90 ML / 6 TBSP / 1/4 CUP PLUS 2 TBSP RED WINE
- OLIVE OIL

PREPARATION TIME: 35 MINUTES

CUT THE LAMB into pieces, each having three ribs.

Wash the savoy cabbage leaves, blanch and plunge into cold water.

Soften up the pork net by dipping into warm water. Coat the lamb cutlets with flour and sear them for two minutes in a little oil in a frying pan.

Remove them and allow to cool for 4 or 5 minutes. Wrap each piece in a cabbage leaf, season with salt and then roll up in a piece of pork net.

Place in a roasting pan with 4-5 tablespoons of oil and a knob of butter and bake in the oven at 220°C (450°F, Gas Mark 8) for 7-8 minutes.

Halfway through, turn the parcels over, dousing with the wine. When the lamb is cooked, remove and keep warm. Reduce the sauce in the pan, add the remaining butter (off the heat) and blend.

Cut the meat into single ribs, mask with the sauce and serve.

Anatra all'arancia

Orange-Flavoured Duck

- A DUCK, ABOUT 1.3KG / 3LB
- 2 ORANGES
- 2 CLOVES OF GARLIC
- A SPRIG OF SAGE
- 60ML / 2 FL OZ / 4 TBSP RED WINE
- 1 ONION
- 1 CARROT
- 1 STICK OF CELERY
- 1/2 TBSP WHITE FLOUR
- 1 TSP SUGAR
- OLIVE OIL

PREPARATION TIME: 1 HOUR 20 MINUTES (PLUS TIME FOR PLUCKING AND TRIMMING THE DUCK)

One of your dinner guests may remark that this is not a dish from Italian cuisine at all, but the very famous *Canard à l'orange*, a cornerstone of the great French culinary school. At that point, with an angelic smile on your face (but with the air of a cat about to pounce on a mouse), suggest that he read up the biography of Catherine de' Medici, born in Florence in 1519, the bride of Henri II de Valois and the mother of two French kings (Henri III and Charles IX). She was regent on behalf of the latter and led her adopted country forcefully through the dark ages of the religious wars. Your guest will thus learn how this magnificent lady and worthy queen, who had been brought up in the refined atmosphere of the Florentine court, introduced haute cuisine into the court of France, which was not accustomed to such delicacies. Along with other delights, she left this refined recipe in inheritance to her subjects. In so doing, she set off France's glorious, secular culinary tradition.

The duck must be plucked, opened out, drawn and singed. Together with the head and claws, do not forget to eliminate the gland which web-footed water birds have at the bottom of their spine, near the tail, and from which, by rubbing their beaks on it, they obtain the grease for preening their feathers with, so that they can then float majestically on the perilous waters which make up their habitat. (Not that we feel the need for it, but this fact is further confirmation of the fact that what one needs in order to survive is not necessarily good to eat.) Put the garlic, the peeled segments of an orange, a few sage leaves, salt and pepper into the stomach cavity of the bird. Fold over the flaps and sew them up with kitchen string. Oil the duck and place in a roasting tin. Cook in a medium oven for an hour, basting frequently with the wine and the cooking juices. Remove the duck from the tin and keep warm, in its place sautéing the very finely-chopped aromatic vegetables, with the addition of the finely-shredded orange zest (after eliminating all trace of the white pith) and the sugar. Bind the sauce with a little flour and let it simmer for 3-4 minutes.

Carve the duck (discarding the filling) and return to the pan. Allow the meat to absorb the flavours thoroughly, then serve masked in the sauce and garnished with slices of orange.

Animelle alla salvia

SWEETBREADS WITH SAGE

- 600G / 1 1/4LB VEAL SWEETBREADS
- 40G / 1 1/2OZ / 1/3 CUP WHITE FLOUR
- 60G / 2OZ / 4 TBSP BUTTER
- A SPRIG OF SAGE

PREPARATION TIME: 35 MINUTES (PLUS SOAKING TIME)

THE SWEETBREADS should be rinsed for half-an-hour under cold running water. Remove the membranes and boil in slightly salted water for twenty minutes.

Drain, allow to cool and cut into slices. Coat lightly with flour and brown over quite a fierce flame (not too high, though) in a frying pan where you have very slowly melted the butter.

Add a few sage leaves and serve.

Arista al forno

ROAST LOIN OF PORK

- 1 1/2 KG / 3 1/4LB LOIN OF PORK ON THE BONE
- 2-3 CLOVES OF GARLIC
- A SPRIG OF ROSEMARY
- PEPPERCORNS
- A FEW WILD FENNEL SEEDS (OPTIONAL)
- OLIVE OIL

PREPARATION TIME: 2 1/4 HOURS

LEGIONS OF GOURMETS, much taken up with lexical questions, have gone to town on trying to discover the etymology of the name of this delicious Tuscan speciality - with little success, however. Still, without worrying too much about the philology involved, we know for certain that the dish was already familiar and appreciated in the fourteenth century.

THE LOIN OF PORK must be boned (I hold that this operation is best left to a butcher), but the bone is then to be reinserted from where it was extracted.

Finely chop the garlic and rosemary and mix with the peppercorns and fennel seeds. Insert pinches of the herbs liberally between the bone and the meat, then tie the loin up with kitchen string, thus returning it to its former shape.

Place the pork in a lightly-oiled roasting tin and put it in the oven at a very moderate setting for about two hours.

Remove the string and bone. Carve into fairly thin slices. Cover with the gravy in the pan (in which you may flavour parboiled vegetables, such as Swiss chard, spinach, turnip tops, kale or cauliflower to serve as your side-plate).

This is delicious even eaten cold.

Bistecca alla fiorentina

T-BONE BEEF STEAK, GRILLED (BROILED) THE FLORENTINE WAY

- 800G-1KG / $1^3/_4$-$2^1/_4$LB PIECE OF SIRLOIN STEAK
- SALT AND FRESHLY-GROUND PEPPER

PREPARATION TIME: $^1/_4$ HOUR

TRUE FLORENTINE BEEF STEAK is taken from the sirloin, cut on the bone, an inch thick (if cut thinner, the result is like leather; if thicker, it remains uncooked in the middle) and complete with its tenderloin and fillet, although the advocates of the so-called entrecôte beefsteak - i.e. without the fillet - maintain (not without reason) that it is tenderer and more flavoursome. Beef steak must be removed from the refrigerator at least two hours before cooking or it will be tough; it is a crime to smother it in oil.

TO DO THINGS "to a T", the beef steak should be cooked over glowing hot charcoal, but with no flame (you can use the oven grill attachment, but the outcome will not be exactly the same). Place the steak in the centre of the grating and keep over the fire for 5 minutes, turning it over (without piercing the meat) to cook on the other side. The meat must be nicely seared on the surface, but rare inside. Season with a pinch of salt and freshly ground pepper.

Bollito misto

MIXED BOILED MEATS

- 400G / 14OZ RUMP STEAK
- 400G / 14OZ BREAST OF VEAL
- HALF A BOILING FOWL
- HALF A CALF'S TONGUE
- 1 SMALL *COTECHINO*, A SPICED PORK SAUSAGE (OPTIONAL)
- 1/2KG / 1LB OX TAIL
- 1 ONION, 1 CARROT, 1 STICK OF CELERY

PREPARATION TIME: 3 1/2-4 HOURS

WIPE AND TRIM the meat and singe the bowling fowl. Heat a large saucepan of salted water with the vegetables. When the water begins to boil, add the rump steak and the ox tail, lower the heat to just simmering point, cover and leave to cook for about an hour. Then add the chicken, the breast and the tongue, put the lid on again and continue cooking a further two and-a-half hours or even three.

If you like *cotechino*, remember that is it cooked separately, following the instructions for the relevant recipe (on page 102). Finally, drain all the meat and carve into slices or cut into chunks, skinning the tongue. Excellent hot, this dish is also delicious cold.

THE MEAT IS ALWAYS ADDED to boiling water. Serve the boiled meats together with a tureen of the broth into which you can dip the meat should it get cold or dry up. Dress with olive oil and *gros sel*, with mustard sauce, piquant green sauce, anchovy sauce and the hot anchovy and garlic dip called *bagna cauda* (see pages 32 and 145).

Cassœula

MIXED PORK CASSEROLE

- 30G / 1OZ UNSMOKED BACON
- 1 PIG'S TROTTER
- 100G / 4 OZ PORK RIND
- 100G / 4OZ PIG'S HEAD
- 100G / 4OZ PORK LOIN
- 4 LEAN PORK SAUSAGES
- HALF A SAVOY CABBAGE
- 1 ONION, 1 CARROT
- 30G / 1OZ / 2 TBSP BUTTER
- 1 STICK OF CELERY

PREPARATION TIME: 3 HOURS

WASH THE SAVOY CABBAGE and wipe the meat (with the exception of the bacon and sausages). In a capacious flameproof casserole (known as *cassoeula* in the Milanese dialect), colour the finely-chopped onion with the diced bacon in the melted butter. Chop up the aromatic vegetables and cut all the meat except the sausages into chunks.

Sauté very gently, stirring with a wooden spoon. Season with salt and pepper and cover with water. Cooking should continue for a good two hours over low heat. Half-an-hour before the end, add the savoy cabbage cut into pieces.

This is traditionally served with a plate of cornmeal or *polenta*.

HERE WE HAVE a meal in itself, and not merely a dish. Only in rugby terminology could we find a word to depict the impact on a sorely-tried digestive system of this noble, ancient Milanese dish (also called *bottaggio*). But just as inexpressible is the pleasure that it furnishes the soul as well as the palate, especially on a wintry day. So then, one day spent in gourmandism is better than a hundred with a poor appetite, don't you agree?

Cibreo di rigaglie

CHICKEN GIBLET CASSEROLE

AN ANCIENT, REFINED DISH which is rarely made.

Clean the livers, trimming them of any bile or parts in contact with it. Blanch briefly in boiling water, together with the cocks' wattles and combs, which, once drained, must be skinned and reduced to tiny pieces.

- 400G / 14OZ CHICKEN LIVERS, COCKS' WATTLES AND COMBS, HEN'S UNLAID EGGS
- 30G / 1OZ / 2 TBSP BUTTER
- 2 EGGS
- 60ML / 2 FL OZ / 4 TBSP MARSALA
- HALF A LEMON
- 1 SCANT TBSP WHITE FLOUR
- HALF A SOUP LADLE / 2 FL OZ / 2 TBSP STOCK

PREPARATION TIME: 3/4 HOUR

Gently colour the combs and wattles in the butter for half-an-hour. A few minutes before the end, add the livers and unlaid eggs, salt and pepper. Stir once more and turn off the heat. Meanwhile, in a separate bowl, beat the two egg yolks with the flour and the lemon juice, adding the warm broth little by little. Turn the giblets in, stir well and serve immediately. It is considered as a first course by some and by others a main dish. As you prefer (though, personally, I would be appalled at having to eat something *after* a delicate *cibreo*). It is, in any case, delicious.

Cima alla genovese

Brisket of Beef, Braised and Stuffed

- 500g / 1lb 2oz brisket of beef
- 2 calf's sweetbreads
- 2 tbsp grated Parmesan
- 2 young bay leaves
- 100g / 4oz breadcrumb, soaked and then squeezed
- 100g / 4oz shelled green peas
- 250g / 9oz lean pork
- pinch marjoram
- 1 egg
- 1 onion
- 1 small carrot
- 1 stick of celery
- knob of butter
- 1 clove of garlic

Preparation time: 3 hours

The meat should be cut thickly enough to withstand a deep lengthways slit down one side to form a kind of pocket for stuffing, the other three sides remaining whole. Let's deal first with the stuffing. Scald the sweetbreads in boiling water and skin them. Transfer to a frying pan with the butter and a tablespoon of oil and add half a clove of garlic and half a finely-chopped onion. Remove before it all colours and dice. Mix the breadcrumb with the cubed pork and cut everything up finely. Add the egg, Parmesan cheese, salt, pepper and a pinch of marjoram. Amalgamate it all thoroughly. Now add the sweetbreads and the peas, which should be of a very small variety. Carefully fill the meat "pocket" with the stuffing and sew the open side up tightly with a needle and some kitchen string to make a clean, trim edge. Put the cima into a saucepan of hot water, together with the carrot, celery, the remaining half onion and the bay leaves. Cook for a couple of hours over moderate heat. When ready, place under a weight on a plate (in the past an iron was used) which will bear well down on the stuffing so that it is nice and firm when the meat is carved up.

A rather bizarre dish which is truly splendid on festive Ligurian dinner tables. In actual fact, that treacherous couple of ounces of lard required in the traditional recipe has here been banned from the stuffing, to the benefit of the more delicate stomach (for your information, the lard is chopped up with the pork). This is excellent both hot and cold, accompanied by a luxurious, home-made mayonnaise, by aspic and by steamed vegetables. The resultant broth is very good and light. Try cooking some fine egg pasta or the famous *bavette* in it and heaven will seem at arm's reach.

Cinghiale in agrodolce

Wild Boar in a Sweet and Sour Sauce

For the marinade:
- 180ml / 12 tbsp / $^3/_4$ cup red wine
- 60ml / 2 fl oz / 4 tbsp vinegar
- 1 onion
- 1 carrot
- 1 stick of celery
- A sprig of parsley
- 3-4 cloves
- 2 bay leaves
- 2 sprigs of thyme
- Peppercorns

- 800g / 1$^3/_4$lb boar meat
- 1 large onion
- 1 carrot
- 1 stick of celery
- 125ml/ 4 fl oz / $^1/_2$ cup white wine
- 2 tbsp white sugar
- 2 tbsp bitter cocoa powder
- 2 tbsp vinegar
- 1 bay leaf
- 1 clove of garlic
- 2 tsp cornflour (cornstarch) or white flour
- Sultanas (white raisins)
- Orange and lemon zest
- 4 dried prunes
- Olive oil

Preparation time: 3 hours, plus marinating time

The day before undertaking this refined recipe, put the wine, the vinegar, the finely-chopped onion, carrot, celery and herbs, the cloves and the peppercorns into a saucepan and bring to the boil. Transfer the marinade to a bowl to cool. Once cold, put in the boar to soak overnight, turning it over, if necessary.

Drain, dry and tie the meat up to keep its shape. Place in a flameproof casserole dish with 6 tablespoons of oil, salt, pepper, the chopped marinade vegetables and half a bay leaf. Sear over fierce heat. When the meat has browned all over, pour over the wine and allow to evaporate. Add half a litre (one pint / two cups) of hot water, put on the lid and cook over a low heat for a couple of hours.

After that, remove the meat from the pan and keep it hot in a little of its sauce. Leave a quantity of not too dense pan juices behind in the casserole, skim off the fat if necessary and keep it all nice and hot.

In a small saucepan, mix together the, sugar, the crushed clove of garlic and the remaining half bay leaf. Dissolve the sugar over low heat, stirring. When the sugar has coloured somewhat, add the vinegar little by little, stirring all the time. Then add the cocoa powder and combine with the other ingredients. Pour this sauce into the gravy left in the bottom of the casserole and return to a faint, vigil flame.

If the sauce seems too runny, add cornflour (cornstarch) or flour. When the desired thickness has been reached, sieve and return to the casserole on the heat. Add the sultanas and the soaked, dried and stoned prunes and allow to blend and reduce considerably.

In the meantime, untie the boar, carve it and serve on a hot serving dish, liberally masked in the sauce.

A triumphant and demanding dish of the Roman cookery tradition, to be attempted only if you have long, idle, serene days ahead of you. Then you can prepare for the visit of those discerning guests who belong to the increasingly restricted confraternity of connoisseurs of the mystic union of savoury and sweet flavours. It is indeed a choice combination which is infrequently used by Italian cooks, both in the catering business and in the home. The classic advice stands for those venturing into undertakings of this type: taste frequently while cooking because we have a proverb which runs "whether savoury or sweet, trust your palate".

The boar can have its rind only if it is young, otherwise it would be more suitable for making up belts, wallets and other articles in leather.

Cinghiale in umido

WILD BOAR STEW

- 800G / $1^3/4$LB WILD BOAR MEAT
- 500G / 1LB 2OZ / $2^1/2$ CUPS TINNED TOMATOES
- 1 ONION
- 1 CARROT
- 1 STICK OF CELERY
- 2 CLOVES OF GARLIC
- 4 BAY LEAVES
- JUNIPER BERRIES
- $^1/2$L / 1PT / 2 CUPS RED WINE
- 2 TBSP VINEGAR
- OLIVE OIL

PREPARATION TIME: $3^1/2$ HOURS, PLUS MARINATING OVERNIGHT

WHEN MAKING this delicious dish, typical of the Maremma district in Tuscany, it is advisable to keep the sauce rather runny. Then at the end of the day, you can serve it up over some excellent *pappardelle* (egg noodles) - the recipe is on page 59. As suggested by the illustration on the right, this stew goes splendidly with *fagioli all'uccelletto* or beans stewed with sage and tomatoes (see page 186).

THE DAY BEFORE, make a marinade with the wine, the vinegar, the cut-up onion, celery and carrot, the bay leaves and the juniper berries.

Trim the tender meat (which should be from a young animal) of nerves, gristle and fat. Cut into medium-sized chunks and marinate overnight.

Drain the vegetables from the marinade, chop finely and sweat them in a fireproof casserole with 5 tablespoons of oil. Add the meat, season with salt and pepper, and brown all over. Pour in a glass of the marinade and evaporate it over fierce heat. Then add the tomatoes, cover with the lid and cook very slowly for two to three hours. If necessary, moisten with a little of the marinade from time to time, perhaps even diluted with a few drops of warm water.

Coda alla vaccinara

BRAISED OXTAIL

- 1KG / $2^1/4$LB OXTAIL
- 800G / $1^3/4$LB RIPE TOMATOES OR TOMATO PULP
- 100G / 4OZ BOILED, UNSMOKED HAM IN A THICK SLICE
- A SPRIG OF PARSLEY
- 1 CARROT
- 1 ONION
- 1 STICK OF CELERY
- 1 CLOVE OF GARLIC
- 60ML / 2 FL OZ / 4 TBSP WHITE WINE
- OLIVE OIL

PREPARATION TIME: $3^1/2$ HOURS

CUT THE OXTAIL INTO chunks and rinse. Cook in boiling water for about twenty minutes, drain and keep to one side. Chop up the garlic, carrot, onion and parsley and sauté in 5 tablespoons of oil in a saucepan. Add the cubed ham and after a moment or so the oxtail. Sear it, season with salt and pepper and moisten with the wine, which you will allow to evaporate over fierce heat.

Add the tomato, stir, put on the lid and continue cooking over a low flame for two-and-a-half hours. Then toss in the sliced celery. Go on cooking for a further twenty minutes, adding some stock, if necessary. This traditional dish from the Lazio region becomes an excellent one-course meal if served with buttered *tagliatelle*.

Coniglio all'umido

STEWED RABBIT

- 1 RABBIT, ABOUT 1.2KG / $2^3/4$LB
- 500G / 1LB 2OZ TOMATOES
- 60ML / 2 FL OZ / 4 TBSP WHITE WINE
- 1 ONION, 1 CARROT AND 1 STICK OF CELERY
- 1 CLOVE OF GARLIC
- ROSEMARY AND SAGE
- OLIVE OIL

PREPARATION TIME: $1^1/4$ HOURS

REMOVE THE HEAD and paws from the rabbit, wash and joint it (into about a dozen pieces, including the liver).

Chop the onion, carrot and celery and sweat them in a saucepan with 6 tablespoons of oil, the garlic and a sprig of rosemary. Throw in the rabbit joints and brown over fierce heat.

When the meat has coloured a little, douse with the wine and allow to evaporate. Then season with salt, pepper and a little sage, stir a couple of times and throw in the coarsely-chopped tomatoes.

Cook slowly for an hour, taking care that the rabbit does not dry up and that there is plenty of flavoursome sauce.

Coniglio con le olive

RABBIT WITH OLIVES

- 1 RABBIT, AT LEAST $1^1/2$ KG / $3^1/4$LB
- 3 CLOVES OF GARLIC
- 4 RIPE TOMATOES
- 60ML / 2 FL OZ / 4 TBSP DRY WHITE WINE
- A HANDFUL OF GARLICKY BLACK OLIVES
- OLIVE OIL

PREPARATION TIME: 1 HOUR

REMOVE THE HEAD and paws from the rabbit, wash and cut into about eleven portions, including the delicious liver. Sauté with 2 cloves of garlic in 4 tablespoons of oil in a flameproof casserole over gentle heat for 5 minutes. When the meat has coloured somewhat, pour in the wine and allow to evaporate. Add the coarsely-chopped tomatoes, the olives, salt and pepper and cook for half-an-hour over a medium flame. The best accompaniments? Boiled or mashed potatoes.

Coniglio in fricassea

RABBIT IN A LEMON SAUCE

- 1 RABBIT, ABOUT 1.2KG / $2^3/4$LB
- 50G / 2OZ / 4 TBSP BUTTER
- 1 ONION
- HALF A CARROT
- 180ML / 6 FL OZ / $^3/4$ CUP VEGETABLE STOCK
- A FEW DRIED MUSHROOMS
- 50G / 2OZ / $^1/3$ CUP WHITE FLOUR
- 2 EGG YOLKS
- 1 LEMON

PREPARATION TIME: 1 HOUR

RINSE AND JOINT the rabbit. Coat with flour. Soak a handful of mushrooms in warm water. Wash the onion and carrot, chop them up finely and sauté gently in the melted butter in a saucepan. Add the rabbit, season with salt and pepper, cover with the lid and cook slowly for 30 minutes, dousing with a little stock, if needed. Now add the drained and dried mushrooms and continue cooking for another quarter-hour. Beat the yolks and dilute with a little stock. Take the pan off the heat and remove the rabbit pieces.

Pour in the egg yolks and amalgamate the sauce carefully with the pan juices. Return the rabbit to the saucepan and stir gently (off the heat) to allow it to absorb the flavours. Serve at once.

Coniglio ripieno

STUFFED RABBIT

- 1 BONED RABBIT (COMPLETE WITH LIVER AND HEART), ABOUT 1.2KG / 2 3/4LB
- 50G / 2OZ UNSMOKED BACON
- 80G / 3OZ BOILED SWISS CHARD
- 300G / 11OZ / 3 CUPS FRESH BREADCRUMB
- 2 CLOVES OF GARLIC
- 2 EGGS
- GRATED ZEST OF HALF A LEMON
- PARSLEY
- 125ML/ 4 FL OZ / 1/2 CUP MILK
- 125ML/ 4 FL OZ / 1/2 CUP WHITE WINE
- 180ML / 6 FL OZ / 3/4 CUP STOCK
- NUTMEG
- POWDERED CINNAMON
- OLIVE OIL

PREPARATION TIME: 1 HOUR 20 MINUTES

BUY THE RABBIT ALREADY boned.

Sauté the liver and heart with the diced bacon and a little oil in a skillet. Soak the breadcrumb in the milk, then squeeze it well and mix into the chopped Swiss chard, the eggs, the lemon zest, the garlic, the parsley, a little grated nutmeg, a pinch of cinnamon, salt and pepper.

Chop it all up in the food processor together with the sautéed offal. Stuff the rabbit and sew up with kitchen string.

Roast for an hour in the oven at 200°C (400°F, Gas Mark 6), basting alternatively with stock and with wine.

Costolette alla milanese

VEAL ESCALOPES, MILANESE STYLE

- 4 VEAL CUTLETS ON THE BONE (CUT FROM THE BEST END)
- 1 EGG
- DRY BREADCRUMBS
- 60G / 2OZ / 4 TBSP BUTTER
- OLIVE OIL

PREPARATION TIME: 1/4 HOUR

FLATTEN THE CUTLETS, dip them first into beaten egg and then into the dry breadcrumbs.

In a frying pan, melt the fat with a couple of tablespoons of oil (to "lighten" the butter and prevent it from blackening).

Brown the cutlets on both sides, two at a time, over a gentle heat.

Arrange on a serving dish and pour over some of the butter they fried in.

Garnish with wedges of lemon and accompany with fried matchstick potatoes.

Costolette alla valdostana

Veal Escalopes with Ham and Cheese

- 4 thick veal cutlets, about 170g / 7oz each
- 100g / 4oz fontina or slices of another processed cheese
- 2 slices of lean, cooked, unsmoked ham
- 50g / 2oz black truffle
- 60g / 2oz / 1/3 cup white flour
- dry breadcrumbs
- 2 eggs
- 100g / 4oz / 1/2 cup butter

Preparation time: 40 minutes

Cut a pocket in the cutlets by slitting them horizontally with a knife blade, but do not divide them in half. Open them out flat, lay a slice of cheese, half a slice of ham, a few slivers of truffle, salt and white pepper on one half and fold over the other.

Beat lightly on the opening so as to seal it, coat sparingly but evenly with flour, dip into the beaten egg and then into the dry breadcrumbs.

Slowly melt the butter in a frying pan (taking care that the butter does not blacken, especially while the meat is cooking, so the flame is to be regulated accordingly). Brown the cutlets slowly, turning them to brown on the other side, too.

Instead of veal cutlets, you may also use two chicken breasts divided in half and opened out like a book. The result is just as delicate.

Cotechino

Spiced Pork Sausage

- 1 *cotechino* of 800g / $1^3/4$lb

Preparation time: $3^1/4$ hours

Pork meat, rind and lard, all minced up fairly coarsely, flavoured with spices and stuffed inside a pig's stomach: such are the requirements for a good *cotechino*. With the name *zampone*, on the other hand, emphasis is placed on the container, consisting of the skin of the pig's fore trotter (with its cloven hoof, as you can see in the illustration on the right), stuffed with rump steak, pork rind, the ears, cheeks and cartilage, all chopped up roughly and aromatised with various spices, among which we have cinnamon, cloves, nutmeg and plenty of pepper. The *zampone* is soaked for a long time (10-12 hours) before cooking. Cut a cross between the cloven hooves and then follow the same procedure as for *cotechino* (including piercing it with a needle).

An exquisite dish, provided that the sausage is of prime quality and it is cooked properly. After pricking it a couple of times with a thick needle being careful not to tear the skin (I do not advise using a fork as there would be too many, too wide holes), wrap the sausage in a white cloth (or parchment) and tie it up. Plunge it into a saucepan of cold water and simmer for barely three hours. Leave it in the cooking water to cool for ten minutes. Drain it, unwrap and serve warm (indeed almost hot), sliced fairly thickly and accompanied by propitious continental lentils (a traditional dish for the New Year), white beans or some mashed potato. Some also like it cold, but that spoils its flavour and charm.

Fagianella tartufata
Pheasant with Truffles

- 1 pheasant hen of about 1kg / 2¼lb
- black truffle
- 100g / 4oz / ⅓ cup lard (or pork net)
- 50g / 2oz / 4 tbsp butter
- 50g / 2oz / 2 tbsp suet or cured ham fat
- a few sage leaves
- 2 bay leaves
- 2-3 juniper berries
- 1 clove, peppercorns
- 60ml / 2 fl oz / 4 tbsp each Marsala and cognac
- 125ml/ 4 fl oz / ½ cup stock
- olive oil

Preparation time: 1 hour, plus time for marinating and resting

The flesh of the female is tenderer, though the dish will also meet with success if males are used. After having "ripened", plucked and drawn the fowl (these are really jobs for the butcher), singe it, wipe it over and dry it. Clean the truffle with a toothbrush, rinse in cold water, then dry it. Scrape off the skin with a small knife, chop it up finely and add to the butter and suet, pounding it all in a mortar (or with a fork in a bowl) so as to get an even, lumpfree paste which you will set aside for a while. Cut the skinned truffle into wedges and place in another bowl to marinate with salt, peppercorns, the spices and herbs, cognac, Marsala and a tablespoon of oil. After an hour, add the marinated truffle to the truffle paste, together with the herbs (tear up the leaves) and 2-3 teaspoons of the marinade. Blend and keep the remaining liquid. Stuff the pheasant, truss with string, bard with lard, tie up the bird and brush with most of the marinade, making sure that a little is left over. Wrap a sheet of aluminium foil around it and allow to rest for a couple of hours. Transfer to a roasting tin and place in a hot oven for half-an-hour. Warm up the stock, pouring in the rest of the marinade. Remove the pheasant from the oven and take off the sheet of foil. Douse with the warm stock and return to the oven for barely a quarter-hour until nice and golden. Serve carved into about a dozen joints, masking with the gravy left in the roasting tin into which you will have amalgamated the filling.

The black truffle, which is the less prized and more economical variety, is more suited to preparations such as this because it only fully expresses its flavour and aroma when cooked.

On the other hand, as is well-known, the white truffle is only used raw and is grated or sliced finely over the food.

Fagiano ai sapori del bosco

PHEASANT WITH RED CURRANT SAUCE

- 4 PHEASANT BREASTS
- 10G / 1/4OZ / 1 TBSP JUNIPER BERRIES
- 50G / 2OZ / 4 TBSP RED CURRANTS
- 1 FULL SHERRY GLASS OF CHERRY BRANDY
- 70G / 3OZ / 1/4 CUP PLUS 2 TBSP BUTTER
- 1 SOUP LADLE / 4 FL OZ / 4 TBSP STOCK
- A FEW ROSEMARY LEAVES

PREPARATION TIME: 3/4 HOUR

DIVIDE THE BREASTS in half and coat with flour. Melt the butter in a frying pan and brown them well on both sides. When they have coloured a little, add the juniper berries, pour over the cherry brandy and allow to evaporate over fierce heat.

Turn down the flame, add the stock and cook over moderate heat for a good half-an-hour. When the bird has finished cooking, take it out and place on a serving dish. Put the red currants in the pan juices over a very low flame for some minutes to obtain a delicious sweet-and-sour sauce with which to mask the fowl.

Serve as you like; whole or carved up.

Fagiano al brandy

BRANDIED PHEASANT

- A PHEASANT, ABOUT 1.3KG / 3LB
- A SPRIG OF SAGE
- BUNCH OF CHIVES
- HALF A STOCK (BOUILLON) CUBE
- 1 SHERRY GLASS OF BRANDY
- OLIVE OIL

PREPARATION TIME: 40 MINUTES

BUY AN OVEN-READY pheasant, otherwise follow the instructions below. Joint and sauté in a flameproof casserole with 3-4 tablespoons of oil, sage, salt and pepper. Add the chopped chives and a glass of water in which you will have dissolved the stock cube. Cover the pan and cook slowly for half-an-hour. Remove the lid for the last ten minutes. Reduce the liquid and transfer the fowl onto a serving dish. Pour the brandy into the cooking juices and, if necessary, bind the sauce over gentle heat with a tablespoon of white flour. Serve the meat masked in its sauce.

IN ORDER TO PREPARE the pheasant for cooking, it must be deprived of the internal organs as soon as possible, or the flavour will be affected. It must ripen for three to four days (one is enough for farm-bred birds). Then pluck the fowl, cut off the claws and head, singe and (if a wild bird) rinse in water and vinegar.

Faraona alle olive

GUINEA FOWL WITH OLIVES

- 1 GUINEA FOWL, ABOUT 1.3KG / 3LB
- 1 ONION, 1 CARROT AND 1 STICK OF CELERY
- 4 RIPE TOMATOES
- A HANDFUL OF BLACK OLIVES
- 50G / 2OZ / 1/3 CUP WHITE FLOUR
- DRIED MUSHROOMS

PREPARATION TIME: 1 HOUR

CLEAN, WASH AND SINGE a guinea fowl. Cut into pieces and coat with flour. Rinse and chop the vegetables and sauté with 4 tablespoons of oil in a large saucepan, then add the guinea fowl and sauté for about ten minutes, turning it over so that it colours evenly on all sides and absorbs the flavours.

Lower the flame, adding salt, pepper, the roughly-chopped tomatoes, the stoned olives and the mushrooms, revived in warm water. Cook slowly for about forty minutes. The sauce should be thick and very flavoursome.

Faraona vignaiuola

GUINEA FOWL WITH GRAPES

- 1 GUINEA FOWL, ABOUT 1.3KG / 3LB
- 1 ONION
- 1 CARROT
- 1 STICK OF CELERY
- 150G / 5OZ SAUSAGE
- 1 STALE BREAD ROLL
- 50G /2OZ / 4 TBSP BUTTER
- 500G / 1LB 2OZ WHITE GRAPES
- 1 SHERRY GLASS MUSCAT WINE
- OLIVE OIL

PREPARATION TIME: 1 1/4 HOURS

BUY A CLEANED, drawn and singed guinea fowl. Wash the grapes and put the bread roll to soak in water. Slice half an onion and sauté it in a saucepan with half the butter, melted. Add the skinned and crumbled sausage and brown briefly. Mix into the squeezed breadcrumb, along with a few grapes, and season with salt and white pepper. Stuff the stomach cavity with this mixture. Wash and chop the celery, carrot and the other half onion and brown, together with the guinea fowl, in a roasting tin with 4 tablespoons of oil and the rest of the melted butter. Turn so that it browns all over. Douse with the wine and roast in the oven at 200°C (400°F, Gas Mark 6) for 45 minutes. Then add more grapes to the tin and return to the oven for another 10 minutes.

Transfer the guinea fowl to a serving dish, cut into pieces (the stuffing may be served apart or even discarded, as you prefer) and garnish with the remaining grapes. Sprinkle with the sieved cooking juices.

This delicate autumnal dish with its unmistakable flavour also works out well if you use a tender little pheasant hen instead of the guinea fowl (seeing that it has a drier flesh, you will have to pep it up with a little stock).

Fegatelli di maiale

TUSCAN PIG'S LIVER

- 600G / 1 1/4LB PIG'S LIVER
- 300G / 11OZ PORK NET (CAUL FAT)
- SLICED BREAD
- FENNEL SEEDS
- BAY LEAVES
- SAGE LEAVES
- OLIVE OIL

PREPARATION TIME: 20 MINUTES

CUT THE LIVER into fair-sized pieces, aromatising with salt, pepper and fennel seeds.

Plunge the pork net into warm water for a few minutes. Drain and dry and cut into squares big enough to wrap around the liver pieces completely, securing them with a wooden toothpick.

Impale the parcels on skewers, alternating a liver parcel with a sage leaf, a slice of bread and a bay leaf, continuing like this until all the ingredients have been used up.

Ideally, the skewers should be cooked in the heat of a charcoal fire, basting from time to time with just a little olive oil. But they are also very good if cooked on top of the stove in a roasting tin, browning them first in a very little oil and basting with a little stock during the brief cooking period.

Serve hot with a nice side-plate of black-eyed beans and the indispensable accompaniment of an excellent red wine.

Fegato alla veneziana

SAUTÉED CALF'S LIVER WITH ONIONS

- 700G / 1 1/2LB CALF'S LIVER
- 400G / 14OZ ONIONS
- 60ML / 2 FL OZ / 4 TBSP STOCK
- PARSLEY
- OLIVE OIL

PREPARATION TIME: 50 MINUTES

SLICE THE LIVER and also slice the onions into fine rings. Together with the finely chopped parsley, sweat them in 4 tablespoons of olive oil in a covered flameproof casserole dish over very low heat for about forty minutes.

Add the liver and the stock, season with salt and pepper and cook for five minutes.

Serve the liver hot with its tasty gravy, with slices of butter-fried bread and not forgetting some mashed potato.

Fettine alla pizzaiola

STEAK WITH A GARLIC, TOMATO AND OREGANO SAUCE

- 600-700G / 1 1/4-1 1/2LB SLICES OF BEEF
- 1 CLOVE OF GARLIC
- 500G / 1LB 2OZ RIPE FRESH OR TINNED (CANNED) TOMATOES
- OREGANO
- OLIVE OIL

PREPARATION TIME: 10-12 MINUTES

SAUTÉ THE GARLIC in a roasting pan with a tablespoon of oil, removing it when it starts to colour. Add the skinned, seeded and roughly-chopped tomatoes, season with a pinch of oregano, salt and pepper and reduce the sauce over fierce heat for 3-4 minutes. Beat the slices out a little, lay them flat in a little oil in a frying pan over a high flame and brown them quickly, turning them over. Season with salt and pepper and place them in the sauce so as to absorb the flavours, finishing off the cooking over a gentle heat.

HAVE THE SLICES cut from the rump where the meat is nice and tender. You may, if you like, add black olives or capers (or both) to enhance the sauce which you will smother the meat in at the moment of serving. Another delicious way of cooking the beef steaks consists in coating them with flour (once they have been flattened) and browning them on both sides in a little melted butter, at the last moment adding a sherry glass of Marsala. Allow the meat to absorb the flavours and serve covered in the sauce.

Filetto alla tartara

TARTAR STEAK

- 400G / 1LB FILLET OF BEEF (OR LEAN, TENDER RUMPSTEAK)
- 4 EGG YOLKS
- 100G / 4OZ / 1/2 CUP CAPERS, DRAINED
- 200G / 7OZ ANCHOVIES
- JUICE OF 1 LEMON
- 1 ONION
- GENEROUS BUNCH OF PARSLEY

PREPARATION TIME: 20 MINUTES

THE MEAT MUST be minced (ground) very finely, but on a low speed to prevent it from overheating and "cooking". It would be better to get the butcher to do this for you; at least he gets the blame if it does not turn out right! Rinse the anchovies and fillet them. Place some meat on each dinner plate, scooping out a hollow in the centre into which you will pop an egg yolk.

Season with salt and pepper (the latter must be white and freshly-ground). Dress with olive oil and lemon (which you will leave on the table, together with Worcestershire and Tabasco sauces, in case someone wishes to help himself to some more). Garnish all around with pieces of anchovy. On the side of the plate, tastefully arrange artistic mounds of chopped onion, parsley and capers for everyone to help themselves to.

Finish the plate off by delicately placing a leaf of parsley on each yolk (careful not to break them) and creating a pleasing effect. Carry through to the table.

Fritto misto

Mixed fry-up

- 4 lamb chops
- Quarter of a rabbit
- 300g / 11oz cubed pork
- 300g / 11oz cubed veal
- 2 sticks of cardoon
- 2 aubergines (eggplants)
- 2 potatoes
- 2 courgettes (zucchini)
- 3 green tomatoes
- 4 small globe artichokes
- 1 bulb Florence fennel
- A quarter of a cauliflower
- 1 onion
- 4 eggs
- A soup bowl of white flour
- A soup bowl of dry breadcrumbs
- 60ml / 2 fl oz / 4 tbsp beer
- Olive oil
- Vegetable or seed oil for frying

Preparation time: 3/4 hour

Blanch the cauliflower in boiling water and drain. Dip the meat pieces into 2 eggs, beaten up with a pinch of salt, then roll in the breadcrumbs and place on a piece of kitchen or yellow paper. Wash and trim the vegetables, eliminating the seeds and any tough or stringy parts. Cut the fennel and artichokes into wedges, the cauliflower into chunks and the other vegetables into slices. Beat the remaining eggs in a large bowl and stir in the beer, a tablespoon of olive oil and one of flour. Season with salt and pepper and blend. Dip the cauliflower, courgettes, onion and tomatoes into the batter. The other vegetables, on the other hand, only need coating with flour (but it is not a crime to use batter, if you prefer). Use a large, deep frying pan, preferably in iron, with plenty of very hot oil (which must not, however, "smoke", or the food will be carbonised). Begin with the meat, the red first, secondly the white and then turn to the vegetables (the cardoons and onion last of all). As soon as each piece is ready, scoop it out with a skimmer onto some kitchen paper to drain. Season. To keep it crisp, put in a hot oven which has been switched off. Serve on yellow paper with lemon wedges.

Galletto alla cacciatora

CHICKEN CACCIATORA

- 1 POUSSIN (OR CHICKEN), 800G - 1KG / 1 3/4 - 2 1/4LB
- 30G / 1OZ / 2 TBSP WHITE FLOUR
- 200G / 7OZ / 1 CUP TOMATO PULP
- 2 CLOVES OF GARLIC
- HALF AN ONION
- 60ML / 2 FL OZ / 4 TBSP WHITE WINE
- A SPRIG OF PARSLEY
- OLIVE OIL

PREPARATION TIME: 3/4 HOUR

THE POUSSIN, PLUCKED and drawn, must be singed and washed, then cut into pieces. Dry well, coat with flour, season with salt and sauté in plenty of olive oil.

Fry the chopped onion in a saucepan with 4 tablespoons of oil and brown the chicken. Pour the wine over, allow to evaporate and add the tomato, the garlic in pieces, the chopped parsley and some ground pepper.

Bring to the boil and simmer over low heat for half-an-hour, without stirring, but shaking the pan from time to time.

THE FLESH OF POUSSINS, tastier and firmer than chicken flesh, is better indicated for this and other preparations of a vigorous, hearty flavour. It is, of course, imperative that the fowl be quite young! But a nice chicken which has been reared properly will certainly cut a fine figure.

Galletto in porchetta

ROAST POUSSIN WITH POTATO STUFFING

- 1 POUSSIN OF 800G - 1KG / 1 3/4 - 2 1/4LB
- 2 CLOVES OF GARLIC
- 50G / 2OZ FENNEL SEEDS
- 200G / 7OZ POTATOES
- A TWIG OF ROSEMARY
- A SPRIG OF SAGE
- OLIVE OIL

PREPARATION TIME: 1 1/4 HOURS

THE DENOMINATION *GALLETTO IN PORCHETTA* which would appear to evoke beasts from Grimm's Fables, alludes to the classic mixture traditionally used to aromatise roast suckling pig, i.e. chopped garlic, rosemary and sage, with the aroma of wild fennel. Truly Mediterranean flavours.

THE POUSSIN, plucked and drawn, must be singed, washed and dried. Peel and dice the potatoes. Sauté in a frying pan with 4 tablespoons of oil the fennel seeds, a little salt and some pepper for 5 minutes. In the meantime, season the chicken with salt and pepper and score the flesh all over, inserting the chopped garlic, sage and rosemary in the slits. Remove the potatoes from the heat, stuff the poussin and place in an oven dish into which you will pour the oil left in the frying pan. Bake the poussin in the oven at 200°C (350°F, Gas Mark 6) for an hour. Serve the poussin divided into quarters (as in the illustration). Keep the potato stuffing well in view.

Involtini di cavolo

STUFFED CABBAGE LEAVES

- 8 LARGE SAVOY CABBAGE LEAVES
- 400G / 14OZ MINCED (GROUND) BEEF
- 1 CLOVE OF GARLIC
- A SPRIG OF PARSLEY
- 1 HARD-BOILED EGG
- A SLICE OF FONTINA CHEESE, 1/4IN THICK (OR SOME PROCESSED CHEESE)
- 300G / 11OZ / $1^1/_2$ CUPS PURÈED TOMATOES (OPTIONAL)
- 90ML / 3 FL OZ / 6 TBSP VEGETABLE STOCK
- OLIVE OIL

PREPARATION TIME: 50 MINUTES

THE LEAVES must be wholesome, large and green. Blanch in salted water, drain and dry on a tea towel, then cut them into approximately rectangular shapes. Mix the meat with the finely-chopped garlic, parsley and egg, the diced cheese and some salt and pepper in a bowl. Put a portion of the stuffing on each leaf, roll it up and tie up the roulades with some kitchen string. Heat 4 tablespoons of oil, mixed in with the stock, in a flame-proof casserole dish, add the roulades, cover and cook over a low flame for half-an-hour.

Then remove the lid, reduce the excess juices and take to the table, masked in the sauce. If your good taste for original wrappings does not let you appreciate a cylindrical shape and if you are intrigued by the addition of tomato, then I suggest you follow the procedure described in *The Complete Illustrated Tuscan Cookery Book* in this series. Without resorting to the use of string, wrap up the cabbage parcels to form a kind of suitcase (as in the illustration at the top); I can assure you that they will stay closed if pressed together well. Brown them gently in oil, add the purèed tomatoes and continue cooking over gentle heat.

With or without tomato, this is a dish fit for a king!

Involtini di manzo al vino

BEEF OLIVES IN WINE

- 4 LARGE SLICES OF BEEF
- KNOB OF BUTTER
- 150G / 5OZ CHICKEN LIVERS
- 2 ANCHOVIES
- SAGE
- 125ML/ 4 FL OZ / 1/2 CUP MEAT STOCK
- 60ML / 2 FL OZ / 4 TBSP RED WINE
- 4 THIN RASHERS OF UNSMOKED BACON
- OLIVE OIL

PREPARATION TIME: ABOUT 1 HOUR

WASH THE CHICKEN LIVERS, discarding the gall bladders. Sauté lightly in the butter. Add the boned anchovies divided into fillets. Season with salt and pepper and douse with the stock. Reduce very slowly. Remove from the heat and chop it all up very finely. Pound the meat slices out and cut them in half. Place a little of the chicken liver stuffing and a sage leaf on each slice, roll up tightly and wrap half a rasher of bacon around the outside, fixing it with a wooden toothpick. Heat 3-4 tablespoons of oil in a flameproof casserole dish and place the beef olives in it to brown. Douse with the wine and lower the flame. Cook them, partially covered, for about ten minutes. Take off the lid, add a little stock, if necessary, and reduce the sauce for another ten minutes.

Involtini in salsa

BEEF OLIVES WITH TOMATO SAUCE

- 4 LARGE SLICES OF BEEF
- 100G / 1/4LB COOKED FRESH HAM IN ONE PIECE
- 1 CLOVE OF GARLIC
- A SPRIG OF PARSLEY
- GRATED PARMESAN
- 1 THICK RASHER OF UNSMOKED SLAB BACON
- 60ML / 2 FL OZ / 4 TBSP WHITE WINE
- 2-3 RIPE TOMATOES
- HALF AN ONION
- HALF A CARROT
- HALF A STICK OF CELERY
- OLIVE OIL

PREPARATION TIME: 1 HOUR

DICE THE HAM, mix in the chopped garlic and parsley, add the grated cheese, a little salt and a pinch of pepper.

Pound out the beef slices and divide them in half. Place some filling on each one, roll them up and fix with the usual toothpicks (but remember to remove them before serving the dish. The parcels will stay rolled up).

Heat 3-4 tablespoons of oil in a flame-proof casserole dish and sear the roulades in it.

Douse with the white wine and allow to evaporate. Take them out when they are evenly browned all over.

Wash the onion, carrot and celery and chop them up finely. Place in the pan with the diced bacon and sauté slowly. Add the tomatoes in pieces and reduce for 6-7 minutes.

Now add the beef olives and allow them to absorb the flavours of the sauce over gentle heat for half-an-hour.

Lepre in salmì

SALMI OF HARE

TO SERVE 6 PEOPLE
- 1 YOUNG HARE OF ABOUT 1.8-2KG (4-4½LB)
- 50G / 2OZ / 4 TBSP LARD
- 60ML / 2 FL OZ / 4 TBSP COGNAC
- ½L / 1PT / 2 CUPS STOCK
- 1 BOUILLON CUBE
- 1 ONION, 1 CARROT, 1 SPRING ONION (SHALLOT)
- A SPRIG OF THYME
- 1 BAY LEAF
- PARSLEY
- PEPPERCORNS
- 60ML / 2 FL OZ / 4 TBSP DRY WHITE WINE
- DRIED *BOLETUS EDULIS* MUSHROOMS
- 60G / 2OZ / 4 TBSP BUTTER
- OLIVE OIL

PREPARATION TIME: 1½ HOURS

FOR THIS RECIPE, the hare should be about a year old. A salmi preparation, a classic which risks passing into oblivion, is suitable for any type of game, furred or feathered (including domestic animals).

THE HARE MUST BE LEFT to ripen, skinned, drawn and the head and paws discarded (this operation is the responsibility of the butcher). Wash, dry and bard it with the lard (though you may use olive oil) and place it in the oven for twenty minutes, being careful that it does not dry out. Joint it, separating the spine and the ribs on the breast from the fleshy parts. Pour the cognac into a flameproof casserole (you should flame it) together with 2-3 tablespoons of boiling stock made with a crumb from the stock cube. Throw in the hare joints, cover and keep warm over a very low flame for all the time necessary to get the sauce ready. Put the chopped onion, carrot, celery and the herbs to flavour in 2 tablespoons of olive oil. Pour on the white wine and, before it completely evaporates, add the remaining stock with the rest of the stock cube. Pound the hare's spinal cord and ribs in a mortar and cook in the casserole for barely a quarter-hour. Sieve the sauce finely, pressing it through with a wooden spoon, then allow to thicken for another ten minutes with the addition of a little flour and a knob of butter. Remove from the heat, strain through the sieve once more, add the remaining butter in flakes and give it a velvety finish by stirring carefully. Pour the sauce into the casserole with the hare and allow the flavours to mingle for a few minutes without boiling, adding the mushrooms, soaked, dried and revived in the butter. Serve the hare hot (but not boiling), masked in its sauce.

Lingua in agrodolce

TONGUE IN A SWEET AND SOUR SAUCE

- 1 OX TONGUE
- TOMATO CONCENTRATE (PASTE)
- 20G / ¾OZ / 1 TBSP BITTER COCOA
- 20G / ¾OZ / 2 TBSP EACH CANDIED CITRON AND SULTANAS (WHITE RAISINS)
- 20G / ¾OZ / 3 TBSP PINE-NUTS
- 50G / 2OZ / ¼ CUP GRANULATED SUGAR
- 60 ML / 2 FL OZ / 4 TBSP VINEGAR
- 1 ONION, OLIVE OIL

PREPARATION TIME: 70 MINUTES

SCALD THE TONGUE and skin it while still hot. Boil in salted water for 20 minutes and slice it. Sauté the finely-sliced onion in a saucepan with 4 tablespoons of oil. Add the tongue. Add 2 tablespoons of tomato concentrate and 180 ml (6fl oz/¾ cup) of stock and cook over a gentle flame for 20 minutes. Dissolve the sugar in the vinegar and pour onto the tongue, together with the pine-nuts, sultanas, diced candied citron-peel and the cocoa. Stir well and bring back to the boil. Cook for another 20 minutes over gentle heat and serve.

Lingua in salsa di lattuga

TONGUE IN LETTUCE SAUCE

- 1 CALF'S TONGUE
- 1 STICK OF CELERY
- 1 CARROT
- 1 ONION
- 2 PARSLEY STALKS
- 5 PEPPERCORNS
- 1 BAY LEAF

FOR THE SAUCE:
- 100G / 4OZ / 1 CUP PINE-NUTS
- 4 TBSP RED WINE VINEGAR
- 2 ANCHOVIES
- 50G / 2OZ BLACK TRUFFLE
- 1 CLOVE OF GARLIC
- 400G / 14OZ LETTUCE
- 1 AUBERGINE (EGGPLANT)
- OLIVE OIL

PREPARATION TIME: $2^1/_2$ HOURS

BEAR THIS EXTREMELY delicate and original cold dish to the table with due deference. It is the ideal complement for a summer's dish of pasta or rice, but it is also perfect to start a dinner off or in fine display at the centre of the buffet table.

COOK THE TONGUE for an hour-and-a-half in boiling, lightly-salted water to which all the ingredients in the first part of the list have been added. Skin it and cool. Sauté the rinsed and filleted anchovies, the chopped garlic and the trimmed and cleaned truffle, sliced finely, in 3 tablespoons of oil. Blanch the lettuce and allow to cool, then blend in the food processor with the pine-nuts, vinegar and the anchovy and truffle sauce. If the outcome is a little too thick, add a little water. Clean, trim and slice the aubergine and toast in a non-stick frying pan until golden on both sides. Arrange the aubergine slices in a circle around the edge of the serving dish. Put the sliced tongue at the centre, masked with the sauce.

Maiale ai marroni

PORK WITH CHESTNUTS

- 1KG / 2 1/4LB PORK LOIN, BONED
- 350G / 12OZ CHESTNUTS
- 50G / 2OZ FENNEL SEEDS
- 2 SOUP LADLES / 8 FL OZ / 1/2 CUP STOCK
- 125ML/ 4 FL OZ / 1/2 CUP MILK
- 1 SHERRY GLASS OF BRANDY
- 1 ONION
- 1 CARROT
- 1 STICK OF CELERY
- SAGE AND ROSEMARY LEAVES
- OLIVE OIL

PREPARATION TIME: 2 HOURS

TIE UP THE MEAT, prick it all over, insert sage and rosemary into the holes and rub *gros sel* and pepper over the surface. Heat 4 tablespoons of oil in a saucepan and sear the meat evenly on all sides in it. Pour the brandy over and allow to evaporate. Add the vegetables in pieces and the fennel seeds.

In the meanwhile, make slits in the chestnut shells and put them in cold water. Bring to the boil for ten minutes. Shell the nuts and remove the skins as well (but leave aside a dozen whole chestnuts as decoration). Add to the meat together with the milk and stock and cook the pork (an hour-and-a-half over gentle heat).

Now remove it from the pan, sieve the sauce and return to the heat to thicken, if necessary with the help of a little flour dissolved in water. Serve the carved loin of pork liberally covered in sauce and garnish with whole chestnuts. Serve oven-glazed vegetables as an accompaniment.

Maiale farcito in crosta

STUFFED PORK IN A CRUST

- 800G / 1 3/4LB PORK LOIN, BONED
- 200G / 7OZ CHICKEN BREASTS
- 250G / 9OZ PÂTE BRISÉE
- 2 CHICKEN LIVERS
- 250ML / 8 FL OZ / 1 CUP WHITE WINE
- 2 ONIONS
- 2 TBSP GRATED PARMESAN
- 2 SOUP LADLES / 8 FL OZ / 1/2 CUP STOCK
- 2 EGGS
- 10 CLOVES
- CINNAMON
- SAGE AND ROSEMARY LEAVES
- 125ML/ 4 FL OZ / 1/2 CUP MILK
- 1 STALE BREAD ROLL
- 1 CARROT
- 1 STICK OF CELERY
- OLIVE OIL

PREPARATION TIME: 2 HOURS

FOR THE BENEFIT of those few who are not aware of the fact and as you will be able to verify in the chapter on desserts, pâte brisée, the cousin of short pastry (though a good deal speedier) consists in two parts of flour to one of butter and cold water. Neither savoury nor sweet, it is the ideal packaging for timbales and refined "crusts" such as this one. Just cut into it and the exquisite stuffed loin will be revealed behind a cloud of delicate aromas, sending bystanders (and perhaps the tenants on the floor above) into ecstasy.

SOAK THE BREAD ROLL in the milk, mince (grind) the chicken breasts, the chicken livers and an onion. Add the egg, the Parmesan cheese, the well-squeezed bread, salt and pepper. Mix well. Cut a sizeable "pocket" in the middle of the loin with a sharp knife, fill it with the stuffing and sew up the opening with kitchen string. Score the meat all over, placing a clove and a little chopped sage and rosemary in the slits.

Season with salt and pepper. Sear the meat all over in 4 tablespoons of oil in a saucepan. Pour the wine over and allow to evaporate over fierce heat.

Now add a vegetable mirepoix (blanched onion, carrot and celery chopped up in the food processor) and the stock. Transfer the pork to a roasting pan, and roast for about an hour in a medium oven, turning it over from time to time and basting with its gravy. Remove from the pan and allow to rest on a rack to drain the fat away properly.

Meanwhile, roll out the pastry with a rolling pin. Place the well-dried loin of pork on it and wrap the pastry around it, overlapping the edges on one side.

Brush the pastry with egg and bake in the oven at 200°C (400°F, Gas Mark 6) for about 20 minutes until the crust has turned an even gold colour.

Ossobuco classico e in salsa

BRAISED VEAL SHANKS IN "GREMOLADA" AND IN TOMATO SAUCE

- 4 PIECES OF VEAL SHIN
- 50G / 2OZ / 4 TBSP BUTTER
- 40G / 1 1/2OZ / 1/4 CUP FLOUR
- 60ML / 2 FL OZ / 4 TBSP DRY WHITE WINE

FOR THE "GREMOLADA":
- A SPRIG OF PARSLEY
- A LITTLE LEMON ZEST
- 1 CLOVE OF GARLIC
- 1 ANCHOVY FILLET

PREPARATION TIME: 1 1/2 HOURS

A TASTY ALTERNATIVE to the *gremolada*? Home-made tomato sauce (as in the illustration on the right). Make a mirepoix of finely chopped herbs, adding a little lemon and orange peel and frying it all in a little olive oil. Add 200g (7oz or 1 cup) purèed tomatoes. Blend the flavours and pour the sauce into the pan with the *ossi buchi* the moment the wine has evaporated. Simmer gently for an hour and serve.

A CLASSIC DISH of Milanese cuisine (together with the risotto, that it goes with so well), it willingly submits itself to a little flavourful experimentation. Coat the *ossi buchi* with flour on both sides and brown in the melted butter in a saucepan. Season with salt and pepper. When they are coloured on one side, turn them over and repeat the procedure on the other side until they are evenly browned. Pour the wine over and allow to evaporate. Then cover and continue cooking over a very moderate heat for a good hour, adding a little water if it looks like drying up.

Meanwhile, get the *gremolada* ready; an indispensable complement to an authentic traditional preparation. Finely chop the parsley, garlic, lemon zest (without the white pith) and half a filleted anchovy. Remove the *ossi buchi* from the pan, add the chopped herbs to the meat juices (which have been kept liquid enough to make the gravy) and blend over very gentle heat. Return the meat to the pan, allow it to absorb the flavours briefly on both sides and serve hot, well-doused with the delicious sauce.

Ossobuco di tacchino

TURKEY SHANKS

- 8 PIECES OF TURKEY SHIN (ABOUT 1KG / 2 1/4LB)
- A SPRIG OF PARSLEY
- 60ML / 2 FL OZ / 4 TBSP DRY WHITE WINE
- 125ML/ 4 FL OZ / 1/2 CUP STOCK
- OLIVE OIL

VEGETABLE SIDE-PLATE:
- 2 COURGETTES (ZUCCHINI)
- 2 CARROTS
- 1 POTATO
- 100G / 4OZ / 1/2 CUP BROWN RICE
- A SPRIG OF SAGE
- OLIVE OIL

PREPARATION TIME: ABOUT 3/4 HOUR

SNIP THE EDGES of the *ossi buchi* so that they do not curl up when they shrink. Coat with flour and brown on both sides in 5 tablespoons of oil. Remove and place on a plate. Drain the oil from the frying pan and pour in the wine instead. Return the *ossi buchi* to the pan and continue cooking over moderate heat for 15-20 minutes, adding the stock a little at a time. Season with salt and pepper. Finally, dust with chopped parsley. Arrange the *ossi buchi* on a serving dish and pour over the gravy from the pan diluted with a little water. How can this appetising and balanced dish (turkey *ossi buchi* are less fatty than veal ones, but just as tasty) be transformed into a full meal? Have ready the rice, boiled for forty minutes. Clean and trim the vegetables, cut into strips and lozenges. Blanch in the pan with a little oil and the sage. Add the drained rice and sauté everything for a few minutes. Place the vegetables on the serving dish, next to the turkey. After this, pass directly onto the sweet course.

Pancetta di maiale "in porchetta"

ROAST JOINT OF BACON

TO SERVE 6 *PEOPLE*

- 3KG / 6¾LB BELLY OF PORK
- 1 CARROT
- 2 STICKS OF CELERY
- HALF AN ONION
- ROSEMARY
- SAGE
- 2 HOT RED PEPPERS
- JUNIPER BERRIES
- OLIVE OIL

PREPARATION TIME: 3 HOURS

GET THE BUTCHER TO BONE THE PORK. Chop up the onion, carrot and celery finely with the herbs and spread over the laid-out meat.

Roll it up on itself tightly and bind with kitchen string at one-inch intervals. Heat 6 tablespoons of oil in a roasting pan and sear the roll on the top of the stove, turning it over from time to time so that it takes on a nice golden brown hue. Roast in the oven at 250°C (500°F, Gas Mark 10) for two-and-a-half hours, until there is a nice crust of crackling. An alternative to whole suckling-pig, excellent served at a dinner party, it is also suitable for cold snacks and buffets.

Piccione arrosto

ROAST PIGEON

- 2 PIGEONS
- 2 THIN UNSMOKED BACON RASHERS
- 1 CLOVE OF GARLIC
- A SPRIG OF SAGE
- A BAY LEAF
- KNOB OF BUTTER
- A FISTFUL OF BREADCRUMB
- 60ML / 2 FL OZ / 4 TBSP WHITE WINE
- OLIVE OIL

PREPARATION TIME: 3/4 HOUR (PLUS THE TIME FOR PLUCKING AND PREPARING THE PIGEONS)

SOAK THE BREAD in the wine. Pluck the pigeons, open them out and draw them, reserving the livers and hearts. Discard the heads and claws and singe the birds. Sauté the garlic, sage and bay leaf in the melted butter in a skillet and add the livers and hearts, browning them briefly. Chop it all up and add to the squeezed bread (but do not throw out the wine). Stuff the pigeons' stomachs and sew over the ends with kitchen string. Wrap each bird in a rasher of bacon, tying it up with string. Roast in a slightly-oiled roasting tin in a hot oven for half-an-hour. Check them half-way through the cooking time and baste with a little wine. At the moment of serving, cut each pigeon into two, discard the stuffing, douse the inside with the gravy and serve each diner with half a fragrant pigeon and a nice vegetable side-plate of Swiss chard with lemon or baked new potatoes.

Pollo alla diavola

GRILLED (BROILED) CHICKEN

- 1 CHICKEN OF ABOUT 1.2KG / 2 3/4LB
- A SPRIG OF SAGE
- 1 LEMON
- OLIVE OIL

PREPARATION TIME: 3/4 HOUR

WASH AND CLEAN the chicken and open it out with a clean cut down the cartilage of the breastbone. Beat it out with a wooden mallet and dust liberally, inside and out (but especially inside), with salt and pepper and finely-chopped sage. When the charcoal fire is ready (red hot but with no flame), lay the chicken on the grating and grill (broil) for a quarter-hour each side, basting frequently with a brush dipped in olive oil which has been mixed with lemon juice.

THE SO-CALLED "Chicken under a brick" is a variant contemplating the use of a clay brick which is generally circular in shape and which flattens out the chicken, enhanced with the aromas of garlic and rosemary. Cooking times do not change as neither does the need to baste the flesh frequently. In both cases, grilling (broiling) is required, which in practice means a fire lit outside the house.

The oven grill attachment can also be exploited, however.

Pollo allo zenzero

GINGER CHICKEN

- 1 CHICKEN OF ABOUT 1KG / $2^1/4$LB
- 80G / 3OZ / $^1/4$ CUP PLUS 2 TBSP MARGARINE
- 2 EGG YOLKS
- 1 TBSP WHITE FLOUR
- 125ML/ 4 FL OZ / $^1/2$ CUP MILK
- 125ML/ 4 FL OZ / $^1/2$ CUP SINGLE CREAM
- 1 TSP GROUND GINGER
- 1 TIN (CAN) SWEETCORN
- 50G / 2OZ / $^2/3$ CUP TOASTED ALMONDS

PREPARATION TIME: $1^1/4$ HOURS

THIS DISH HAS A RATHER oriental air about it owing to the presence of the ginger. This spice is the underground stem of the Zingiber plant, which, as can be seen in the illustration, has a pale flesh and a pungent aroma, used everywhere in oriental gastronomy, both in the fresh or powdered form, to exalt the flavours of dishes (and not to make them piquant).

Ginger has carminative and digestive properties to complement its distinctive flavour.

DIVIDE THE CLEANED and singed chicken into quarters. Melt half the margarine in a flameproof oven dish and sear the chicken for ten minutes, turning it to brown on all sides.

Dilute the ginger in the milk, melt the rest of the margarine, blend in the flour and stir in the milk to obtain a thick sauce. Coat the chicken with it and sprinkle the sweetcorn over. Beat the egg yolks with the cream, salt and pepper and pour onto the fowl. Bake in the oven at 200°C (400°F, Gas Mark 6) for 45 minutes. Garnish with coarsely-chopped almonds and serve.

Pollo in tegame

CHICKEN CASSEROLE

- 1 CHICKEN OF ABOUT 1KG / $2^1/_4$LB
- 1 SLICE CF COOKED, UN-SMOKED HAM
- 1 CLOVE OF GARLIC
- PINCH OF CHIVES, MARJORAM
- 60ML / 2 FL OZ / 4 TBSP RED WINE
- 4 RIPE TOMATOES (OR PUREED TOMATOES)
- 90ML / 3 FL OZ / $^1/_4$ CUP + 2 TBSP STOCK

PREPARATION TIME: $^3/_4$ HOUR

CLEAN, RINSE AND SINGE the chicken. Joint it and sauté the pieces in a saucepan where the ham has been gently sweated in 3-4 tablespoons of oil.

Season with salt and pepper. When the chicken is evenly browned all over, add the chopped garlic, the rinsed and chopped herbs and the red wine, evaporating it over a fierce flame.

Add the washed, seeded and roughly-chopped tomatoes and lower the flame. Cook for twenty minutes, only if necessary moistening with a little stock (vegetable stock, which does not impart too strong a flavour).

Serve at once in the nice, thick sauce.

Polpette

CROQUETTES

- 400G / 14OZ BOILED BEEF
- 2 EGGS
- A SPRIG OF PARSLEY
- 2 CLOVES OF GARLIC
- 1 BOILED POTATO
- A HANDFUL OF BREADCRUMB
- 180ML / 6 FL OZ / $^3/_4$ CUP MILK
- DRIED BREADCRUMBS
- OIL FOR FRYING

PREPARATION TIME: $^1/_2$ HOUR

SOAK THE BREADCRUMB in the milk (or in stock, if you prefer). Mince (Ground) the boiled beef (meat balls came about to use up left-overs; you could also replace it with raw minced (ground) meat, but, honestly…). Place in a bowl with the squeezed breadcrumb, the potato, the eggs, the chopped parsley and garlic, salt and pepper. Combine everything together well in your fingers and roll the mixture into balls, flattening them a little. Coat in the dry breadcrumbs. Deep fry a few at a time in plenty of oil in a deep frying pan, drain and serve them nice and crisp with lemon wedges. Delicious! They can be flavoured for five minutes in some tomato sauce in a casserole, made by simmering 400g (14oz /2 cups) tomato pulp with a clove of garlic and oil.

Polpettone

Meat Roll

- 400g / 14oz minced (ground) beef
- a thick slice of mortadella with pistachios, about 50g / 2oz
- 2 eggs
- a handful of breadcrumb
- 350ml / $^3/_4$pt / $1^1/_2$ cups stock
- 3 tbsp flour
- dry breadcrumbs
- 60ml / 2 fl oz / 4 tbsp red wine
- olive oil

Preparation time: 50 minutes

You may replace the minced (ground) beef by boiled beef chopped up; in actual fact, half and half would be the utmost in flavour. The *polpettone* is also excellent if 400g (14oz or 2 cups) puréed tomato is added once the surface has been seared and the sauce then reduced. It is delicious simmered and served with mayonnaise. The cookery expert, Pellegrino Artusi, relished it with lemon-and-egg sauce: when cooked, turn off the heat and add one whole egg and a yolk, beaten with half a squeezed lemon.

Soak the breadcrumb in the stock. Dice the mortadella and mix with the meat, the eggs, the squeezed breadcrumb (but keep the stock it soaked in), salt and pepper. Combine the mixture in your hands and shape into a dumpy sausage. Coat it lightly in flour and roll in the dry breadcrumbs. Sear in 6 tablespoons of oil, turning it over to brown on all sides. Pour over the wine and evaporate. Cook for about half-an-hour over a moderate flame, diluting the gravy with a little stock, if needed.

Allow the *polpettone* to cool somewhat before slicing it up and serving it masked in its gravy.

Quaglie alla grappa

QUAILS COOKED IN GRAPPA

- 4 QUAILS
- 4 UNSMOKED BACON RASHERS
- A HANDFUL OF JUNIPER BERRIES
- A TWIG OF ROSEMARY
- A SPRIG OF SAGE
- 60ML / 2 FL OZ / 4 TBSP GRAPPA (ITALIAN EAU DE VIE)
- A KNOB OF BUTTER
- 180ML / 6 FL OZ / 12TBSP/ 3/4 CUP VEGETABLE STOCK
- OLIVE OIL

PREPARATION TIME: 3/4 HOUR

IF THE QUAILS are not bought oven-ready, you will need to pluck, draw, clean and singe them as usual.

Chop up the rosemary and sage together, along with a seasoning of salt and pepper and put a large pinch in the stomach cavity of the fowl.

Lay a rasher of bacon across each breast securing it with kitchen string. Sear the quails in a frying pan with 4 tablespoons of oil and the melted butter for a good quarter-hour, turning the birds on all sides. When they have coloured a little, moisten with the *eau-de-vie* and flame them off the heat (remember that spirits are more easily ignitable when hot).

Add a twig of rosemary and the juniper berries, cover the pan and cook very slowly, if necessary basting with some stock, for another 25 minutes.

Mask the quails with the gravy and serve with plain boiled rice.

Rognoni in gratella

GRILLED (BROILED) KIDNEYS

- 2 OX KIDNEYS
- OLIVE OIL
- JUICE OF A LEMON
- A SPRIG OF PARSLEY

PREPARATION TIME: ABOUT 1/4 HOUR, PLUS 1 1/2 HOURS FOR SOAKING AND MARINATING

BEFORE COOKING THEM, the kidneys must be immersed for half-an-hour in cold, running water, then trimmed of fat and the central core. Cut them in half lengthways and divide again into two slices. Leave them for about an hour on a plate with a trickle of oil and a seasoning of salt and pepper.

Stoke up a charcoal fire or heat the grill attachment and cook on both sides over moderate heat (a few minutes are enough). Serve very hot, with a sprinkling of lemon juice and a dusting of chopped parsley.

Rognoni trifolati

SAUTÉED KIDNEYS

- 2-3 CALF'S KIDNEYS
- WHITE FLOUR
- GARLIC AND PARSLEY
- JUICE OF HALF A LEMON
- 1 ANCHOVY FILLET
- KNOB OF BUTTER
- OLIVE OIL

PREPARATION TIME: 15 MINUTES, PLUS SOAKING TIME

WASH AND TRIM the kidneys as described in the recipe above. Slice them finely. Sweat the garlic in 4 tablespoons of oil in a frying pan, removing it when it starts to colour. Add the kidney pieces, lightly coated in flour, and raise the flame immediately to sear the meat and prevent it from "weeping". Add the filleted anchovies, season with salt and pepper, shake the pan a couple of times and turn off the heat. Kidneys need very little cooking, in fact, otherwise they will harden. Add the butter, sprinkle with lemon juice, dust with parsley, stir carefully and serve them tantalisingly fragrant.

Salsicce e fagioli

SAUSAGES AND BEANS

- 400G / 14OZ DRY, WHITE BEANS
- 300G / 11OZ RIPE FRESH OR TINNED (CANNED) TOMATOES
- 5 CLOVES OF GARLIC
- A SPRIG OF SAGE
- 4-5 FRESH SAUSAGES
- PEPPERCORNS
- OLIVE OIL

PREPARATION TIME: 1 1/2 HOURS, PLUS SOAKING TIME

SOAK THE BEANS for two hours. Cook them over a low heat for three quarters-of-an-hour in a covered saucepan with a clove of garlic, some sage and a few drops of oil. Drain them while still firm to the tooth. Sweat 4 cloves of garlic with a sage leaf or two in a saucepan with 5-6 tablespoons of oil, add the tomato, salt and pepper and cook for 10 minutes. Add the beans, stir and cook over a low flame for a quarter-hour, then add the sausages, pricked over. Cook another 10 minutes.

Saltimbocca alla Romana

Veal with Ham and Sage

- 400g / 14oz veal cut into 8 thin slices
- 8 slices of prosciutto, totalling about 80g / 3oz
- 8 sage leaves
- 50g / 2oz / 4 tbsp butter

Preparation time: 15 minutes

Take note: *saltimbocca* are not veal birds, so they do not get rolled up. Instead, having spread out and pounded the slices of veal, lay a slice of ham and a sage leaf on each one, securing them with toothpicks.

Melt the butter in a flameproof casserole and cook the barely-salted (remember there is the ham!) and peppered *saltimbocca* in it over a high flame. Turn them over as soon as they have coloured, completing the cooking quickly on the other side.

Serve them very hot, masked with the cooking juices diluted in a spoonful of water and thickened with a pinch of flour.

Why veal necessarily and not beef? Because the rapid cooking over a high flame would make any meat which was not quite tender uneatable. Then, of course, the flavour is provided by the ham. After all, *saltimbocca* do not require much more time and care than a hamburger. But if you choose the former, you will finally see regard and consideration in your family's eyes…

Scottiglia

Mixed Meat Stew

- 200g / 7oz stewing lamb
- 200g / 7oz chicken
- 200g / 7oz duck
- 200g / 7oz rabbit meat
- 1 stick of celery
- 1 onion
- 1 carrot
- tinned (canned) tomatoes
- 2 tbsp white flour
- 1 clove of garlic
- sage and rosemary
- hot red pepper
- olive oil

Preparation time: 40 minutes

Trim the meat and cut into chunks. Roll in flour and brown in 3-4 tablespoons of oil with a clove of garlic and a sprig of rosemary. Sauté the chopped onion, carrot and celery in a little oil in a roasting tin.

Drain the oil off the meat and transfer the pieces to the roasting tin with the vegetables. Add the tomatoes, salt, white pepper, hot red pepper and sage. Cover and stew in the oven at 220°C (425°F, Gas Mark 7) for 25 minutes. Serve the *scottiglia* hot, accompanying it with pieces of grilled (broiled) polenta.

What better solution is there to use up meat left-overs which would otherwise be difficult to utilise with results satisfactory to the palate?

A wine which goes very well with this red and white "meat cacciucco" and which is typical of the district around Arezzo and the Casentino area in Tuscany, especially (but with some variations it is also found in the Maremma district) is a Cabernet di Montalcino.

Spezzatino con le patate

Beef Stew with Potatoes

- 600g / 1 1/4lb stewing steak
- 5-6 ripe tomatoes
- 500g / 1lb 2oz potatoes
- 1 onion
- 1 carrot
- 1 stick of celery
- 125ml/ 4 fl oz / 1/2 cup red wine
- A few sage leaves
- Olive oil

Preparation time: 2 hours 20 minutes

Cut the stewing steak into fair-sized chunks. Wash the aromatic vegetables and herb, chop them finely and fry gently in a saucepan with 4-5 tablespoons of oil. Add the steak and brown over fierce heat. Pour in the wine and allow to evaporate. Lower the flame, season with salt and pepper and add the rinsed and roughly-chopped tomatoes. Cook with the lid on for at least a couple of hours over a low flame, adding a little warm water if the meat should show signs of drying out. About twenty minutes before the end of the cooking time, add the peeled potatoes cut into chunks and stir. Do not make the mistake of making this stew with veal, thinking that it would be more delicate and tenderer. First and foremost, without the well-defined flavour of beef, you will not get a real stew, but a rather insipid mush. In the same way, the long, gentle cooking will make the stewing steak tender enough and also suitably nourishing.

Spiedini delicati

Spit Roast of White Meats

- 200g / 7oz loin of pork
- 200g / 7oz chicken breast
- 200g / 7oz veal
- 4 quails
- 1 red sweet (bell) pepper
- A sprig of sage
- 4 slices of white bread
- Olive oil

Preparation time: 3/4 hour

Wash and trim the sweet pepper. Cut into inch squares. Likewise the slices of bread. Cut the meat into mouth-sized pieces. Leave the quails whole and clean and singe them. Place a little salt and a sage leaf inside the stomach cavity.

Thread the ingredients one by one onto the skewers, alternating a cube of meat with a square of pepper, a chunk of bread, a sage leaf and so on, making sure that the quail finishes up in the middle. Brush with oil and grill (broil) over charcoal, red-hot but not flaming. Turn the skewers over frequently, basting with more oil if they should show signs of drying out. A moment before taking them off the fire, season judiciously with salt and pepper. If you do not possess a rotisserie, line them up in a well-oiled roasting tin and roast in the oven. In this case, season with salt and pepper beforehand.

Stinco di vitella al forno

BAKED VEAL SHANK

TO SERVE 6 PEOPLE

- 1 VEAL SHIN
- 1 STICK OF CELERY
- 1 ONION
- 1 CARROT
- A SPRIG OF SAGE
- A TWIG OF ROSEMARY
- A FEW BAY LEAVES
- 125ML/ 4 FL OZ / 1/2 CUP WHITE WINE
- 180ML / 6 FL OZ / 3/4 CUP VEGETABLE STOCK
- A KNOB OF BUTTER
- OLIVE OIL

PREPARATION TIME: ABOUT 2 HOURS

GET YOUR BUTCHER to bone the shank, asking him to remove superfluous fat and cut into the tendons with a knife point. Finely chop up together some bay leaves, sage and rosemary and distribute pinches of the herbs inside the shank. Tie up tightly with kitchen string, season the outside with salt and coat with flour. Heat 5 tablespoons of oil in a roasting pan and sear the shank, turning it over so that it colours evenly. Add the vegetables, washed and coarsely chopped and put the pan in the oven, heated to 250°C (500°F, Gas Mark 10), for ten minutes. When they have wilted, lower the oven temperature to 220°C (425°F, Gas Mark 7) and continue cooking for an hour-and-a-half, basting with the stock from time to time. Remove the shank from the pan and carve it into slices which you will arrange on a serving dish. Strain the cooking juices back into the pan and blend in a knob of cold butter. Pour this gravy over the meat and serve.

Stracotto

Braised Beef

TO SERVE 6 PEOPLE

- 400G / 14OZ / 2 CUPS TOMATO PULP
- 2.3KG / 5LB LEAN BEEF IN ONE PIECE
- PAPRIKA
- 125ML/ 4 FL OZ / 1/2 CUP WHITE WINE
- MIXTURE OF CINNAMON, SAGE, ROSEMARY, PEPPERCORNS AND JUNIPER BERRIES, CHOPPED
- 1 ONION
- OLIVE OIL

PREPARATION TIME: 2 1/4 HOURS

Trim the beef of any gristle and surface fat. Spread the chopped herb mixture liberally over one side. Roll the meat up tightly and tie with kitchen string. Coat with flour.

Sweat the finely-chopped onion in 8 tablespoons of olive oil in a roomy saucepan.

Place the meat in the pan and sear it on all sides until it turns a nice dark brown all over.

Season with salt and douse with the white wine which you will allow to evaporate. Add the tomato pulp, dusting with plenty of paprika.

Cover and leave to simmer gently for at least two hours.

The best thing for serving with it? Why, *fagioli all'uccelletto* (white beans stewed with tomatoes, sage and garlic); refer to the recipe on page 186. As with the beef stew on page 128, the same principle also applies here: long, slow cooking makes the meat easier on your teeth, while maintaining it rich and juicy for the palate.

Tacchinella d'autunno

TURKEY WITH CHESTNUTS AND PRUNES

TO SERVE 6 PEOPLE

- 1 TURKEY-HEN OF ABOUT 3KG / $6^3/4$LB
- PORK NET (CAUL FAT)
- 1 FRESH SAUSAGE
- 1 RASHER FATTY BACON
- 1 COOKING APPLE (RENETTA)
- 200G / 7OZ BREADCRUMB
- 125ML/ 4 FL OZ / $^1/2$ CUP MILK
- 125ML/ 4 FL OZ / $^1/2$ CUP CREAM
- 20 CHESTNUTS
- 100G / 4OZ DRIED PRUNES
- 50G / 2OZ TRUFFLE
- A SPRIG OF SAGE
- A TWIG OF ROSEMARY
- KNOB OF BUTTER
- OLIVE OIL

PREPARATION TIME: 4 HOURS

SOAK THE PRUNES in warm water and boil the chestnuts for an hour. Drain the former and skin the latter. Peel the apple and, squeeze the bread (previously soaked in milk) dry. In a food processor, blend the prunes, chestnuts, apple and breadcrumb with the cream, the heart and liver of the turkey (sautéed with a little oil and a sage leaf in a skillet), the sausage and bacon roughly chopped up, grinding it all for some time on a low speed. Stuff the turkey with the forcemeat seasoned with salt, pepper and the truffle in pieces. Score the flesh and fill with some chopped rosemary and sage, salt and pepper. Sew up the bird and wrap it in the pork net, previously softened in warm water. Place in a roasting tin with a knob of butter and 4 tablespoons of oil, roasting in a medium oven until nicely golden (two-and-a-half to three hours), basting with the cooking juices. As an alternative, the stuffing could consist of mushrooms, to be cut up by hand. The other ingredients remain the same, but a little minced (ground) veal is added.

Tacchino arrosto

Roast Turkey

- 1kg / $2^1/4$lb turkey breast or other turkey meat
- enough pork net (caul fat) to hold it in
- a sprig of sage
- a large twig of rosemary
- 100g / $^1/4$lb unsmoked bacon
- 1 sherry glass brandy (optional)
- olive oil

Preparation time: 1 hour

In the oven - Score the turkey flesh and insert pinches of chopped bacon, rosemary and sage, seasoned with some salt and pepper. Soften the pork net in warm water and wrap the bird in it, securing it with toothpicks. Place in a roasting tin with 4-5 tablespoons of oil, a clove of garlic and a twig of rosemary and roast in the oven at 200°C (400°F, Gas Mark 6) for 35-40 minutes, turning it over and basting with the juices in the pan to keep it moist. A stylish touch? Remove from the oven , put on a serving dish, souse with brandy and flame. *On top of the stove* - As an alternative to oven roasting, pan roasting guarantees excellent results. Instead of the pork net, wrap the bird in 3-4 thin bacon rashers, held in place with some kitchen string. Put the turkey to brown in a flameproof casserole dish with 5 tablespoons of oil, garlic and rosemary. Pour over the brandy and allow to evaporate, then continue cooking over low heat for twenty minutes, dousing with a little stock, if necessary. Untie the turkey, remove the bacon and break it up in the pan juices. Cook for another quarter-hour, colouring the bird on all sides.

Tagliata all'aceto

Steak with a Vinegar Dressing

- 800g / $1^3/4$lb fillet of beef
- olive oil
- balsamic vinegar
- chicory leaves
- grains of *gros sel*

Preparation time: 20 minutes

Balsamic vinegar (*aceto balsamico*) is originally from the countryside around Modena and Reggio Emilia, and is produced in small quantities thanks to a technique perfected over the centuries. This method dictates that the "boiled" and fermented must be allowed to mature for a total of 5 years in the barrel, one year each in oak, chestnut, cherry, ash and mulberry woods, without the addition of spices.

Grill (Broil) the fillet on both sides for 5 or 6 minutes over a medium heat, barely seasoning with salt.

Cut it into diamond shapes, so as to obtain slices of even thickness, which are placed on a serving dish and dressed with olive oil, drops of balsamic vinegar (how many? as you like, without thinning down too much) and a few grains of *gros sel*.

Serve the *tagliata* on a hot serving dish, surrounding it with a nice fresh chicory salad.

Terrina delicata ai fegatini

WHITE MEAT AND CHICKEN LIVER TERRINE

- 200G / 7OZ / $1^{2}/3$ CUPS POTATO STARCH
- 300G / 11OZ / $1^{1}/2$ CUPS SOFTENED BUTTER
- 350G / 3/4LB / $2^{1}/3$ CUPS WHITE FLOUR
- 1 EGG

FOR THE FILLING:

- 80G / 3OZ WHITE BREAD
- 100G / 4OZ SINGLE CREAM
- 300G / 11OZ CHICKEN BREAST
- 300G / 11OZ VEAL
- A SPRIG OF SAGE
- A TWIG OF ROSEMARY
- 1 SMALL NEW ONION
- 1 STICK OF CELERY
- A BAY LEAF
- 1 CLOVE OF GARLIC
- 90ML / 3 FL OZ / 6 TBSP WHITE WINE
- 250G / 9OZ CHICKEN LIVERS
- 30G / 1OZ / 2 TBSP WHITE FLOUR
- 50G / 2OZ / 4 TBSP BUTTER
- OLIVE OIL

PREPARATION TIME: 1 $^{1}/2$ HOURS

MOISTEN THE STARCH with a decilitre of water (7 tablespoons or just under half a cup) and amalgamate with the egg and butter. Add the flour, all at once, and knead the dough well. Shape into a ball and leave in the refrigerator for half-an-hour. Meanwhile, wash and trim the onion, celery and herbs, chop them finely and sauté in a little oil, dousing with the wine which is evaporated over a high flame.

Mince (grind) the chicken and veal finely twice and blend in the food processor with the cream, vegetable mixture and a pinch of salt and pepper. Then clean the chicken livers, coat with flour and brown in a knob of butter in a small frying pan for 4 minutes. Butter a terrine dish and line it with a layer of the pastry rolled out to a uniform thickness of an eighth of an inch.

Spoon in a third of the filling, followed by a layer of chicken livers. Continue layering until all the ingredients have been used up. Close up the terrine with the remaining pastry, sealing it at the edges and pricking the top over. Bake in the oven at 220°C (425°F, Gas Mark 7) for about half-an-hour. Remove from the heat, allow to rest a while, turn out of the dish and serve. As the illustration opposite suggests, you can let your imagination run wild and think up various shapes for this dish.

Trippa alle bietole "inzimino"

TRIPE WITH SWISS CHARD

- 800G / $1^{3}/4$LB TRIPE
- 600G / $1^{1}/4$LB SWISS CHARD
- 500G / 1LB 2OZ FRESH OR TINNED (CANNED) TOMATOES
- 2 CLOVES OF GARLIC
- 125ML/ 4 FL OZ / $^{1}/2$ CUP WHITE WINE
- PARSLEY
- 1 HOT RED PEPPER
- OLIVE OIL

PREPARATION TIME: $^{3}/4$ HOUR

CLEAN AND TRIM the Swiss chard and boil in a little water. Drain and squeeze the liquor out. Sauté the garlic with 4 tablespoons of oil in a frying pan, then remove it and add the roughly-chopped chard. Chop up the other clove of garlic with the parsley and sauté in 6 tablespoons of oil. When it begins to colour, add the washed and dried tripe, cut into strips. Pour the wine over, allow to evaporate, season with salt. Break up the hot red pepper in the saucepan and, when the flavours have blended, add the tomatoes and cook over low heat for half-an-hour. Add the chard, stir well and cook slowly for a quarter-hour. Differently to tripe cooked the Parmesan or Florentine way, it is best to avoid cheese.

A RATHER UNUSUAL way of serving tripe. Inzimino, a sauce based on Swiss chard and tomatoes, is traditionally used to flavour cuttlefish, but it manages to enhance the ox offal with a particular taste. For better results, choose assorted cuts (the term 'tripe' refers to various parts of the digestive apparatus of ruminants).

Trippa alla fiorentina

Florentine Tripe

- at least 1kg / 2 1/4lb tripe
- 40g / 1 1/2oz unsmoked bacon
- 1 onion
- 1 stick of celery
- 1 carrot
- 500g / 1lb 2oz tinned (canned) tomatoes
- 180ml / 6 fl oz / 3/4 cup white wine
- grated pecorino cheese
- hot red pepper
- 4 slices of toast (optional)
- olive oil

Preparation time: 2 hours

Wash the tripe and cut into even strips. Blanch in boiling water with a glass of white wine. Allow to cool and then dry. Sauté the diced bacon with the finely-chopped aromatic vegetables in 6 tablespoons of oil in a flameproof casserole dish. Add the tripe and brown it well, leaving it to cook for 10 minutes. Douse with the remaining white wine, allow to evaporate and add the tomatoes, salt, pepper and hot red pepper.

Cover the dish and cook over low heat for 30-40 minutes, adding stock or water if the tripe seems to be drying out. Serve it hot (over slices of toast, if you like), dusted liberally with grated pecorino cheese.

The secret which makes this "hearty" dish rather more delicate lies in the initial blanching. Replacing the traditional Parmesan with the more zingy pecorino cheese is a personal touch which I hope you will appreciate (likewise the addition of slices of toast).

Vitello tonnato

Cold Braised Veal with Tuna Sauce

To serve 6 people

- 800g / 1 3/4lb lean veal
- 1 small onion
- 2 anchovies
- a bay leaf
- 1 stick of celery
- 1 carrot
- a sprig of parsley
- 250ml / 8 fl oz / 1 cup dry white wine
- peppercorns

For the sauce:
- 2 anchovies
- 150g / 5oz tuna fish in oil, drained
- 1 lemon
- a handful of pickled capers, drained
- olive oil

Preparation time: 3 hours, including cooling period

Pour the wine into a saucepan of lightly salted water and heat. Toss in the bay leaf, onion, celery, carrot, parsley, pepper and the cleaned and filleted anchovies. When the water boils, add the tied-up meat and cook slowly for just under two hours. Allow to cool in the broth, then remove, untie and carve. Strain the stock and put the solids (with the exception of the bay leaf) into a mortar (or food processor) together with the tuna fish, the rinsed and filleted anchovies, the lemon juice and the capers. Pound (or blend) to a fine, soft paste, moistened with a generous tablespoon of oil and a little stock. The result will be a thick, coating sauce. Serve the cold (but not chilled) meat, evenly covered in sauce.

The secret of this delicate dish - suitable for dinner on the terrace on a placid summer's evening - lies in adding the meat to boiling water to seal off the fibres and keep the flavour in.

Some people are convinced that it is enough merely to whip up a little commercially-bottled mayonnaise with a chunk of tuna and a few capers for spreading on slices of boiled beef (this is what they do in some slapdash restaurants), but I can assure you that the result has nothing to do with a plate of authentic *vitello tonnato*.

If you like the taste of egg, you may, at the most, add the yolk of a hard-boiled egg to the ingredients of the sauce.

A view of the Amalfi coastline, renowned for its beauty spots and its delicious fish dishes

Special Dishes

Ideas for carefree, one-course meals

Arancini e Supplì

RICE PATTIES AND CROQUETTES

BLANCH THE PEAS in a little water, along with a drop of olive oil and a parsley leaf.

Clean, trim and sauté the chicken giblets in a little butter in a frying pan. Cook the rice,

drain while still firm and dress with butter, Parmesan cheese and meat sauce (for convenience, we refer you to our own recipe, but any meat stewed in a sauce will do fine). Chop up

the braised meat finely and divide it evenly between two bowls. In the first one (where you will make up the patty filling), mix in the saffron powder, egg yolk, drained peas and cheese. Dress with half a soup ladle or 2 tablespoons of *pommarola*. Add the egg to the meat in the second bowl, along with the chopped chicken giblets, the cut-up ham and the diced mozzarella. Season both mixtures with salt and pepper. Take a handful of rice, make a hollow in the centre, stuff liberally with the patty filling and close it up to make a spherical shape the size of a tennis ball.

Repeat the operation until all the ingredients are used up, then make up the croquettes in the same way. Dip patties and croquettes in dry breadcrumbs and deep fry, a few at a time, in oil in a frying pan over a medium flame. Serve hot, but not before dipping the *arancini* into the remaining tomato sauce.

- 450G / 1LB / 2 CUPS ITALIAN ARBORIO RICE
- 2 SLICES OF BRAISED MEAT WITH PLENTY OF SAUCE (SEE PAGE 131)
- 40G / 1 1/2OZ / 3TBSP BUTTER
- GRATED PARMESAN CHEESE
- DRY BREADCRUMBS
- OIL FOR FRYING

FOR THE PATTIES:

- 1/4TSP POWDERED SAFFRON
- 1 EGG YOLK
- 1 1/2 SOUP LADLES / 6 TBSP POMMAROLA (SEE PAGE 33)
- 100G / 4OZ SHELLED GREEN PEAS
- MILD PROVOLONE CHEESE, FLAKED
- PARSLEY LEAVES
- OLIVE OIL

FOR THE CROQUETTES:

- 1 EGG
- 100G / 4OZ CHICKEN GIBLETS (LIVERS, HEARTS, COCKSCOMBS, GIZZARDS, UNLAID EGGS, ETC.)
- KNOB OF BUTTER
- A THICK SLICE OF COOKED, UNSMOKED HAM
- 1 BALL OF MOZZARELLA

PREPARATION TIME: 1 1/2 HOURS

WE HAVE LUMPED together two specialities (one Sicilian and the other Roman) in just one recipe, simplifying it a little and adapting it to the contemporary housewife's kitchen (where everything needs to be done well in a hurry, without rehashing the usual old things). This fare is the mainstay of delicatessens and fast food places.

Both are very tasty, though not at all easy to digest. But once or twice in life a little exaggeration is called for, whatever dietologists say. Quantities are sufficient to calm the hunger pangs of four people without twinges of remorse or guilt, backed up by a nice mixed salad.

Cacciucco

FISH SOUP

- 800G / $1^3/4$LB FISH IN SMALL PIECES (SCORPION FISH, SEA BASS OR GURNARD, GREY MULLET, CONGER EEL, GARPIKE, WEEVER, SEA BREAM, ETC.)
- 200G / 7OZ DOGFISH
- 200G / 7OZ GROPER
- 4 SURMULLET, RED MULLET OR GOATFISH
- 8 MANTIS SHRIMPS
- 400G / 1LB CUTTLEFISH, YOUNG SQUID AND BABY OCTOPUS
- 500G / 1LB 2OZ RIPE TOMATOES
- 5 CLOVES OF GARLIC
- 2-3 HOT RED PEPPERS
- A SPRIG OF PARSLEY
- 1 ONION
- 1 SMALL CARROT
- 1 HEART OF CELERY
- 60ML / 2 FL OZ / 4 TBSP RED WINE
- UNSALTED WHITE BREAD, SLICED
- OLIVE OIL

PREPARATION TIME: 2 HOURS

BLANCH THE TOMATOES, skin and seed them. Scrub and wash the shellfish and (with the exception of the mantis shrimps) cut into serving pieces. Clean and gut the fish, scrape off the scales and discard the ink sacs (fish can usually be bought already cleaned; however, just in case...). Remove heads, fins and bones (except where the mullet are concerned), but do not throw them away. Boil the trimmings with the onion, carrot, celery and a few parsley leaves for half-an-hour. Gather them up in a slotted spoon and reduce to a paste in a *mouli légumes* or vegetable mill. Keep their cooking liquor warm, too. Brown two garlic cloves and one hot red pepper in 4-5 tablespoons of oil in a large saucepan. Pour in the purée of fish trimmings, allow the flavours to blend and sauté the pieces of shellfish (except the mantis shrimps) in it. Douse with the wine, allow to evaporate, cover the saucepan and simmer for another 20 minutes over low heat, thinning out the soup with a little fish stock to which you have added a pinch of salt. Now add all the other fish (excluding the red mullet and mantis shrimps), cut into serving pieces. Allow the flavours to blend, then add the roughly-chopped tomatoes, the two remaining cloves of garlic and the remaining hot red peppers. Put on the lid and continue cooking slowly for a further half-hour, adding more fish stock as necessary to keep the soup quite thin. Add the mantis shrimps whole and, 5 minutes later, the red mullet as well. After 10 minutes of cooking with the lid off, reduce the liquid a little (though not too much). The tougher fish should now be very tender, with the flesh almost falling apart. In each soup bowl, place two slices of toasted bread, rubbed over with garlic. Spoon the soup over and cover with the fish and shellfish, distributing the whole fish equally and attractively among the bowls. Sprinkle with chopped parsley and serve.

ANYONE WHO HAS TRIED *cacciucco* in a restaurant will, perhaps, wonder at the absence of mussels. Without any intention of picking a quarrel, I wish to point out that the flavour of this delicate shellfish would not even be noticed in the bombshell of flavours which make up this soup. At the most, their function is to catch the eye with the black of their valves standing out against the red soup. If you really cannot do without, buy half a kilogram or a pound of mussels, wash and scrub and them, removing the filament, and add to the soup together with the red mullet. They will open up and cook in just a few minutes. *Cacciucco* cannot be treated as just any old fish soup. It constitutes the first and second course. (To round off your meal, I would soothe the flaming palates of your guests with a sorbet (sherbet) or creamy dessert). The quantities in our recipe will be enough for four people, even though, all-in-all, the ingredients go to make up a rather more refined dish than the hearty one which represents the greatest source of culinary glory for the city of Livorno. (Admittedly, to go by my fine friend and mentor, Mario Cardinali, the restaurants in the Livorno district where a *cacciucco* can be tasted *comme il faut* are becoming rarer and rarer. If he says that, well...

Carpaccio

RAW BEEF, FINELY-SLICED

- 250G / 9OZ SIRLOIN OF BEEF
- 2 *BOLETUS EDULIS* OR CULTIVATED MUSHROOMS
- JUICE OF HALF A LEMON
- FRESHLY-GROUND PEPPER

PREPARATION TIME: 15 MINUTES (PLUS REFRIGERATION PERIOD)

THE MEAT MUST be compact so it can be sliced very thinly.

It is a good idea to get your butcher to slice it in his machine.

On a serving dish (which has been lightly sprayed with olive oil and lemon), overlap the meat slices slightly and season as little as possible with salt.

The mushrooms are cleaned by scraping them with the tip of a knife and wiping them over with a damp cloth. Slice them up finely and arrange tastefully over the meat slices. Pour 3 tablespoons of oil, the lemon juice, salt and pepper into a small bowl and whisk briskly.

Spoon the dressing evenly over the carpaccio.

Allow the dish to rest in the refrigerator for twenty minutes, then serve it fresh and appetising.

IT HAS BECOME the general habit to enhance the dish with tiny slivers of Parmesan cheese and rocket salad (the Mediterranean plant *Eruca sativa*) or a mixed salad of chicory or endive. Every cook is free to add or subtract ingredients at will. For

example, my family go wild for artichokes sliced finely, salted capers (rinsed, of course), finely-chopped chives and (at least as regards the more elderly members of the family) multicolour peppercorns. I, myself, prefer finely-chopped carrot and celery, or else ultra-thin slices of baby white onions, red radishes and raw courgettes (zucchini), with a condiment of cider vinegar instead of the lemon and a dash of mustard seeds and juniper berries, or else half a clove of garlic, to be removed before dressing the meat. *Carpaccio di mare*, made with very fresh sword fish (such as in the illustration opposite), is, without doubt, enhanced with a quantity of multicoloured peppercorns, oregano and lashings of lemon.

"Flan" di patate

POTATO PIE

- 600G / $1^1/_4$LB POTATOES
- 80G / 3OZ / $^1/_4$ CUP + 2 TBSP BUTTER
- 3 THIN SLICES OF COOKED, UNSMOKED HAM
- 3 SMALL MOZZARELLA BALLS
- 2 EGGS
- NUTMEG
- 70G / 3OZ / 9 TBSP GRATED PARMESAN
- 250ML / $7^1/_2$ FL OZ / 1 CUP MILK
- 100G / 4OZ / $^1/_2$ CUP BUTTER
- DRY BREADCRUMBS

PREPARATION TIME: $^3/_4$ HOUR

BOIL THE POTATOES and peel them. Mash with a potato ricer and combine with the butter, milk, cheese, egg, salt, pepper and a little grated nutmeg in a bowl. Mix well.

Butter a pie dish and sprinkle with dried breadcrumbs. Half fill it with the potato mixture.

Make a layer of ham and mozzarella slices on top, then sandwich with the rest of the potato.

Sprinkle some dry breadcrumbs over and bake in the oven at 180°C (350°F, Gas Mark 4) for 20 minutes. When a nice golden crust has formed, remove the pie from the oven, allow to rest for five minutes and serve.

The most suitable drink to accompany it? Why, beer!

"Fonduta"

MEAT FONDUE

- 600G - 800G / $1^1/_4$ - $1^3/_4$LB FIRST-GRADE BEEF
- $^1/_2$L / 1PT / 2 CUPS VEGETABLE OR SEED OIL
- A SPRIG OF THYME OR A BAY LEAF
- AN ARRAY OF ASSORTED SAUCES EACH IN ITS OWN BOWL (ANCHOVY, GARLIC, CURRY, HOLLANDAISE, PIQUANT AND GREEN PARSLEY SAUCES AND MAYONNAISE, SEE OPPOSITE)
- VARIOUS QUALITIES OF MUSTARD, KETCHUP, CAPERS, GHERKINS AND BABY ONIONS IN BOWLS, AS WELL AS TABASCO, WORCESTERSHIRE AND SOYA SAUCES

PREPARATION TIME: $^1/_4$ HOUR (PLUS TIME TO PREPARE THE SAUCES)

CUT THE MEAT (trimmed of fat and gristle) up into inch-sized cubes and take to the table in one or more tureens. Pour the oil (if you can rise to a crystal-clear olive oil, so much the better) into a small copper saucepan and heat, adding a sprig of thyme or a bay leaf, according to your taste. The container must be placed on a small sprit stove at the centre of the table to keep the oil boiling hot. You can find assembled fondue sets with the equipment you need in the shops. Each dinner guest will spear a cube of meat on his special fork and will plunge it into the oil for a few seconds, until cooked to the degree desired. He then withdraws it and dips it in one of the previously-prepared sauces, finishing off with a drop of the commercially-available sauces, if wished. So as to avoid your guests burning themselves on their hot forks, it is a good idea to provide some long wooden toothpicks (or some more forks) for actually eating with.

TO ACCOMPANY THE MOST classical and convivial of one-plate meals (you just need to back it up with a *pinzimonio* or salad dip and there is your dinner ready), choose a nice bright red wine, a young French wine of recent vintage, for example, or even, as favoured by some, an oriental one. In fact, under the name of Tempura, Japanese culinary tradition includes a delicious fondue of meat, fish and shellfish, where the role played by vegetable oil may be fulfilled by broth, with excellent results. It is superfluous to note that, as an alternative to the "mono-

Sauces

AIOLI - In a mortar, pound 4-5 sizeable cloves of garlic and add a pinch of salt and an egg yolk. Whisk the sauce by hand (much better than in a food mixer) and pour in the oil a little at a time, just as you do with mayonnaise (see below). Delicious, though not to be recommended if close encounters are intended!

CURRY - There is a huge variety of Indian, curry-based sauces. This one is rather tame and mild, but some very hot, aggressive ones do exist. Cut up a new onion finely and sweat over gentle heat in 4 tablespoons of oil, without allowing it to colour. Dilute a tablespoon of curry powder in a drop of milk and add to the onion, blending in the flavours for a minute. Add some stock and allow to reduce for a quarter-hour. Serve warm.

MAYONNAISE - Break an egg into a deep bowl, add an egg yolk, a teaspoon of mustard and a pinch of salt. Add a drop of oil and emulsify, always slowly stirring in the same direction with a wooden spoon, or else use the mayonnaise fixture of a food mixer.

As the mayonnaise gradually thickens, pour in a little oil at a time (100ml, or 3 fl oz, or 1/3 cup in all) and lastly the juice of half a lemon.

Excellent, though a couple of teaspoons of mustard amalgamated once the mayonnaise is ready will improve it, as will finely-chopped capers, gherkins and baby onions.

HOLLANDAISE SAUCE - In a small saucepan in a *bain marie*, heat 80g (3oz / 1/4 cup plus 2 tbsp) butter in pieces. As soon as it starts to melt, add an egg yolk and whisk briskly over a very low flame.

When the sauce has thickened, add the juice of half a lemon and a pinch of salt and amalgamate thoroughly.

Once ready, the sauce may also in this case be "adjusted" with a little mustard and a pinch of tarragon.

PIQUANT SAUCE - This must be prepared well in advance. In a frying pan, sauté a handful of hot red peppers, stripped of their seeds, and purée them with a teaspoon of vinegar, a pinch of curry powder (optional) and a sprig of parsley.

Pour into a small ovenproof dish and, stirring well, add as much vinegar as necessary (you may dilute it, if you wish) to make a thick, pouring sauce. Place the covered dish in a slow oven for an hour. Cool before serving.

PIQUANT GREEN PARSLEY SAUCE - Wash a bunch of parsley and cut up finely (or put in a food mill) with 50g (2oz / 1/2 cup) of drained capers, a hard-boiled egg, a little thyme (if you wish, you may add a few herbs such as catmint, garden mint and basil) and a tablespoon of vinegar. Transfer to a small bowl and add 4 tablespoons of olive oil, mixing thoroughly and allowing to rest a while.

graphic" version, it is an excellent, truly agreeable idea to propose a variety of meats (chicken, pork, lamb, beef) or else of fish and shellfish. Someone may, quite rightly, find that cooking in broth is lighter and more respectful of the intrinsic flavour of meat. In short, if you wish to experiment with these variations, you have my blessing. And if you feel like splashing out, prepare two little stoves, one for oil and one for broth, and *chacun à son goût*. Here above are given indications for preparing some of the fundamental sauces (others will doubtlessly require imagination and experience, useful in other circumstances, too). Remember that the recipe for the anchovy sauce can be found elsewhere (on page 32) and that the quantities are suitable for the *fonduta* and may therefore need adjustment for use with other dishes.

Insalata di Pollo

CHICKEN SALAD

- 1 CHICKEN BREAST
- 1 STICK OF CELERY
- 1 SMALL ONION
- 1 CARROT
- 1 HEAD OF LETTUCE
- 1 HARD-BOILED EGG
- TINNED (CANNED) SWEET CORN
- BLACK AND GREEN OLIVES
- MAYONNAISE (SEE PAGE 145)
- MUSTARD
- OLIVE OIL
- CIDER VINEGAR

PREPARATION TIME: 1 HOUR (INCLUDING THE CHICKEN COOKING TIME)

REMOVE THE GRISTLE and wishbone from the chicken breast and boil it with the onion, carrot and celery in slightly salted boiling water (the resultant stock will be useful in the preparation of other dishes). Allow to cool and cut into strips. Mix them with 8 tablespoons of mayonnaise in a bowl. Wash the lettuce, tear it up with your fingers and add to the chicken, together with the stoned olives, the sliced egg and the drained sweet corn. Dress with 2-3 tablespoons of olive oil, emulsified with a pinch of strong mustard and a teaspoon of vinegar. Blend well and serve.

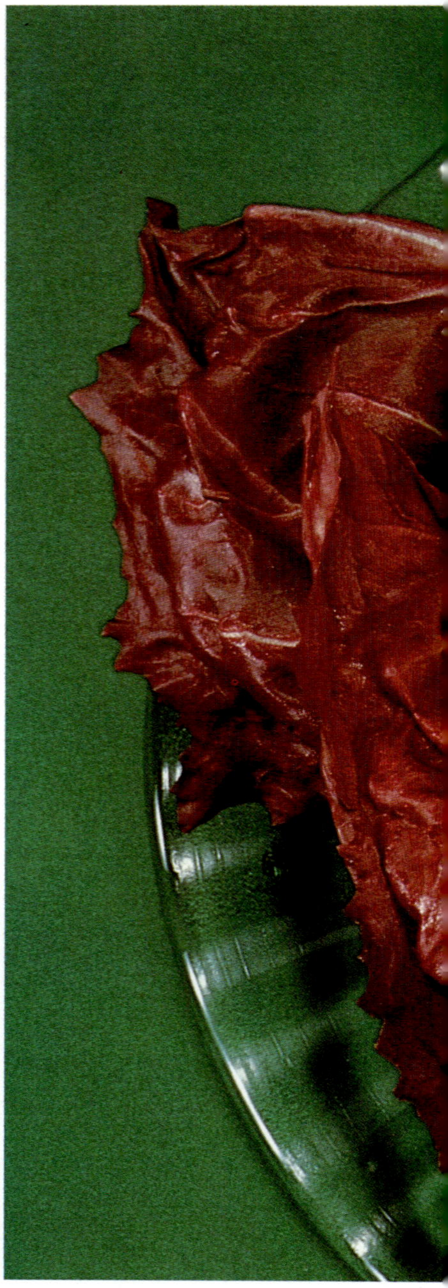

THIS "BASIC" VERSION can, of course, be integrated and modified as you will, depending on the occasion and your own imagination. Examples of possible additions or variations? From the green grocery counter: a boiled potato, a small onion cut into rings, a diced fennel bulb, a very tender stick of celery cut into short lengths, shelled and blanched spring peas, a diced courgette (zucchini), a sliced gherkin, a segment of chopped, steamed cauliflower, or strips of sweet pepper and so on. As far as the lettuce is concerned, some prefer curly-leafed endive, some the rather bitter chicory (witloof), some radicchio rosso while others prefer rocket salad and lamb's lettuce. From the delicatessen counter: artichoke hearts and baby mushrooms under oil,

onions in vinegar, gherkins in brine, drained capers, palm hearts, little scalded shrimps, filleted anchovies, diced Emmental, slivers of Parmesan, flakes of soft cream cheese or curls of creamy full-fat, fresh *mascarpone* cheese. From the gourmet counter: *Boletus edulis* or even fresh finely-sliced Caesar's mushrooms, slivers of truffle, slices of avocado pear and anything else you can afford. As you can see - and you will know by experience - you can give vent to your imagination. In any case, chicken salad is eaten cold and, therefore, preferably in summer (even in the hottest hours of the day, because it is light and appetising), after half-an-hour in the fridge.

Insalata di riso

RICE SALAD

- 250G / 9OZ / 1 CUP LONG-GRAIN RICE
- BLACK AND GREEN OLIVES
- ARTICHOKE HEARTS AND MUSHROOMS IN OIL
- VEGETABLE PICKLES
- 100G / 4OZ / 1/2 CUP TUNA FISH IN OIL
- 1 RIPE TOMATO
- 1 EGG, HARD-BOILED
- CAPERS, DRAINED
- 1 ANCHOVY, FILLETED
- 1 SLICE OF FONTINA CHEESE
- 1 THICK SLICE OF COOKED, UNSMOKED HAM
- PARSLEY
- HALF A LEMON
- OLIVE OIL

PREPARATION TIME: 20 MINUTES

THE SAME SUGGESTIONS hold for rice salad as for chicken salad. However, with rice we are catapulted into the world of fish (anchovies, sardines, sole or swordfish), of molluscs and crustaceans (cuttlefish, squid, *moscardini*, scampi, prawns, mantis shrimps, crayfish) and shellfish (mussels, Venus clams and baby clams). To make a rice salad which has the aroma of the sea, take 200g (7oz) of fish suitable for frying (e. g. whitebait, baby cuttlefish, shrimps), 100g (1/4lb) cooked scampi, 400g (1lb) mussels or clams. Cook the whitebait with a little garlic, parsley and a trickle of oil and fillet them. Flavour the shellfish and molluscs in a little oil with the chopped garlic and parsley, until the shells open up and you can extract the flesh from them (leave some for garnish). Break up the ingredients, mix into the rice, add the scampi, dress with olive oil and lemon, add a drop of Tabasco sauce and cool in the refrigerator.

THE RICE SHOULD BE the quick-cooking kind (6 - 7 minutes) with grains which stay fluffy and separate. Boil in salted water, drain and put under running cold water to halt the cooking. Turn into a bowl and stir in all the other ingredients, after reducing them to small pieces or thin slices (the pickles and vegetables in oil included, if they are in rather too big pieces). Dress with a little oil emulsified with the juice of half a lemon, salt and pepper. Add some mayonnaise, if you like (personally, I do not).

Insalata tiepida di coniglio

RABBIT SALAD

- 2 FLORENCE FENNEL BULBS
- 4 ORANGES
- 200G / 7OZ RABBIT MEAT
- OLIVE OIL

PREPARATION TIME: 30 MINUTES

HERE IS A SALAD of white meat which can stand up to any *carpaccio* (finely sliced raw, prime beef), even as far as taste and aroma are concerned, and the two go together splendidly on the buffet table. Peel three oranges and divide into segments, carefully and patiently removing all trace of the white pith. Steam the rabbit for 7-8 minutes and wait for it to cool until just warm. In the meanwhile, wash the fennel thoroughly and slice it very finely. Arrange the salad on the dinner plates, artistically alternating fennel, orange segments and the rabbit, sliced paper thin. Make a dressing for the salad with the juice of the remaining orange, olive oil and salt, blending it all thoroughly. If you reduce the amounts, this dish is a delicate, original *antipasto*.

Mozzarella in carrozza

FRIED MOZZARELLA CANAPÉS

- 500G / 1LB 2OZ MOZZARELLA FROM BUFFALO MILK
- 16 SLICES OF WHITE BREAD
- 2 EGGS AND 1 EGG YOLK
- 250G / 9OZ / 1 2/3 CUP WHITE FLOUR
- 4 ANCHOVIES (OPTIONAL)
- 1 TBSP DRAINED CAPERS (OPTIONAL)
- OIL FOR FRYING

PREPARATION TIME: 1/2 HOUR

CUT THE MOZZARELLA cheese balls (not the variety in plaits) into fairly thick slices. The bread should have the same round shape as the cheese; with the aid of an upturned cup, you may press out discs of crustless bread of the size you need from each slice of bread. Place a slice of mozzarella on top of each one.

If you like the flavour, slip half a fillet of anchovy and a caper under the cheese. Plunge each "open sandwich" into the egg which has been beaten with a pinch of salt, coat with flour on either side and dip into the egg once more.

Deep fry a couple at a time in plenty of oil in a deep frying pan. Turn them over with two forks until golden on both sides.

A PLATE OF CRISP MOZZARELLA in carrozza and a light rice or chicken salad will thoroughly delight your guests. Alternatively, pair a *mozzarella in carrozza* up with a dish of rice patties and croquettes (see page 140). You will notice how your guests will not be shy about coming forward, either.

Polenta e osei

Cornmeal with little birds

If ordered in good time, it is not difficult for the local butcher in Italy to get hold of little birds, already plucked, drawn and singed, especially in the hunting season.

Those fortunate enough to have the acquaintance of a hunter who can shoot the birds for them (a rare circumstance nowadays) will no doubt know that they must be plucked as soon as possible, left to ripen for a couple of days and drawn only just before cooking. If you simply cannot find these little birds, I rather hesitatingly suggest falling back on the acceptable farm-bred quails on sale in many supermarkets. If you really want the most ex-

- 500G / 1LB 2OZ / 3 CUPS CORNMEAL
- 12 - 16 SMALL BIRDS (PREFERABLY THRUSHES)
- 150G / 5OZ THIN BACON RASHERS
- BUNCH OF SAGE
- OLIVE OIL

PREPARATION TIME: 45 MINUTES

BRING A SAUCEPAN (preferably one in copper) with 2 litres (4 pints / 8 cups) of water to the boil, season with salt and sprinkle in the cornmeal, stirring briskly to prevent lumps from forming.

Cook slowly, stirring continuously, for at least 40 minutes.

Lard the little birds by wrapping each in a rasher of bacon (held together with a

toothpick) after seasoning the body cavity with a little salt and pepper and a sage leaf.

Roast on the rotisserie attachment for 20 minutes, basting frequently with oil (carefully collecting the fat that runs off), or else roast in a well-oiled meat tin in the oven for 40 minutes, turning the birds over frequently.

When the *polenta* is ready, spread it out over a large wooden board and lay the birds on top. Douse them lavishly with their cooking juices.

quisite delicacy, another piece of advice is to pour four or five soup ladles (1-1 1/4 cups) of a good, freshly-made meat or mushroom sauce onto the prepared *polenta*, then lay the birds on top.

Use a length of string to cut the set *polenta*, after letting it cool a minute or so.

This dish is typical of the northern region of Veneto (*osei* is the local term for *uccelli*, i. e. birds).

Sartù di riso

Timbale of Rice

For the filling:
- 150g / 5oz minced (ground) meat
- 100g / 1/4lb chicken giblets
- 2 tbsp white flour
- 2 small pork sausages
- 50g / 2oz / 4 tbsp butter
- 50g / 2oz / 4 tbsp dried mushrooms
- 50g / 2oz / 1/2 cup fresh breadcrumb
- 50g / 2oz shelled peas
- 1 egg white
- olive oil

For the sauce:
- 100g / 1/4lb pig's cheek or streaky bacon (unsmoked)
- half an onion
- 800g / 1 3/4lb / 4 cups ripe or tinned (canned) tomatoes
- knob of vegetable margarine
- 350g / 12oz / 1 1/2 cups Italian Arborio rice
- 2 tsp white flour
- 100g / 4oz / 1/2 cup butter
- 60ml / 2 fl oz / 4 tbsp milk
- dry breadcrumbs
- grated Parmesan cheese
- 1 whole egg and 1 egg yolk
- 1 mozzarella cheese ball

Preparation time: 2 to 3 hours

This was once considered a rather substantial *entrée*. Today it reasonably appears as an appetising and memorable single-dish meal for a carefree supper among friends, preceded by a refreshing vegetable dip. There is no trace of either oil or butter (even less of margarine) in the original Neapolitan recipe; mention was only made of very refined suet (and lard instead of the pig's cheek or bacon). I beg forgiveness for the inevitable adaptation to contemporary dietary habits. But…

Let's get started with the sauce, first of all (but remember to put the dried mushrooms and breadcrumb to soak for the filling). Sauté the chopped onion in the margarine in a saucepan, together with the diced pig's cheek or bacon (how's that for lightness!). Add the roughly-chopped tomatoes and cook slowly until the sauce is nice and thick. In the meanwhile, assemble the stuffing. Squeeze the mushrooms and strain their water through some kitchen paper. Place them in a small frying pan to fry with a knob of butter, a tablespoon of the liquor, salt and pepper. Clean and rinse the chicken giblets and brown these in the butter, as well, then break them up into small pieces. The sausages, on the other hand, will be crumbled and sautéed in a little olive oil. Wash the peas and blanch in boiling water with a little salt. Mix the minced (ground) meat with the squeezed breadcrumb, a little butter, the egg white, salt and pepper. Make tiny meatballs, roll them in flour and fry in 2 tablespoons of oil. Turn everything into a saucepan and blend the flavours in a spoonful of the tomato sauce over low heat, stirring well. Keep warm. Meanwhile, cook the rice as for a risotto with the remaining tomato sauce in a saucepan (go easy on the salt and pepper), keeping it nice and moist with the addition every now and then of a tablespoon of warm stock. After cooking for about a quarter-hour over a moderate flame, turn off the heat and dress the rice with an egg and a liberal sprinkling of Parmesan cheese, stirring well. While it is resting, melt a knob of butter in a small saucepan and make a roux with the flour. When it begins to colour, add the milk, egg yolk and a pinch of salt, allowing the sauce to amalgamate well over a gentle flame and keeping it of a pouring consistency. Butter a deep, square baking dish, sprinkle liberally with dry breadcrumbs and, aiding yourself with a spatula, line it with a thick layer of rice, leaving about a quarter aside with which to finish off the timbale. Arrange the filling on this bed of rice, mixing in the diced mozzarella, the white sauce, some grated Parmesan and flakes of butter. Cover with the rest of the rice and dredge with dry breadcrumbs, dotting with flakes of butter here and there. Bake in the oven at 180°C (350°F, Gas Mark 4) for 30 minutes, until a nice, golden crust forms. Remove from the oven and allow to cool slightly. Loosen the timbale by sliding the blade of a knife all around the edges of the dish, turn it out onto a serving dish and serve it nice and hot. After so much hard work, the admiration and wonder of your guests are guaranteed.

Torta Pasqualina

GENOESE EASTER PIE

TO SERVE SIX PEOPLE

FOR THE PASTRY:
- 500G / 1LB 2OZ / 3 1/3 CUPS WHITE FLOUR
- PINCH OF SALT
- OLIVE OIL

FOR THE FILLING:
- 3 BUNCHES OF SWISS CHARD (THERE WILL BE ABOUT 1/2KG OR 1LB ONCE CLEANED, BOILED AND DRAINED)
- 1 WHITE-SKINNED ONION
- 100G / 4OZ DRIED MUSHROOMS
- 2 CLOVES OF GARLIC
- A PINCH OF MARJORAM
- A SPRIG OF PARSLEY
- 150G / 5OZ / 1 1/4 CUPS GRATED PARMESAN
- 8 FRESH EGGS
- 300G / 11OZ RICOTTA CHEESE
- 60ML / 2 FL OZ / 4 TBSP MILK
- 3 TBSP WHITE FLOUR

PREPARATION TIME: 3 HOURS

EXCELLENT EATEN cold or warm, this is well worth the considerable effort and care required. Traditionally the dish prepared for Easter Day in Liguria, it can be offered as the delicious climax to a refined, light luncheon, starting off with titbits served warm or cold and finishing off with a Bavarian berry cream and set off with a good dry white wine or - why not? - a good Venetian sparkling wine, prosecco or Cartizze. It can also be made with other vegetables such as spinach and globe artichokes.

ACT ONE: SOAK THE MUSHROOMS. Wash the Swiss chard and strip of the white midribs. Scald in very little water. Drain, cool in running water, squeeze the moisture out and chop up finely.

Sauté the chopped onion in a saucepan with 2 tablespoons of oil. Chop up the drained and dried mushrooms, a clove of garlic and the parsley and add to the onion with a pinch of marjoram when it starts to colour.

Put on the lid and leave to cook for a good quarter-hour, moistening with water, if necessary.

Take the saucepan off the heat, add the Swiss chard, half the Parmesan, two beaten eggs and season with salt and pepper.

Mix well and leave to rest. Turn the ricotta into a bowl and, with a wooden spoon, blend in two beaten eggs, the rest of the Parmesan, the milk, salt, pepper and a tablespoon of flour. The mixture should be thick and creamy. Allow to stand a while.

Heap the flour onto a board. Hollow out the top and pour into it a scant tablespoon of oil and a pinch of salt, adding enough water to make a soft dough.

Knead at length, until the pastry is nice and springy. At this point, allow it to rest a quarter-hour under a tea towel. Take an interval break.

Act two: divide the dough into ten equal portions and flour them. Oil a round, shallow oven dish, 12 inches in diameter.

Take a portion of dough and, with a rolling pin, roll it out on a floured pastry board to a quarter-inch thickness. Then, with the manual technique for making pizzas, widen the disc of dough, whittling it down to gossamer thickness. Lay the pastry on the oven dish, allowing it to flow over the edges. Oil it lightly.

Repeat the operation with three more pastry sheets, then spoon the filling on top, starting with the chard and finishing up with ricotta. Level off the top and leave an inch space free all round.

Hollow out four symmetrical cavities in the filling into each of which you will break an egg. Season each with salt and pepper and a dot of butter.

Cover the whole lot with the same number of pastry sheets, even thinner than the previous ones if at all possible. Make sure they do not stick one to the other.

Cut off the pastry overlapping the dish. Roll the pieces up to make a cord to put around the edges of the pie, forming a rim. With the prongs of a fork, mark out notches in it.

Bake in a medium oven. Remove the pie after an hour, when the pastry is a nice, golden colour.

THE DIFFERENCE BETWEEN the true *Torta Pasqualina* and other types of pie lies mainly in the thickness of the pastry.

If you have the patience and skill to succeed in rolling it out paper-thin until almost transparent (just like strudel pastry, which tradition requires you should be able to read the paper through), go straight ahead.

Otherwise, fall back on something simpler, such as an ordinary vegetable pie, even though you will thus deprive yourself of something special!

Torta salata

Savoury Pie

- 200g / 7oz / $1^1/_3$ cups white flour
- 100g / $^1/_4$lb / $^1/_2$ cup butter
- 1 egg yolk

For the filling:

- 200g / 7oz smoked bacon
- 2 eggs and 2 egg yolks
- 400ml / $^3/_4$pt / $1^1/_2$ cups cream
- 125ml/ 4 fl oz / $^1/_2$ cup milk

Preparation time: 1 hour

The generous quantities and substantial ingredients make this delicious pie (the Italian version of the *quiche lorraine* which crossed the border some time ago to settle down on the other side of the Alps) an excellent winter meal in itself.

Put flakes of the butter, the egg yolk and a pinch of salt in the hollowed out "crater" of the mounded flour. Knead briefly and briskly to obtain a soft, springy dough, with the addition of a scant glass of water.

Allow to rest under a damp tea towel while you get the filling ready.

Discard the rind and cut the bacon into strips. Scald in boiling water. Whisk the yolks and the whole eggs in a bowl, then add salt, pepper, the cream and the milk.

Roll out the pastry to a sheet a quarter-inch thick. Butter an oven dish or baking tin and line it with the pastry. Cut off any pastry overlapping the edges and prick the bottom with the prongs of a fork.

Lay the strips of bacon across, pour in the egg-and-cream mixture and dot with butter. Bake in a medium hot oven until the surface is nicely golden.

Serve warm.

Fish and Shellfish

Anguille alla salvia

Sage-Flavoured Eel

Clean the eels, open them out, remove the heads, gut and cut into chunks. In an oven dish, heat 4-5 tablespoons of oil and sweat the sage and garlic very slowly. Roll the eel chunks in the dry breadcrumbs and sauté them. Add the wine, allow to reduce a little and bake in a hot oven for a good half-hour, basting with the cooking juices.

- 1kg / 2 1/4lb medium-sized eel
- 2 cloves of garlic
- 80g / 3oz / 3/4 cup dried breadcrumbs
- 6-8 sage leaves
- 125ml/ 4 fl oz / 1/2 cup white wine
- Olive oil

Preparation time: 3/4 hour

Eel can only be skinned if it is of sizeable proportions, otherwise it is sufficient just to draw it.

How does one skin an eel? Cut all around the skin under the head of the eel, pull it up a little and then, with one hand gripping the head, rip the skin down and off with one tug, turning it inside out like a glove. By the way, it is better to wear gloves or hold the eel with a dishcloth because is indeed notoriously slippery!

While you are at it, if you have a large eel, grill (broil) it over charcoal, basting it with oil and dusting with salt and pepper while it is cooking.

Baccalà alla livornese

Salt Cod, Livorno Style

- 800g / 1 3/4lb salt cod, previously soaked
- 2 leeks
- 300g / 3/4lb / 1 1/2 cups tinned (canned) or puréed tomatoes
- 4 cloves of garlic
- Parsley
- White flour
- Olive oil

Preparation time: 1/2 hour

This dish works out very well with stockfish, too. Indeed, I understand that the original recipe specified the use of dried and not salted cod. Sautéed leek instead of the usual onion renders a rather "aggressive" dish a little milder. If you double the quantity of tinned tomatoes to 500 or 600 grams, crumbling in the fried *baccalà* and reducing the sauce very gradually, you then have a delicious sauce to pour over your spaghetti, vermicelli and what have you.

Purée the tomatoes. Sauté the sliced leeks and chopped garlic in 4-5 tablespoons of oil, add the tomato and cook very slowly for a quarter-hour. Meanwhile, cut the fish (skinned and boned) into 6 chunks, coat with flour and fry over medium heat, allowing to colour nicely on both sides. Drain and dry and flavour by adding to the tomato sauce for ten minutes with a little ground pepper or red hot pepper Serve the *baccalà* hot, dredged with chopped parsley.

Baccalà alla messinese

SALT COD BAKED IN A RICH TOMATO SAUCE

- 800G / $1^{3}/4$LB SALT COD
- 5 RIPE TOMATOES
- 1 ONION, 2 POTATOES
- PINE-NUTS AND SULTANAS (WHITE RAISINS)
- A HANDFUL BLACK OLIVES, STONED
- 1 HOT RED PEPPER
- 60ML / 2 FL OZ / 4 TBSP WHITE WINE
- OLIVE OIL

PREPARATION TIME: $1^{1}/2$ HOURS

SOAK THE COD, SCALD THE TOMATOES, skin and purée, discarding the seeds. Slice the onion finely and sauté in a pan with 4-5 tablespoons of oil. When the onion has become translucent, add the puréed tomatoes and allow the flavours to blend for about ten minutes, keeping the flame moderate. Add the fish in small chunks, the pine-nuts, the sultanas (revived in water, then squeezed), the stoned olives, the peeled and sliced potatoes, the hot red pepper and the wine. Season sparingly with salt.

Stirring, allow the fish to absorb the flavours, put on the pan lid and bake in a medium oven for half-an-hour.

Baccalà alla vicentina

WINE-BAKED SALT COD

- 800G / $1^{3}/4$LB SALT COD, PREVIOUSLY SOAKED
- 50G / 2OZ / $^{1}/3$ CUP WHITE FLOUR
- GRATED PARMESAN CHEESE
- HALF AN ONION
- 1 CLOVE OF GARLIC
- 2 ANCHOVIES
- A SPRIG OF PARSLEY
- 125ML/ 4 FL OZ / $^{1}/2$ CUP WHITE WINE
- 1 CUP OF MILK
- KNOB OF BUTTER

PREPARATION TIME: $^{1}/2$ HOUR

RINSE THE ANCHOVIES, bone them, remove the head and cut into small pieces. Cut the fish into large chunks, coat with flour and arrange in an oven dish, sprinkling with pepper and Parmesan. Chop the garlic and onion and sauté in a pan with 3-4 tablespoons of oil, adding the anchovies gradually and mixing them in. Pour in the wine and add the milk and butter. Blend the sauce over gentle heat, mixing carefully. Turn into the oven dish and bake in a medium oven for twenty minutes, until the sauce has been completely absorbed. Dust with chopped parsley and serve. The original recipe requires stockfish, but the modification makes no difference (do be careful of the salt, though). The same may be said for the preceding recipe, *Baccalà alla messinese*.

Baccalà con i ceci

SALT COD AND CHICKPEAS

- 700 -800G / $1^{1}/2$-$1^{3}/4$LB SALT COD, PREVIOUSLY SOAKED
- 250G / 9OZ CHICKPEAS (GARBANZOS)
- PARSLEY AND AROMATIC VEG.
- COARSE SEA SALT
- PEPPERCORNS
- OLIVE OIL

PREPARATION TIME: 2 $^{1}/2$ HOURS

SOAK THE CHICKPEAS overnight in cold water with a pinch of bicarbonate of soda and one of coarse sea salt. Drain and then boil in fresh water for two hours. When they are three-quarters done, heat some water with a piece each of leek, celery and carrot in a fish kettle. When the water comes to the boil, add the salt cod and cook over moderate heat for ten minutes, until the flesh breaks up. Drain and place on a serving dish, surrounded by the hot chickpeas. Season with salt, pepper, parsley and olive oil.

Buridda

GENOESE FISH CASSEROLE

- 1 CONGER EEL OF ABOUT 1.5KG / 3 1/4LB
- 1 WHITE-SKINNED ONION
- A SPRIG OF PARSLEY
- 1/2L / 1PT / 2 CUPS DRY WHITE WINE
- 300G / 3/4LB / 1 1/2 CUPS RIPE OR TINNED (CANNED) TOMATOES
- 500G / 1LB MUSSELS
- 500G / 1LB BABY CLAMS
- PEPPERCORNS
- OLIVE OIL

PREPARATION TIME: 1 HOUR

THIS IS THE ORIGINAL, fully-guaranteed Genoese recipe for a fragrant, very delicate fish dish (there are those who interpret this dish as a soup). Some people sauté the onion and parsley in a saucepan first, together with a fillet of anchovy, a clove of garlic and a handful of pine-nuts, then they brown the eel and only afterwards pop it into the oven with the wine. A tasty variation, though it is rather heavier than the traditional recipe.

CLEAN AND WASH the conger eel thoroughly. Slice, rinse and dry the pieces on a tea towel. Get the shell fish to open their shells by putting them in a pan with a little boiling water. Shell them (or as an alternative, it is possible to use frozen mussels and clams).

Arrange the eel slices on the bottom of a small, deep oven dish together with 3 tablespoons of oil. Scatter chopped onion and parsley over, adding a little of the seafood and seasoning with salt and pepper. Now put down another layer of eel and continue like this until all the fish ingredients are used up. Put pieces of tomato and a tablespoon of oil on the final layer. Pour over the wine to cover everything and place the dish in a medium oven. The *buridda* is ready when almost all the wine has evaporated.

Cozze al forno

BAKED MUSSELS

- 1.8KG / 3 3/4LB MUSSELS
- 2 CLOVES OF GARLIC
- A SPRIG OF PARSLEY
- 3 TBSP DRY BREADCRUMBS
- JUICE OF HALF A LEMON
- 50ML / 3 TBSP WHITE WINE
- OLIVE OIL

PREPARATION TIME: 1/2 HOUR

CLEAN THE MUSSELS, tearing off their rope-like "beards" and scraping the shells. Put them with a little water in a pan over the heat so that they open their shells. Eliminate those which remain closed, discard the empty shell of each one and arrange those with the mollusc inside on the bottom of a roasting-pan. Pre-heat the oven. In a bowl, thoroughly mix together the chopped garlic and parsley, the wine, the lemon, the liquor from the shell-fish, salt and pepper. Distribute the dressing among the full shells, dredging with dry breadcrumbs. Put the mussels in the oven to cook for a bare ten minutes.

Dentice all'ortolana

SEA-BREAM WITH COURGETTES

- 1 DENTEX OR SEA BREAM OF ABOUT 1KG / $2^1/_4$LB
- 4 RIPE TOMATOES
- 3 COURGETTES (ZUCCHINI)
- 1 TSP GRATED LEMON RIND
- 1 LIQUEUR GLASS DRY MARTINI VERMOUTH
- 60ML / 2 FL OZ / 4 TBSP WHITE WINE
- 4 TBSP FISH OR VEGETABLE STOCK
- KNOB OF BUTTER
- 20G / 1OZ / 2TBSP WHITE FLOUR
- OLIVE OIL

PREPARATION TIME: 35 MINUTES

CLEAN THE FISH, discarding the head and guts and divide into 4 fillets. Place in an oven dish and moisten with the vermouth, wine and 2-3 tablespoons of oil. Season with salt and white pepper. Bake the dish in the oven at 250°C (500°F, Gas Mark 10) for 6-7 minutes. Remove the fillets and keep warm. Work the butter into the flour and incorporate into the cooking juices in the dish, making a thick sauce. Wash and trim the vegetables and sauté the sliced courgettes in a pan with 4-5 tablespoons of oil, after refreshing them in the stock. Add the roughly-chopped tomatoes. Mix, season with salt and pepper and the lemon zest. Spoon the sauce into a serving dish and lay the fillets on top.

Grongo alla genovese

GENOESE CONGER EEL

- 1 CONGER EEL OF ABOUT 800G -1KG / $1^3/_4$-$2^1/_4$LB
- HALF AN ONION
- 4 ANCHOVIES
- 50G / 2OZ DRIED MUSHROOMS
- 60ML / 2 FL OZ / 4 TBSP DRY WHITE WINE
- 1 CLOVE OF GARLIC
- 600G / $1^1/_4$LB / $2^1/_2$ CUPS GREEN PEAS
- TOMATO SAUCE, OLIVE OIL

PREPARATION TIME: $^1/_2$ HOUR

SOAK THE MUSHROOMS. Clean, gut and wash the conger eel under running water, then cut into small chunks. Sauté the chopped onion in a pan with 6 tablespoons of oil and the rinsed and filleted anchovies.

Add the eel, drained and dried, and brown well on all sides. Drain and dry the mushrooms and add to the eel, together with the garlic, shelled peas, salt, pepper and wine (which you will allow to evaporate). Add a liberal tablespoon of tomato sauce, cover with the lid and cook for a quarter-hour, duly allowing it all to reduce.

Moscardini inzimino

Baby Squid with Chard

- 1kg / 2¼lb small squid or *moscardini*
- 2 bunches Swiss chard
- 2 cloves of garlic
- 220g / 8oz / 1¼ cups home-made tomato sauce
- Hot red pepper
- 125ml/ 4 fl oz / ½ cup white wine
- A sprig of parsley
- Olive oil

Preparation time: 1 hour

For those not in the know, the *moscardino* is an eight-armed cephalopod which is rather like an octopus in miniature. It has various dialectal names in Italian and there is even a variety of inferior quality which goes under the name of *moscardino bianco*. It admirably replaces octopus, squid or cuttlefish in any kind of recipe and is, in fact, a lot more delicate and tender. It can stand up boldly to our snub in the face of tradition which dictates the use of cuttlefish with *inzimino* sauce. Nobody knows exactly what the etymology of *inzimino* is, but luckily this does not detract from the absolute deliciousness of this characteristic preparation, based on molluscs, vegetables and aromas.

Trim and wash the chard (stripped of the tough, white midribs) and blanch briefly in boiling water. Drain, squeeze the water out and chop coarsely. Clean, gut and rinse the squid, cutting the inksac into fairly thick rings and halving the tentacles. Sauté gently in 3 tablespoons of oil in a pan with the garlic and pour over the wine, allowing it to evaporate slowly. Season with salt and pepper. Now add the chard and allow to absorb the flavour for about ten minutes. Add the tomato and hot red pepper and cook slowly for about twenty minutes. Dredge with finely-chopped fresh parsley at the moment of serving.

Orata al forno

Baked Gilthead

- 2 small gilthead or other varieties of white fish, e.g. dentex, bass, etc. (400g / 1lb each)
- 3-4 potatoes
- 1 leek
- rosemary
- half a lemon
- 2 cloves of garlic
- a sprig of parsley
- olive oil

Preparation time: 35 minutes

Wash, scale and gut the gilthead, opening them out. Stuff the stomach of each fish with a twig of rosemary, a slice of lemon, a clove of garlic, just a little salt and a pinch of pepper. Peel the potatoes, trim the leek and slice both vegetables. Arrange in a greased oven dish, sprinkle with salt and pepper and bake in a preheated, medium oven.

After ten minutes, oil the fish and lay it on the bed of potatoes and leeks. Cook for twenty minutes, turning the fish over half-way through. Finally, skin the fish and fillet it, discarding all the bones. Place the fillets on each dinner plate and garnish with the leeks and potatoes arranged artistically in a crescent. Add a wedge of lemon and a sprig of parsley.

Polpo alla luciana

Octopus Salad

- about 1kg / 2$^{1}/_{4}$lb octopus
- a sprig of parsley
- 1 lemon
- olive oil

Preparation time: 1 hour (plus cooling time)

Clean the octopus and place in a pan of barely-salted cold water and cook for three quarters-of-an-hour. The secret to make it nice and tender? Allow it to cool completely in its liquor. Drain, cut into pieces and place in a bowl with first-quality olive oil, salt, pepper and chopped parsley. Leave in a cool place for quite a few hours to rest and absorb the flavours (e.g., make it at mid-day for eating in the evening). A delicious, simple and superb recipe from the Neapolitan cuisine.

Polpo in galera

OCTOPUS STEWED IN TOMATO SAUCE

- ABOUT 1KG / 2 1/4LB OCTOPUS (PREFERABLY SMALL ONES)
- 125ML/ 4 FL OZ / 1/2 CUP WHITE WINE
- 400G / 14OZ / 2 CUPS TINNED (CANNED) TOMATOES
- 1 HOT RED PEPPER
- 2 CLOVES OF GARLIC
- A SPRIG OF PARSLEY
- OLIVE OIL

PREPARATION TIME: ABOUT 1 HOUR 10 MINUTES

IN A SAUCEPAN with 5 tablespoons of oil, sauté the crushed cloves of garlic and the chopped parsley very gently. Add the washed and trimmed octopus, with the eyes removed. Allow three or four minutes to absorb the flavour, then pour the wine over and turn up the flame to evaporate.

Lower the heat, add the roughly-chopped tomatoes, salt to taste and the hot red pepper. Cover with the lid and cook very slowly for 40-50 minutes (depending on the size of the octopus).

Once cooked, allow to cool a little in the saucepan and serve, garnishing with fresh parsley, if liked.

THE SAUCE OBTAINED from this octopus dish is excellent for serving over pasta. Indeed, I suggest you try it (see the recipe for *pennette alla corsara* on page 64). However, you will then need to increase (almost doubling) the quantity of tomato and dredge the finished pasta with very finely-chopped fresh parsley.

Rana pescatrice alla melagrana

ANGLER FISH WITH POMEGRANATE

- 600G / 1 1/4LB FILLET OF ANGLER FISH
- 60G / 2OZ / 4 TBSP BUTTER
- 125ML/ 4 FL OZ / 1/2 CUP CREAM
- 2 LEMONS
- 1 POMEGRANATE
- A SPRIG OF PARSLEY
- A TWIG OF WILD FENNEL
- 60ML / 2 FL OZ / 4 TBSP MARTINI DRY VERMOUTH
- 1/2L / 1PT / 2 CUPS REDUCED FISH STOCK
- 3-4 TBSP WHITE FLOUR

PREPARATION TIME: 35 MINUTES

COAT THE FILLETS with flour and colour in the melted butter in a frying pan until both sides are golden. Douse with the Martini and allow to evaporate. Put the fillets with the fish stock in an oven dish and bake for 20 minutes. Meanwhile, blend the cream, lemon juice, parsley and chopped fennel. Season with salt and white pepper. Arrange the fillets on a serving dish and mask with the sauce. At the moment of serving (absolutely not beforehand, or they will discolour), scatter the pomegranate seeds over and grate a little lemon zest on top.

Sgombri "in scaveccio"

Mackerel in a Vegetable Sauce

- 4 mackerel fillets
- 2 carrots
- 2 sticks of celery
- 2 courgettes (zucchini)
- 1 potato
- 185ml / 6 fl oz / 3/4 cup white wine
- 125ml/ 4 fl oz / 1/2 cup wine vinegar
- 30g / 1oz / 2 tbsp butter
- olive oil

Preparation time: 3/4 hour

Arrange the mackerel fillets in an oven dish with salt and pepper, and pour over 4 tablespoons of white wine and 4 of olive oil (of pure quality but not too sharp on the palate) so as to submerge the fish. Chill the dish in the refrigerator. Clean the vegetables and cut them up finely. Sauté in the butter in a frying pan and pour on the remaining wine and the vinegar. Cook over gentle heat for half-an-hour. Then sieve it all (or put through a *mouli légumes*) to make a sauce, regulating the density by adding a little flour, if needs be. Place the dish of fillets in a medium oven for 15-20 minutes. Pour the sauce into the centre of the serving dish, lay the fillets on top, drizzle a little oil over and serve.

Sogliole alla lattaia

Soles Poached in Milk

- 4 soles
- 1/2l / 1pt / 2 cups milk
- 125 ml / 4 fl oz / 1/2 cup fish stock
- 1 small white-skinned onion (or chives)
- 60g / 2oz / 4 tbsp butter

Preparation time:25 minutes

Clean the soles by slitting them across near the tail. Pull up the dark skin, grasp it firmly and drag it up and off the fillets. Poach in the milk diluted with the stock for 10-12 minutes, after seasoning them with salt and pepper. Meanwhile, pound the skinned onion to reduce it to a paste. With a fork, blend it into the butter.

Remove the soles from the heat, drain and serve very hot, decorating each one with a good-sized flake of aromatised butter which will slowly melt. Serve with chunks of boiled potatoes dusted with parsley.

Sogliole al vino

SOLES IN A WINE AND CHEESE SAUCE

- 4 SOLES
- 1 EGG
- DRY BREADCRUMBS
- KNOB OF BUTTER
- 125 ML / 4 FL OZ / 1/2 CUP WHITE WINE
- FONTINA OR SHARPER ASIAGO CHEESE
- PARSLEY
- VEGETABLE OIL

PREPARATION TIME: 30 MINUTES

CLEAN THE SOLES, remove the heads and fillet by cutting down the spine. Immerse the fillets in a bowl with the beaten eggs, salt and pepper and leave them for an hour or two. Rub both sides in the dry breadcrumbs and fry in boiling oil. Drain them and lay in the frying pan to colour in a little of the oil they were fried in, together with the butter and season to taste with salt and pepper. Pour in the wine and blend for five minutes, adding a little chopped parsley. Serve the fillets masked with their sauce and dusted with flakes of a good cheese (you can also use slices of processed cheese). To resolve the problem of a vegetable plate in one "sole" sweep, lay the sole on some boiled spinach.

Sogliole fritte

FRIED SOLE

- 4 SOLES
- A SOUP PLATE FULL OF MILK
- WHITE FLOUR
- VEGETABLE OIL FOR FRYING

PREPARATION TIME: 25 MINUTES

CLEAN THE SOLES. Leave to soak briefly in the milk. Drain and coat lightly with flour.

Colour the fish on both sides in boiling oil, drain and season sparingly with salt.

Serve nice and crisp with lemon wedges and parsley sprigs. Accompany with fried or mashed potatoes.

Spiedini di mare

Seafood on the Spit

- 4 sole fillets
- 200g / 1/2lb prawn tails
- 200g / 1/2lb red mullet fillets
- 200g / 1/2lb cuttlefish, cleaned
- 1 lemon
- 1 courgette (zucchini)
- olive oil

Preparation time: 20 minutes

Get the fishmonger to clean the fish, molluscs and crustaceans. Cut them into pieces small enough to thread onto a skewer. Wash the courgette and slice. Scrub the lemon and cut into wedges and slices. Take a skewer and impale on it a chunk of prawn, a slice of courgette, a portion of cuttlefish, a slice of lemon, a piece of sole, another slice of courgette, a length of mullet, a slice of lemon, and so on. Grease each skewer with a drop of oil and cook over charcoal (or under the electric grill attachment) for about ten minutes, adding a pinch of salt at the end.

Spigola al piatto

Steamed Bass

- 700-800g / 1 1/2 - 1 3/4lb bass
- 2 cloves of garlic
- a sprig of parsley
- 4 tiny cherry tomatoes
- olive oil

Preparation time: 25 minutes

Scale, clean, gut and open out the bass, eliminating the fins, head and bones and reducing them to fillets. Lay them side by side on a large plate, trickle some oil over, dust with salt and white pepper. Place a sprig of parsley and a clove of garlic on each one and arrange the tomatoes at one side. Put the plate over a suitably-sized saucepan which is three quarters' full of water. Cover the fish with another plate without squashing it or letting it escape at the sides. Bring the water to the boil and steam slowly for a quarter-hour. Skin the fillets, divide them in half, arrange on the dinner plates, garnish with a baby tomato and a sprig of parsley.

A dressing of mayonnaise would be customary, otherwise dribble a little oil over. There is no better way to savour bass.

Tonno coi piselli

Tuna with Green Peas

- 1kg / 2 1/4lb fresh tuna
- half a white-skinned onion
- 1 clove of garlic
- 2 anchovies
- 400g / 14oz / 2 cups tomatoes
- 60ml / 2 fl oz / 4 tbsp white wine
- 600g / 1 1/4lb green peas
- olive oil

Preparation time: 1/2 hour

Sauté the finely-chopped garlic and parsley with the boned anchovies, torn to pieces, in 5 tablespoons of oil in a saucepan. Gently fry the tuna fish, turning it over to brown on both sides. Pour over the wine and allow to evaporate.

Add the roughly-chopped tomatoes, cover and reduce over a medium flame for ten minutes.

Rinse and drain the shelled peas and add to the fish. Stir carefully and, leaving the pan uncovered, continue cooking slowly for another ten minutes.

Triglie alla livornese

Red Mullet, Livorno Style

- 800g / 1 3/4lb medium-sized red mullet
- White flour
- Half an onion
- 2 cloves of garlic
- 400-500g / 14oz - 1lb 2oz / 2-2 1/2 cups fresh or tinned (canned) tomatoes
- Parsley
- Olive oil

Preparation time: 1/2 hour

Clean, gut and rinse the mullet. Coat with flour and brown in 6 tablespoons of oil in a frying pan. Take out the fish and leave to dry on a sheet of kitchen paper. Sauté the chopped onion and the whole garlic in the pan, then remove them and flavour the skinned, roughly-chopped tomato in the oil, seasoning with salt and pepper. Barely ten minutes later, add the mullet and allow to absorb the flavour over very gentle heat. Turn them over carefully because this is a very fragile fish. Continue cooking until the sauce has reduced. Serve hot in the sauce, with a dusting of parsley.

Triglie all'erbe fini

Red Mullet with Fines Herbes

- 4 red mullet, 250g / 9oz each
- Bunch of fines herbes (dill, chervil, tarragon and marjoram), chopped
- 125ml/ 4 fl oz / 1/2 cup white wine
- 4 potatoes
- A little vegetable or fish stock
- Knob of butter
- Olive oil

Preparation time: 1/2 hour

Peel the potatoes and slice finely. Wash and trim the mullet. Heat 6 tablespoons of oil in an oven dish and lay a layer of potatoes on the bottom. Arrange the mullet on top, sprinkle the fines herbes over (remember to keep a little aside), season lightly with salt and freshly-ground pepper and moisten with the wine. Cover the dish with a sheet of aluminium foil and bake in the oven at 220°C (450°F, Gas Mark 8) for 5 minutes. Take the dish out of the oven, remove the foil, if necessary moisten with a little stock and return to the oven for another 5-6 minutes. Remove the fish and potatoes and arrange them on a hot serving dish (you cannot see it in the illustration opposite, but I can assure you it is hot!). Blend the cooking juices, the remaining herbs and a few pieces of cold butter in the food processor. Pour this sauce over the mullet and serve.

Trota al cartoccio

Trout Baked in Foil

- 4 trout, each about 250g /9oz
- 300g / 11oz (clean weight) mussels, baby clams, squid and shrimps (frozen, if you prefer)
- Half a lemon
- A sprig of parsley
- A twig of rosemary
- Olive oil

Preparation time: 1/2 hour

Clean, gut and wash the trout. Dip them in a bowl with 5 tablespoons of oil into which the lemon juice has been whisked.

Lay four sheets of aluminium foil out on the kitchen table and grease them with the oil left in the bowl.

Place a trout on each one, dust with salt and pepper. Put rosemary and a strip of lemon peel in the stomach of the fish.

Arrange the seafood on and around the trout, seasoning with a little salt and a few parsley leaves.

Close up the parcels well and bake in a medium oven for barely twenty minutes.

Serve each diner with a trout still enclosed in its parcel, for him to unwrap himself, discarding the foil.

Trote al pepe tricolore

Trout with Tricoloured Pepper

- 4 fillets of salmon trout
- 4 small potatoes
- 50g / 2 oz top of the milk or single (light) cream
- 80g / 3oz / 4 tbsp butter
- 2 tbsp white, red and green peppercorns
- 125ml/ 4 fl oz / 1/2 cup vermouth (Martini dry) or dry white wine
- White flour

Preparation time: 20 minutes

Flour the trout fillets and brown in a frying pan with a large knob of butter (three minutes each side). Drain the fat off from the pan and moisten the fish with the vermouth. Season with salt and ground white pepper.

Immediately add the tricoloured peppercorns and the cream, completing the brief spell of cooking. Separately, peel the potatoes and slice finely into rings. Colour them on both sides in a pan with a little butter.

Arrange them tastefully on a serving dish, together with the trout, covered in its sauce and the peppercorns. Carry the dish through to the dining table, not neglecting to remark nonchalantly to the company that this is a truly Italian dish...

Fishing boats and nets on the calm, blue waters of the small port of Mazara del Vallo

OMELETTES

Fricassea aromatica di patate

HERBY POTATOES IN A LEMON SAUCE

- 1 KG / 2¼LB POTATOES
- 2 ONIONS
- 30G / 1OZ / 2 TBSP WHITE FLOUR
- 40G / 1½ OZ / 3 TBSP BUTTER
- 50G / 2OZ CURED HAM
- JUICE OF 1 LEMON
- ½L / 1PT / 2 CUPS BOILING MEAT STOCK
- HALF A LEEK
- 125ML / 4 FL OZ /½ CUP MILK
- A BUNCH OF FRESH (OR A PINCH OF DRIED) HERBS: CHIVES, TARRAGON, WATERCRESS, THYME AND DILL

PREPARATION TIME: ½ HOUR

PEEL THE POTATOES and slice. Take the outer skin off the onions and the external leaves off the leek, slice finely and place in a pan to brown in the butter with the potatoes and the diced cured ham. Dredge with flour, stir gently and pour the broth over, adding salt, white pepper and the lemon juice. Stir again and finally pour in the milk, allowing the sauce to thicken after five minutes on a moderate boil. Turn off the heat. Wash and pick over the herbs, cut them up finely and toss into the saucepan. Serve immediately.

THIS IS A GREAT DISH even served up as a side-plate. Watercress with its rather bitter flavour is not difficult to come by and can even be cultivated on your balcony in the city. Thyme, scattered all along the Mediterranean coast, is easy to find dried and it still keeps its aroma in that state. Dill, which can also be dried, is a Mediterranean shrub similar to wild fennel. The sprouts and more tender leaves are gathered just before the flowering period when their aroma is at its most intense.

Frittata all'ortolana

VEGETABLE OMELETTE

- 8 EGGS
- 200G / 7OZ POTATOES
- 1 ONION (OR LEEK)
- 1 SALAD TOMATO
- 1 CLOVE OF GARLIC
- 125ML / 4 FL OZ / 1/2 CUP VEGETABLE STOCK
- BASIL
- PARSLEY
- PARMESAN CHEESE, IN FLAKES
- OLIVE OIL

PREPARATION TIME: 3/4 HOUR

WASH AND PEEL the potatoes and slice into chunks. Sweat the sliced onion and garlic in 4 tablespoons of oil in a frying pan. Add the potatoes and the roughly-chopped tomato, cover with the lid and allow the flavours to blend, moistening the vegetables every now and then with the stock, until the potatoes soften up. Beat the eggs with a little salt and pepper, adding the Parmesan cheese and the contents of the pan. Stir. Oil a frying pan and pour in the mixture. Let the omelette set on one side, then, helping yourself with a plate, turn it over to cook on the other side. In Liguria they make it with parboiled Swiss chard and marjoram.

PELLEGRINO ARTUSI, the Italian cookery expert, suggested the eggs should not be whisked too much for omelettes. Break them up with a fork and when the egg whites mingle in with the yolks, stop whisking.

Frittata alla contadina

COURGETTE (ZUCCHINI) OMELETTE

- 5 EGGS
- 2 COURGETTES (ZUCCHINI)
- 1 RIPE TOMATO
- 2 CLOVES OF GARLIC
- A SPRIG OF PARSLEY
- HARD PECORINO CHEESE, GRATED
- OLIVE OIL

PREPARATION TIME: 1/2 HOUR

WASH THE COURGETTES and slice into rounds. Put in a covered saucepan and, for barely a quarter-hour over a low flame, sweat in 3 tablespoons of oil with a clove of garlic cut in half. Beat the eggs in a bowl with a little salt and pepper. Add the courgettes, the roughly-chopped tomato, a whole clove of garlic, the sprig of parsley and a dusting of grated pecorino cheese.

Heat a frying pan with a little oil covering the bottom and toss in the mixture. Cook the omelette on both sides, using a plate to turn it over.

Frittata alle erbe aromatiche

HERB OMELETTE

- 8 EGGS
- A SPRIG OF PARSLEY
- A BUNCH OF CHERVIL
- A FEW CHIVES
- 4 TWIGS OF TARRAGON
- OLIVE OIL

PREPARATION TIME: 20 MINUTES

BEAT THE EGGS in a bowl, season with salt (sparingly) and the herbs, washed, trimmed and finely-chopped. Heat the oil in a skillet and pour in the eggs and allow to set. When the omelette has coloured on one side, turn it over with the aid of a plate and finish cooking on the other side. Serve hot.

CHERVIL, a plant similar to parsley but more delicate, originated in the Mediterranean area. Tarragon is also known by the French term *estragon*. An excellent omelette may be made with basil and garden mint (or catmint).

Frittata con gli zoccoli

BACON OMELETTE

- 4 EGGS
- 200G / 7OZ UNSMOKED SLAB BACON
- OLIVE OIL

PREPARATION TIME: 1/4 HOUR

DICE THE BACON and brown it slowly in an oiled frying pan. Meanwhile, beat the eggs, seasoning with salt.

When the bacon is golden, pour the eggs into the pan and allow to set just enough to enable you to fold half the omelette over and finish cooking on the other side.

Frittata di cipolle

ONION OMELETTE

- 6 EGGS
- 1 LARGE WHITE-SKINNED ONION
- KNOB OF BUTTER
- OLIVE OIL

PREPARATION TIME: 1/2 HOUR

ALTHOUGH ONIONS are delicious and good for your health, a strong stomach is needed to digest them. For more delicate stomachs and the less accommodating members of the family, I suggest a substitution with the more agreeable leek or even changing the vegetable component altogether; blanch some green peas with some garlic, parsley and a *soupçon* of oil in a little water, then add to the omelette. An expedient of great social and peptic efficacy!

TRIM THE ONION, quarter and slice finely. Sauté in butter in a skillet until golden, barely seasoning with salt.

Meanwhile, beat the eggs in a bowl and, when the onions are coloured, pour into the pan.

Cook the omelette on one side only, leaving the centre creamy and unset.

Frittata di pasta

PASTA OMELETTE

- 4 EGGS
- 200G / 7OZ COOKED PASTA
- A SPRIG OF PARSLEY
- PARMESAN CHEESE
- OLIVE OIL

PREPARATION TIME: ABOUT 20 MINUTES

IF YOU HAVE a little pasta left over (whether covered in sauce or not, or whether of the short or long type, though in the latter case, cut in half), do not even think of throwing it all out, but prepare this delicious omelette. It is the umpteenth demonstration - as if there were any need - of Neapolitan genius. Beat the eggs in a bowl, dust with cheese, salt and pepper and throw in the pasta (separating the pieces out if some have stuck together) and the chopped parsley and stir. Set aside to rest for ten minutes. Heat a well-oiled frying pan and pour in the mixture, stirring. Allow the egg to set over reduced heat, turn over the omelette with the aid of a plate and finish off cooking on the other side. A delicious crust will have formed here and there on the pasta.

Tortino di carciofi

ARTICHOKE OMELETTE

- 4 GLOBE ARTICHOKES
- 2 TBSP WHITE FLOUR
- 6 EGGS
- 30G / 1OZ / 2 TBSP BUTTER
- 60ML / 2 FL OZ / 4 TBSP MILK

PREPARATION TIME: 1/2 HOUR

UNLIKE THE USUAL omelettes which are generally solid and well-set, the consistency of these so-called *tortini* must be quite creamy.

CLEAN AND TRIM the artichokes.

Cut them into wedges and dip in water acidulated with some drops of lemon to prevent them from blackening.

Roll them in flour and fry in 8 tablespoons of oil in a frying pan until they are crisp. Beat the eggs in a bowl, adding the milk, salt and pepper. Butter an oven dish and arrange the artichokes in it.

Cover with the beaten egg and allow to set in a slow oven for ten minutes.

Tortino di spinaci

SPINACH OMELETTE

- 400G / 14OZ SPINACH
- 4 EGGS
- 30G / 1OZ / 2 TBSP BUTTER
- OLIVE OIL

PREPARATION TIME: 35 MINUTES

WASH AND PICK over the spinach and parboil in very little water. Squeeze the liquor out and chop the vegetable up finely. Heat 2-3 tablespoons of oil with a clove of garlic in an oven dish and let the spinach absorb the flavour. Add the eggs, beaten up with a little salt and pepper, add flakes of butter and allow to melt. Transfer the dish to a preheated, very hot oven (220°C / 450°F / Gas Mark 8) and leave it for about fifteen minutes. Take it out a moment before the eggs set in the centre of the *tortino*.

Tortino di zucchini

COURGETTE (ZUCCHINI) RAMEKINS

- 6 ELONGATED COURGETTES
- 3 EGGS
- 50G / 2OZ PARMESAN CHEESE
- GARLIC AND PARSLEY
- 50G / 2OZ TOP OF THE MILK (MEDIUM CREAM)
- 50G / 2OZ / 4 TBSP BUTTER
- OLIVE OIL

PREPARATION TIME: 1 HOUR

SLICE THE COURGETTES into thin rings and sauté gently with a clove of garlic in 2-3 tablespoons of oil in a covered frying pan.

Beat the eggs in a bowl and add the courgettes, the top of the milk, the chopped parsley, the grated Parmesan, salt and pepper.

Butter some individual ramekins, pour in the mixture and cook in a water bath for 40 minutes in the oven at 180°C (350°F / Gas Mark 4).

Uova bazzotte al pomodoro

LIGHTLY-BOILED TOMATO EGGS

- 8 EGGS
- 500G / 1LB 2OZ FRESH OR TINNED (CANNED) TOMATOES
- 1 ONION, 1 CARROT, 1 STICK OF CELERY
- 2 CLOVES OF GARLIC
- HOT RED PEPPER
- BASIL, PARSLEY, OREGANO, WILD FENNEL LEAVES, MARJORAM
- OLIVE OIL

PREPARATION TIME: 3/4 HOUR

MAKE A RATHER THICK tomato sauce by sweating the clove of garlic in 4 tablespoons of olive oil in a saucepan. Remove and toss in the roughly-chopped tomatoes, the finely-sliced herbs, and the other whole clove of garlic with the whole hot red pepper. Season with salt, cover with the lid and allow to reduce over gentle heat. In the meantime, boil the eggs (four minutes once the water starts to bubble), allow to cool, then shell them. When the tomato sauce is ready, turn off the heat, trickle over a little raw olive oil and sprinkle with the washed and finely-chopped aromatic herbs. Arrange the eggs symmetrically on the serving dish and mask with the sauce. Serve immediately.

THESE EGGS, WHICH also go under the incorrect name of *mollette* from the French *oeufs mollets*, are cooked in their shells in boiling water for 4 or 5 minutes at the most. With their lovely creamy yolk, they are halfway between *oeuf à la coque* (boiled for 3 minutes at the most) and hard-boiled eggs (7 minutes at least). As

an alternative to the tomato sauce, you may serve them with a nice green sauce (based on garlic, parsley, capers, anchovies and olive oil), home-made mayonnaise, or else blanched and liquidised vegetables (spinach, Swiss chard, carrots, celery) which have been sautéed in butter or olive oil with garlic.

Uova in cocotte al pomodoro

POACHED EGGS WITH TOMATO

A *COCOTTE* (which is nothing to do with certain young ladies known to be immune to undue prejudice - the appellation goes back a few years because nowadays the relevant terminology has become much coarser), is a round container, usually in porcelain, fitted with a lid and particularly suitable for cooking in a *bain marie* or in the oven.

In this specific case, tiny individual *cocottines* will be needed - one for each diner. An egg will be broken into each one and cooked for just as long as necessary to set the white without it hardening (the egg will then be served in the same container).

PREPARE THE tomato sauce by following the instructions in the previous recipe, but reduce the quantities by half. Butter each cocotte dish and place in it a tablespoon of sauce, an egg, salt and pepper. Mask with more sauce, a leaf of basil and a knob of butter. Put on the lid and bake in a *bain marie* in a medium oven for 6-7 minutes.

- 4 EGGS
- FRESHLY-MADE TOMATO SAUCE
- BASIL
- 100G / 4OZ / 1/2 CUP BUTTER

PREPARATION TIME: 3/4 HOUR

AN *EN COCOTTE* preparation can be varied in a thousand ways: besides using tomatoes, try dressing the eggs with diced prosciutto and fontina cheese, as well as a fair amount of pepper. Or else, put some crumbled sausage and a knob of *stracchino* soft cream cheese. Yet another alternative is a quarter of a clove of garlic, parsley, gorgonzola cheese and a teaspoon of celery parboiled and liquidised.

Salads and Vegetable Dishes

Asparagi alla fiorentina

ASPARAGUS, FLORENTINE STYLE

- 1KG / 2 1/4LB ASPARAGUS
- 4 EGGS
- 80G / 3OZ / 1/4 CUP PLUS 2 TBSP BUTTER
- GRATED PARMESAN
- FRESHLY-GROUND PEPPER

PREPARATION TIME: 3/4 HOUR

TRIM AND SCRAPE the asparagus. Tie into bundles and cook upright in a covered saucepan in enough cold water to cover the white part. After a quarter-hour, test how firm the vegetables are; they must be cooked *al dente*. Allow to cool a little, drain and discard the white part. Place the green tips in a frying pan where you have melted the butter. Sauté the asparagus over low heat for 5 minutes, then remove from the pan, where you will now fry the eggs, seasoning them with salt and pepper. Arrange the asparagus on a serving dish, lay the eggs on top and dust with Parmesan cheese.

THIS IS QUITE a hefty side-dish, almost a meal in itself. It could, perhaps, be followed by a delicate *stracciatella* (egg and cheese flakes in broth) to make a tasty, but light, luncheon. It must be pointed out here that there is a secret even to the common fried egg. First of all, the frying pan must not be too large and the butter should be hot, but not smoking. Once the egg is broken, slip only the white (without any salt or pepper) into the fat, adeptly keeping the yolk back in a shell half. When the white has set and is practically cooked (some turn it over with a spatula to get it 'done' all over), place the yolk, seasoned with salt and pepper, in the centre. It should remain under-cooked; rather runny and turning slightly pearly.

Caponata

AUBERGINE (EGGPLANT) APPETISER

- 2 SMALL FRESH ONIONS
- 2 AUBERGINES (EGGPLANTS)
- 500G / 1LB 2OZ RIPE TOMATOES
- 500G / 1LB 2OZ COURGETTES (ZUCCHINI)
- 2 SWEET (BELL) PEPPERS
- 1 CLOVE OF GARLIC
- PINE-NUTS (OPTIONAL)
- OLIVE OIL

PREPARATION TIME: 50 MINUTES

ORIGINALLY FROM SICILY, this flavoursome mixture of vegetables (which, with a variation or two, is known under the name of *ratatouille* in the South of France) could even, together with plain boiled rice or fresh egg noodles, be proposed as a meal in itself, especially in the summer.

Wash and trim the vegetables, removing the seeds from the tomatoes and peppers. Heat 6 tablespoons of oil in a large frying pan, add the finely-chopped onions, the skinned tomatoes cut into pieces, the diced aubergines, the peppers in strips, the rounds of courgettes and the garlic.

Sauté everything over a fierce heat, season with salt and pepper and lower the flame. Simmer for about twenty minutes, adding pine-nuts, if you wish. During the cooking time, it may be necessary to add a little more oil.

Serve hot, though it is also very good when eaten cold. Indeed, it is consumed exclusively so by some people in Sicily.

Cardi in umido

BRAISED CARDOONS

- 800G / $1^3/4$LB CARDOONS
- 5 TBSP WHITE FLOUR
- 1 CLOVE OF GARLIC
- 5 FRESH, RIPE TOMATOES (OR THE SAME TINNED WEIGHT)
- OLIVE OIL
- OIL FOR FRYING

PREPARATION TIME: ABOUT $^1/2$ HOUR

BLANCH, SKIN AND SEED the tomatoes. Pick over the cardoons, removing the leaves and tough parts, and parboil in salted, boiling water.

Cut into short lengths, coat with flour and deep fry in oil. Drain. Sauté the garlic in a saucepan with 4 tablespoons of oil, then remove. Add the roughly-chopped tomatoes. Blend over a gentle heat.

Now add the fried cardoons and allow them the absorb the flavour. What more is there to say? Just staggering!

Fagioli all'uccelletto

WHITE BEANS WITH TOMATO AND GARLIC

- 1KG / $2^1/4$LB FRESH TOSCANELLI BEANS (400G / 14OZ IF DRIED)
- 400G / 14OZ / $2^1/2$ CUPS TINNED (CANNED) TOMATOES
- 3 CLOVES OF GARLIC
- FRESH SAGE
- OLIVE OIL

PREPARATION TIME: $^3/4$ HOUR

IF THE BEANS are dried, they must be soaked, unless you are willing to wait longer for them to cook than the usual half-hour of this recipe. Once the beans are cooked, heat six tablespoons of olive oil in a saucepan and sauté the garlic and sage. Add the beans and stir to allow them to absorb the flavours. Throw in the tomatoes, roughly-chopped. Season with salt, cover the pan and cook for about a quarter-hour. Serve nice and hot with a sprinkling of freshly-ground pepper.

Fagiolini in salsa verde

RUNNER BEANS IN PARSLEY SAUCE

- 600G - 700G / $1^1/_4$ - $1^1/_2$LB RUNNER BEANS
- 2-3 CLOVES OF GARLIC
- BUNCH OF PARSLEY
- CAPERS
- OLIVE OIL

PREPARATION TIME: ABOUT 20 MINUTES

TOP, TAIL AND STRING the runner beans. Boil in salted water for a quarter-hour until nice and crisp.

In the meanwhile, finely chop the garlic and a lot of parsley. Add the drained beans, dress with olive oil, salt and pepper. Mix in some drained capers.

These are very easy to prepare and delicious, even better if eaten when in season (frozen beans tend to be rather mushy). Served with a sliced hard-boiled egg, they are better still.

They should be served hot.

Fagiolini in fricassea

RUNNER BEANS IN A LEMON SAUCE

TOP, TAIL AND STRING the runner beans and immerse in boiling salted water for about twenty minutes.

Drain and place in a saucepan with the melted butter, sprinkling with the Parmesan cheese. Stir and, after 3-4 minutes, turn off the heat. Beat the yolks well and mix in the lemon juice.

Add this sauce to the runner beans (remember, always off the heat). Stir and serve warm. A simple but delicious side plate

- 600G / 1LB 5OZ RUNNER BEANS
- KNOB OF BUTTER
- GRATED PARMESAN CHEESE
- 2 EGG YOLKS
- JUICE OF HALF A LEMON

PREPARATION TIME: ABOUT 30 MINUTES

Fave stufate

BRAISED BROAD BEANS

- $1^1/_2$-2KG / 3-4LB FRESH BROAD BEANS
- 1 ONION
- 50G / 2OZ UNSMOKED BACON
- $^1/_2$- TBSP TOMATO CONCENTRATE (PASTE)
- OLIVE OIL

PREPARATION TIME: ABOUT $^3/_4$ HOUR

HULL THE BROAD BEANS (i.e., take them out of the green pod which contains the delicious seeds: the overall weight also depends on the freshness, in other words, how much water there is in the vegetable fibre). There should 600-700g ($1^1/_4$-$1^1/_2$lb) beans left.

Slice the onion and sauté until golden, together with the diced bacon, in 4 tablespoons of oil in a saucepan. Add the beans, salt and pepper. Allow the flavours to blend slowly; there is no hurry. Dissolve the tomato paste in a very little water and pour into the saucepan. Cover and simmer slowly for half-an-hour, adding a little more water if needs be.

Fiori di zucca fritti

Courgette Flower Fritters

- About 20 courgette (zucchini) flowers
- 2 whole eggs and 1 egg white
- 180g / 7oz / 1 cup 3 tbsp white flour
- Vegetable oil for frying

Preparation time: about 1 hour

Beat the whole eggs and the egg white in a bowl, gradually whisking in the flour until you have a fairly runny, lump-free, coating batter (if necessary, add about 60ml / 2 fl oz / 4 tbsp water or beer). Put aside for half-an-hour. The courgette flowers should not be rinsed; if (quite rightly so) you do not trust their freedom from grit, limit the contact with water to the minimum and dry them very, very well. After removing the pistil and the little green leaves, dip them into the batter, draining off any excess. Fry in plenty of oil, making sure that they are evenly golden all over. Serve them very crisp. The flowers can only be found in late spring and summer.

Funghi trifolati

Mushrooms with Garlic and Parsley

- 500g / 1lb 2oz *Boletus edulis* mushrooms
- 1 clove of garlic
- A sprig of parsley
- A sprig of catmint (or garden mint)
- Olive oil

Preparation time: 45-50 minutes

Clean the mushrooms: remove any lumps of earth and other impurities with the tip of a knife blade, brushing off grit and dirt with a toothbrush, and wash them by wiping them over with a damp cloth.

They absolutely must not be rinsed under running water, as some part-time gourmet may suggest. Not only are they quite simply not cleaned in this way, but the soaking takes away their delicate aroma and gives them a decided taste of dish water!

Prepare the mushrooms by cutting them, stems included, into pieces and lay them on a dry tea cloth. Chop the garlic and parsley finely and sauté very slowly in a small saucepan with 5 tablespoons of oil. Add the mushrooms, season with salt and pepper and put on the lid. Cook over very low heat for a good quarter-hour. Remove the lid, add some catmint leaves (though careful not to exaggerate) and cook for another ten minutes.

Insalata di Caterina

Red Chicory Salad

- 2 bunches of *radicchio rosso*
- 200g / 7oz fresh pecorino cheese
- Fillets of anchovy
- Capers
- A fistful of black olives
- Olive oil
- Vinegar

Preparation time: 1/4 hour

Rinse and dry the red chicory. Add the diced cheese, the anchovy fillets (broken up), the stoned olives and the capers. Season with salt and pepper, olive oil and vinegar (the latter may be the pure, naturally sweet grape product called *aceto balsamico*, if you prefer). The red, ivory and black of the ingredients contrast beautifully (see opposite page). Of the two types of this 'lettuce', you should really choose the Chioggia one (at the southern tip of the Venetian lagoon), with curly leaves growing in a ball, and not the Treviso variety (north of Venice) which forms a bunch of leaves.

Insalata di rinforzo

Cauliflower Salad

To serve 6 people

- 1 cauliflower
- 6-7 anchovies
- A fistful of black olives
- A fistful of capers
- Olive oil
- Vinegar

Preparation time: 1/2 hour (plus "resting" time)

Rinse the anchovies, eliminating head and bones, and fillet them. Trim the cauliflower, discarding the core and tough leaves. Boil in salted water for barely 15 minutes, putting a piece of bread in the pan so that the whole house does not become impregnated with the persistent smell. Remove while still crisp, drain, allow to cool and break it up. Mix in the roughly-chopped anchovies, the stoned olives and the drained capers. Dress with salt, pepper, olive oil and vinegar. Leave to rest before serving. This side dish is poetic and sober; it "backs up" the traditional Neapolitan eel on Christmas Eve.

Lenticchie stufate

Stewed Lentils

- 250g / 9oz dried continental lentils
- 1 onion
- 1 carrot
- 1 stick of celery
- 1 tsp tomato concentrate (paste)
- A sprig of parsley
- Olive oil

Preparation time: about 1 hour (plus the soaking time)

Soak the lentils in water for 3-4 hours. Drain and boil them in salted water for half-an-hour, draining the seeds before they get mushy. Make a mirepoix with the coarsely-chopped vegetables sautéed in 4 tablespoons of oil. Add the lentils, salt (very little) and pepper, and allow the pulses to absorb the flavours. Add the tomato concentrate and dilute with a little of the lentil liquor. Cover and cook over low heat for half-an-hour, adding more water, if necessary. Then remove the lid, reduce the liquid and garnish with a few parsley leaves. Lentils are a fine foil for *cotechino*, the spiced pork sausage served boiled. It is believed that, eaten on New Year's Day, they bring good luck and especially money. Let's hope so!

Melanzane al funghetto

AUBERGINE (EGGPLANT) SAUTÉ

- 3 ROUND AUBERGINES (EGGPLANTS)
- 1 CLOVE OF GARLIC
- A PINCH OF OREGANO
- CHOPPED PARSLEY
- 2 RIPE OR TINNED (CANNED) TOMATOES

PREPARATION TIME: 25 MINUTES

WASH THE AUBERGINES and cut each into six wedges without peeling them. Remove a little of the central flesh, full of seeds, and cut the wedges into strips.

Sauté the garlic in 4 tablespoons of oil in a frying pan, removing it before it colours.

Add the aubergines and season with salt, pepper and oregano (and, if you like the aroma, some catmint leaves, no more than just a couple). Halfway through cooking (about 8-10 minutes), add the tomatoes, cleaned, skinned and roughly-chopped.

Dredge with the chopped parsley and serve. Elongated aubergines may be used at the cook's discretion (just as the round ones may also be used in the following recipe).

Melanzane farcite

STUFFED AUBERGINES (EGGPLANTS)

- 4 ELONGATED AUBERGINES (EGGPLANTS)
- 2 MOZZARELLA BALLS
- 10 STONED BLACK OLIVES
- BASIL
- OREGANO

PREPARATION TIME: ABOUT 3/4 HOUR

RINSE AND TRIM thoroughly the aubergines and cut in half lengthways. With a teaspoon, scoop out most of the flesh, leaving little "shells" which you will season with salt and will place upside down for half-an-hour to drain, so that the vegetables lose that bitter flavour which would compromise your family and guests' appreciation of this dish. Chop one ball of mozzarella, the olives, basil and oregano all up together, season with salt and pepper and fill the aubergines with this mixture. Cover each "shell" with a slice of mozzarella. Bake in a hot oven at 200°C (400°F, Gas Mark 6) for half-an-hour and serve the aubergines hot on a platter (like in the illustration) rich with other stuffed vegetables, such as the potatoes in the following recipe, globe artichokes, sweet peppers, tomatoes and courgettes (zucchini). Of course, just as the vegetable "shell" may vary according to taste, so may the filling. Instead of cheese, there may be meat (as in the courgettes on page 199) or rice (which blends well with tomato).

Patate farcite

STUFFED POTATOES

- 4 LARGE POTATOES
- 50ML / 3 TBSP CREAM
- 60G / 2$^{1}/_{2}$ OZ / 4 TBSP BUTTER
- GRATED PARMESAN CHEESE
- 1 EGG
- GROUND NUTMEG

PREPARATION TIME: 1 HOUR

WASH THE POTATOES, brush the earth off them with a toothbrush, but do not peel. Cut them in half. Chop off the end of the potato halves to get a kind of drum with a more or less hemispheric lid. Assemble the potatoes again and bake them upright in an oven dish at 160°C (300°F, Gas Mark 2) for half-an-hour. Now scrape out as much of the flesh as you can without marring the shape of the vegetable "drum". Liquidise the flesh with the cream, butter, 2 tablespoons of Parmesan, the egg, a pinch of ground nutmeg, salt and white pepper in the food mill.

Blend at length so as to obtain a smooth paste. Fill the potato shells, put on their lids and return to a very hot oven at 220°C (450°F, Gas Mark 8) until golden.

Peperoni gratinati

SWEET PEPPERS AU GRATIN

- 6 YELLOW, RED AND GREEN SWEET (BELL) PEPPERS
- 100G / 4OZ ANCHOVIES
- 50G / 2OZ / 1/3 CUP GARLICKY BLACK OLIVES
- 1 CLOVE OF GARLIC
- 1 TBSP CAPERS
- A FEW OREGANO LEAVES
- OLIVE OIL

PREPARATION TIME: 3/4 HOUR

WASH AND TRIM THE PEPPERS and bake in the oven until the skins peel off easily. Cut them into wide strips. Meanwhile, bone and fillet the anchovies. Arrange a layer of peppers on the bottom of a well-oiled baking dish. Put some anchovy, olives, capers and oregano on top and sprinkle with dry breadcrumbs, finishing off with a little olive oil.

Make another layer of peppers and repeat the whole operation until all the ingredients have been used up. Bake in a slow oven for about twenty minutes. Allow to cool before serving.

Peperoni ripieni

STUFFED SWEET / BELL PEPPERS

- 4 SWEET (BELL) PEPPERS
- 1 TBSP CAPERS
- 4 ANCHOVY FILLETS
- 200G / 7OZ MINCED (GROUND) BEEF
- 2 TBSP GRATED PECORINO CHEESE
- 1 MOZZARELLA
- GARLIC, BASIL, OREGANO
- 2 EGGS
- DRY BREADCRUMBS
- OLIVE OIL

PREPARATION TIME: 3/4 HOUR

WASH AND DRY the peppers. Divide in half crossways, discarding the seeds and stringy pith. Heat 5 tablespoons of oil in a frying pan and sauté the garlic with the anchovies. When the garlic has turned golden, remove it and add the meat. Stir and season with salt and pepper.

When the meat has absorbed the flavours, place it in a bowl and add the eggs, capers, pecorino, diced mozzarella and the basil. Blend the ingredients thoroughly and stuff the pepper halves with the mixture. Line them up in an oiled baking dish, sprinkle with oregano and dry breadcrumbs and bake in a pre-heated oven at 180°C (350°F, Gas Mark 4) for half-an-hour.

Pinzimonio

OLIVE OIL DIP

- 1 FENNEL BULB, 2 GLOBE ARTICHOKES, 2 CARROTS, 2 SWEET (BELL) PEPPERS
- 2 STICKS OF CARDOON, 2 CELERY HEARTS, 2 CHICORY SPROUTS
- 1 HEAD OF CHICORY (AMERICAN ENDIVE)
- 12 RADISHES
- OLIVE OIL

PREPARATION TIME: 1/4 HOUR

WASH AND TRIM the vegetables, tearing them up or chopping them up roughly, if necessary. Arrange them attractively on a serving dish and pour the dip (a dressing based on good quality extra-virgin olive oil, salt and pepper) into the individual bowls. Take to the table.

Depending on personal taste and, above all, the particular season, you may add or detract vegetables as you wish. It is important that they be fresh and tastefully displayed (as in the illustration opposite). A delicious, quick and coloured complement to dishes which are rather more demanding.

Piselli all'olio

GREEN PEAS IN OIL

- 1KG / 2¹/4LB FRESH GARDEN PEAS (PREFERABLY SMALL ONES)
- 100G / 4OZ UNSMOKED BACON OR NOT TOO SALTY CURED HAM
- 2 CLOVES OF GARLIC
- OLIVE OIL
- A SPRIG OF PARSLEY
- 1/2 TSP SUGAR (OPTIONAL)

PREPARATION TIME: 3/4 HOUR

SHELL THE PEAS without rinsing them and place in a deep saucepan with the diced bacon (or ham), the garlic, two tablespoons of oil, salt, pepper and the roughly-chopped parsley.

If you will accept my advice, add some sugar, because peas are good when they are sweet. If, however, the idea bothers you, do not worry about it.

Cover the peas with cold water and bring gently to the boil. Cook them for half-an-hour over a slow flame (better if you keep the lid on, so that their delicious liquor does not go up in steam - just try it on bread!).

Pomodori al forno

BAKED TOMATOES

- 8 FIRM, MEDIUM-SIZED TOMATOES
- 16 STONED BLACK OLIVES
- 1 CLOVE OF GARLIC
- 1 SPRIG OF PARSLEY
- DRY BREADCRUMBS
- OLIVE OIL

PREPARATION TIME: 1/2 HOUR

WASH THE TOMATOES and cut off the tops, scooping out most of the flesh. In the food processor, blend 5 tablespoons of dry breadcrumbs with the olives, the garlic, the parsley, salt and pepper. Add 6 tablespoons olive oil and blend thoroughly. Fill the tomatoes with the mixture. Oil an oven dish, line up the tomatoes in it, cover with the tomato lids and bake in a pre-heated oven at 200°C (400°F, Gas Mark 6) for a quarter-hour. Serve warm, though they are also good eaten cold.

Porri alla Parmigiana

PARMESAN LEEKS

- 4 LARGE LEEKS
- 125ML / 4 FL OZ / 1/2 CUP BÉCHAMEL SAUCE (SEE PAGE 52)
- 1 SOUP LADLE / 4TBSP TOMATO SAUCE (SEE PAGE 33)
- GRATED PARMESAN CHEESE
- KNOB OF BUTTER

PREPARATION TIME: 40 MINUTES

TRIM THE LEEKS, eliminating the green part. Cut the white stems into two equal chunks and blanch in boiling salted water. Drain and dry.

Follow the instructions on page 52 to make a liquid béchamel sauce (not too runny, however, because it must set in the oven without "weeping" dismally onto the bottom of the oven dish).

Butter an oven dish, arrange the leeks in it, pour over the béchamel sauce mixed with the home-made tomato sauce, dust liberally with grated Parmesan and a pinch of salt and pepper. Put under the grill (broiler) for about a quarter-hour.

Take to the table steaming hot, with a further sprinkling of grated Parmesan.

Sedani ripieni

STUFFED CELERY

- 1 HEAD OF CELERY + 1 STICK
- 1 ONION
- 1 CARROT
- 100G / 1/4LB MINCED (GROUND) VEAL
- 100G / 1/4LB MINCED (GROUND) LAMB
- 100G / 1/4LB CHICKEN LIVERS, CHOPPED
- 50G / 2OZ PROSCIUTTO
- 50G / 2OZ MORTADELLA SAUSAGE
- 2 WHOLE EGGS AND 2 YOLKS
- 50G / 2OZ / 6 TBSP GRATED PARMESAN CHEESE
- 60G / 2OZ / 1/3 CUP WHITE FLOUR
- 1/2L / 1PT / 2 CUPS TOMATO PURÉE
- 125ML/ 4 FL OZ / 1/2 CUP WHITE WINE
- OLIVE OIL

PREPARATION TIME: 1 1/4 HOURS

STRIP THE LEAVES from the celery. Rinse the tenderest stalks and blanch for a few minutes in boiling, salted water. Drain and place on a tea towel to dry.

Cut into chunks four inches long. In a bowl, thoroughly mix the chopped cured ham and mortadella sausage, the yolks and the cheese with the two types of meat.

Open out the sticks of celery, flatten them and then stuff with the mixture. Close them up carefully. Coat with flour, dip them in the beaten egg and fry in 4 full tablespoons of oil in a frying pan over gentle heat for 20 minutes.

In a separate pan, make a mirepoix with the aromatic vegetables and 4 tablespoons of oil, adding the chopped chicken livers and the wine. Sauté for 10 minutes, then add the tomato purée.

Bring the stuffed celery stalks slowly to the boil again in this sauce. Season with salt and pepper.

Serve very hot. This is a hearty side-plate, almost a full meal (especially if you proportionately increase the doses both of the celery and the stuffing).

Sformato di cavolo

CAULIFLOWER PUDDING

TRIM AND CLEAN THE CAULIFLOWER and broccoli. Boil in salted water for about twenty minutes, then drain and chop in the food grinder. Make a pouring béchamel (but not too runny) and mix into the cauliflower purée.

- 1 MEDIUM-SIZED CAULIFLOWER
- 4 WHITE-SPROUTING BROCCOLI
- BÉCHAMEL SAUCE (SEE PAGE 52)
- 1 EGG
- GRATED PARMESAN CHEESE
- 80G / 3OZ / 1/4 CUP PLUS 2 TBSP BUTTER

PREPARATION TIME: 1 HOUR 10 MINUTES

Now blend in the egg yolk, the cheese and lastly the stiffly-beaten egg white.

Butter an oven dish thickly and turn the mixture into it. Dot with flakes of butter. Bake the pudding in a medium oven for about forty minutes, until the top is nicely golden.

This delicately flavoured dish goes nicely with roast meat or scaloppine.

Sformato di finocchi

FENNEL PUDDING

- 800G / $1^3/4$LB FLORENCE FENNEL
- KNOB OF BUTTER (PLUS ANOTHER ONE IF OVEN-BAKED)
- 125ML/ 4 FL OZ / $^1/2$ CUP MILK
- 90ML / 6 FL OZ / 6 TBSP BÉCHAMEL SAUCE (SEE PAGE 52)
- GRATED PARMESAN CHEESE
- PINCH OF GROUND NUTMEG
- 3 EGGS

PREPARATION TIME: ABOUT 1 HOUR

WASH AND TRIM the bulb fennel, discarding the core and the tougher exterior leaves. Cut into segments and parboil in boiling salted water for 5-6 minutes. Drain and brown gently in a knob of melted butter in a saucepan over gentle heat. Moisten with the milk and then, once it has all been absorbed, add the béchamel sauce. Allow the flavours to mix for a few more minutes, then blend it all in the food processor, adding the beaten egg, cheese, salt, pepper and a pinch of nutmeg. Pour the mixture into a smooth-sided mould and cook in a water bath in the oven for half-an-hour. If you prefer, you may butter the mould and bake in a medium oven for about forty minutes until there is a nice golden crust on top.

IN THE CASE OF COOKING in a *bain marie* and if you serve it warm, this side-plate is just right for boiled meats or dishes based on giblets or offal.

Should you prefer to bake it in the oven, it is ideal for eating as a light supper-dish which is not too airy-fairy, covered with a beef or (even better) rabbit meat sauce. In both these cases, it is important not to purée the fennel too finely, so that the pudding keeps a certain solidity. If you use artichokes instead of the fennel (following the same procedure, more or less, and in the same time), the pudding will turn out just as delicious and delicate.

Zucchine ripiene

STUFFED COURGETTES

- 8 ROUND COURGETTES
- 100G / $^1/4$LB FONTINA OR OTHER SEMI-SOFT CHEESE IN 4 SLICES
- 200G / 7OZ MINCED (GROUND) BEEF
- 1 EGG
- GRATED PARMESAN CHEESE
- OLIVE OIL

PREPARATION TIME: 1 HOUR

BLANCH THE COURGETTES for 2-3 minutes in boiling salted water. Drain and allow to cool. Cut in half lengthways and scoop out the flesh from the skins with the aid of a teaspoon. Put the flesh with the minced meat, the egg and 2 tablespoons of the grated Parmesan cheese. Season with salt and pepper to taste and mix well.

Spoon the mixture into the skins and arrange in a well-oiled oven dish with 4 tablespoons of oil. Top each one with half a cheese slice and place in a medium oven for about twenty minutes.

ROUND COURGETTES are more suitable for filling. They are good when eaten cold, too. When the weather is very hot, I advise you to use 50g (2 oz / $^1/4$ cup) of boiled and sparingly-buttered long-grain rice, 100g (4 oz) green peas, 50g (2 oz) fresh cooked ham and the same amount of diced fontina cheese. Season with salt and pepper, stuff the courgette shells, bake twenty minutes in the oven and cool. A spring-time version? 100g (4 oz) mortadella, a spring onion, a clove of garlic, chopped parsley, some breadcrumb soaked in milk (then squeezed) and a roughly-chopped tomato, all mixed up with the minced (ground) meat and an egg, salt and pepper. Bake for forty minutes in a slow oven and cool. Here is a version preferably to be relished hot: mix the ingredients of the basic recipe with a few tablespoons of béchamel sauce (not too runny) and half a chopped leek. Dredge with flakes of Emmenthal and ovenbake.

A splendid view of full-blown summer in the Tuscan countryside of the Mugello valley

Desserts, Cakes and Pastries

Babà

RUM BABÀ

- 200G / 7OZ / 1 1/3 CUPS FLOUR
- 100G / 4OZ / 1/2 CUP BUTTER
- 5G / 1 TSP BREWER'S YEAST
- 50G / 2OZ / 1/3 CUP SULTANAS (WHITE RAISINS)
- 3 EGGS
- 1 TBSP CASTER (FINELY GRANULATED) SUGAR
- PINCH OF SALT

FOR THE SYRUP:

- 3 TBSP GRANULATED SUGAR
- 60ML / 2 FL OZ / 1/4 CUP RUM

PREPARATION TIME: 3/4 HOUR (PLUS OVER 2 HOURS LEAVENING)

SOAK THE SULTANAS in warm water. Dissolve 50g (2oz / 1/3 cup) flour together with the yeast in four tablespoons of warm water in a bowl and set aside for twenty minutes (remember not to leave the bowl in a draughty or cold place, a rule which goes every time you leave dough to rise). Transfer the mixture to a bowl with the remaining flour, 80g (3 oz / 1/3 cup) butter, the eggs and salt, and knead thoroughly for six to seven minutes. When the dough is soft and springy, blend in the sugar and the squeezed dried fruit, kneading all the time.

Butter a baba mould (a deep tin with a hole in the centre) and fill it just about half-full with the dough. Cover with a tea cloth and leave to prove for one-and-a-half hours, until the dough has risen to the edges of the mould.

Bake in a medium-to-hot oven for twenty minutes. Meanwhile, make the rum syrup: pour an inch of water into a small saucepan and heat to dissolve the sugar. Bring to the boil, take off the flame and stir in the rum. When the baba is the colour of antique gold, remove it from the oven and douse with the hot syrup. Scrumptious!

DO NOT GET CARRIED away when dosing the rum as some cooks tend to do. This cake must be pleasantly moistened, not soaking like a sponge. To give the eye its fill, dilute four tablespoons of icing (confectioners') sugar in a little cold water, adding a little at a time and stirring gently. Pour the rather liquid glacé icing (frosting) over the rum-impregnated baba and return to the unlit (but still warm) oven just long enough to to set it.

Befanini

ORANGE BISCUITS (COOKIES)

- 3 EGGS
- 80G / 3 OZ / 1/3 CUP BUTTER
- 180G / 7OZ / 3/4 CUP PLUS 2 TBSP GRANULATED SUGAR
- 350G / 3/4LB / 2 1/3 CUPS WHITE FLOUR
- 7.5G / 1 TSP BAKING POWDER
- 60ML / 2 FL OZ / 4 TBSP MILK
- GRATED ORANGE ZEST
- LIQUEUR GLASS OF RUM

PREPARATION TIME: 3/4 HOUR

BEAT TWO EGGS in a bowl. Add the flour and the softened butter, mixing in thoroughly. Add the spirit, a little grated rind and the baking powder, blend well and leave to rest for ten minutes.

With a rolling pin, roll the dough out into a thin sheet about a quarter-inch thick. Use a biscuit cutter or an upturned glass to cut out the biscuits (cookies).

Brush with beaten egg and place in a slow oven for about twenty minutes until they have turned a nice hazelnut colour.

The biscuits look more appealing if, once they are all lined up on the baking tray just before baking, they are decorated with pieces of almond or candied peel.

Biscotti all'avena

Oatmeal Biscuits (Cookies)

- 50g / 2oz / 1/2 cup sultanas (white raisins)
- 100g / 4oz / 2/3 cup oatmeal
- 100g / 6oz / 1/2 cup light brown sugar
- 125g / 4oz / 1/2 cup plus 1 tbsp butter
- 250g / 9oz / 1 3/4 cups white flour
- 1 tbsp honey
- handful of pine-nuts
- 15g / 2 tsp baking powder
- vanilla-0.5g / 1/4 tsp powder or 1/2 tsp extract
- vanilla sugar

Preparation time: 3/4 hour

Work the sugar, honey and vanilla flavouring with the butter, blending everything well. Add the sultanas (raisins), pine-nuts, oatmeal, baking powder and flour. Knead the mixture until smooth and leave to rest for about twenty minutes.

Roll into little balls the size of walnuts and flatten them on one side. Place on a baking tray lined with baking parchment and bake in the oven at 180°C (350°F, Gas Mark 4) for 20 minutes. Just before serving, sprinkle the biscuits with vanilla sugar.

This recipe is merely a modest example of the practically endless range of sweet things that can be concocted with cereals, all of them simple, delicious and healthy into the bargain. The use of honey as a sweetener makes these biscuits easier for the body to metabolise.

Biscotti al mais

CORN FLAKE BISCUITS (COOKIES)

BEAT THE EGGS, SUGAR, salt and vanilla flavouring into the softened butter. Work in the flour, sultanas, corn flakes and a pinch of baking powder. Leave to rest for about twenty minutes.

Roll the mixture into little balls the size of walnuts and flatten the bottom. Bake in the oven at 180°C (350°F, Gas Mark 4) on a baking tray lined with baking parchment for 15 minutes.

- 2 EGGS, A PINCH OF SALT
- 250G / 9OZ / $1^3/4$ CUPS WHITE FLOUR
- 100G/ 2OZ / $^1/2$ CUP BUTTER
- 120G / 5OZ / $^1/2$ CUP PLUS 2 TBSP GRANULATED SUGAR
- 80G / 4OZ / $1^1/2$ CUPS CORN FLAKES
- 50G / 2OZ / $^1/2$ CUP SULTANAS (WHITE RAISINS)
- $1^1/2$ TSP BAKING POWDER
- VANILLA-0.5G / $^1/4$ TSP POWDER OR $^1/2$ TSP EXTRACT

PREPARATION TIME: $^3/4$ HOUR

Just as with the above recipe for cereal biscuits, here is another one with simple ingredients, easy to prepare and immensely satisfying to the palate, as well as to the eye. No panning shot over this type of biscuit would be complete if we omitted the suggestion of finishing off your biscuits with walnut kernels, pine-nuts and dried fruit.

Budino di ricotta

RICOTTA PUDDING

- 50G / 2OZ / $1/2$ CUP SEMOLINA
- 350G / 12OZ RICOTTA CHEESE
- 50G / 2OZ / $1/4$ CUP GRANULATED SUGAR
- 2 EGGS
- 1 TBSP MIXED CANDIED FRUIT
- HANDFUL SULTANAS (WHITE RAISINS)
- 1 LIQUEUR GLASS OF RUM
- DRY BREADCRUMBS
- KNOB OF BUTTER
- VANILLA SUGAR

PREPARATION TIME: ABOUT $1^1/2$ HOURS

SOAK THE SULTANAS in warm water. Heat an inch and-a-half of water in a small saucepan and sprinkle in the semolina, stirring constantly.

Allow to thicken. Remove from the heat after 2-3 minutes and spread the "porridge" over a wooden board to cool. In the meanwhile, put the ricotta in a bowl and work it delicately with a fork for some time. Mix in the sugar, the finely-chopped candied peel, a whole egg and one yolk, the sultanas squeezed of their soaking water and the rum. The mixture should be very soft and smooth.

Beat the remaining egg white until stiff and fold into the cheese mixture, along with the "porridge". Turn into a capacious buttered mould, evenly lined with breadcrumbs.

Bake your pudding in a medium oven for an hour. Remove, allow to cool slightly for a quarter-hour and turn it out onto a serving dish. Serve cold, dredged with vanilla sugar.

Budino Medici

MEDICI PUDDING

- 4 EGGS
- 30G / 1OZ / 3 TBSP SULTANAS (WHITE RAISINS)
- 30G / 1 OZ / 4 TBSP PINE-NUTS
- 200G / 7OZ / 1 CUP GRANULATED SUGAR
- 60ML / 2 FL OZ / 4 TBSP *VIN SANTO*
- $^1/_2$L / 1PT / 2 CUPS MILK
- 1 TBSP HONEY
- VANILLA EXTRACT

PREPARATION TIME: 1 HOUR

BRING THE MILK to boil in a small pan with half the sugar and the vanilla. Beat the eggs thoroughly with the other half of the sugar. Remove the pan from the heat, dissolve the honey in the milk, add the beaten eggs and blend. Caramelise some sugar in some individual moulds. In each one, place the sultanas, the pine-nuts, the almonds and the egg and milk mixture. Cook in a *bain marie* in the oven at 180°C (350°F, Gas Mark 4) for 50 minutes.

SERVE THESE DELICIOUS individual puddings with a *vinsanto* sauce (the typical Tuscan liqueur-like raisin wine) which transforms them into a true delight for the palate.

You will need 2 egg yolks, 2 tablespoons granulated sugar and a tablespoon of *vinsanto*. Beat the sugar into the yolks well. When the mixture is frothy, add the wine. Place the container in a *bain-marie* and cook slowly over boiling water, continually stirring, until the sauce has thickened.

If you cannot get hold of any *vinsanto*, use another liqueur-like raisin wine, or failing that, some Sicilian Marsala, but, make sure it is not too sweet or the flavour will override the others.

Castagnaccio

CHESTNUT CAKE

- 500G / 1LB 2OZ CHESTNUT FLOUR
- PINCH OF SALT
- OLIVE OIL
- MUSCATEL RAISINS OR SULTANAS (WHITE RAISINS)
- PINE-NUTS
- WALNUT KERNELS
- SPRIG OF ROSEMARY

PREPARATION TIME: ABOUT 1/2 HOUR

SIEVE THE FLOUR and turn into a bowl, adding the salt, 2 tablespoons of olive oil and enough cold water to make a rather liquid mixture.

While this is resting, put the rosemary with 3 tablespoons of olive oil in a small saucepan to heat up gently. Lightly oil a shallow baking tin or oven dish and pour in half-an-inch of the chestnut mixture. Sprinkle some sultanas, pine-nuts and roughly-chopped walnuts on the top and drizzle the rosemary oil over.

Bake in the oven at 220°C (450°F, Gas Mark 8) for 30 minutes. The chestnut cake is ready when the top has turned the nice brown colour of the chestnut shells and the crust has cracked.

HOW DELICIOUS chestnut flour is! My grandmother used to put a little of the flour in the thimble she used for sewing with and she would place it on the ashes in the warming pan. After a few minutes, there was a very simple and delicious morsel ready for eating. Yes, not more than forty years ago heating was indeed a makeshift affair in many houses (even those in the city), but there was a positive

side to it which offered other advantages, such as being able to roast chestnuts. If chestnut flour is good, so are chestnuts! Get hold of a kilogram (2 1/4 lbs) of chestnuts, put them in a pan of cold water with a few bay leaves and a twig of wild fennel. Boil for an hour and you will have a tasty dessert, especially if served with a little ricotta cheese and a tablespoon or two of raisin wine.

Cavallucci

ANISEED BISCUITS

- 400G / 14OZ / 2 2/3 CUPS WHITE FLOUR
- 150G / 5OZ / 1/2 CUP HONEY
- 100G / 4OZ / 1/2 CUP GRANULATED SUGAR
- 50G / 2OZ / 4 TBSP CANDIED ORANGE PEEL
- PINCH OF ANISEED
- 15G / 1/2OZ / 2 TSP BAKING POWDER
- 6 WALNUT KERNELS
- PINCH OF SALT

PREPARATION TIME: 35 MINUTES

POUND THE ANISEED, dice the candied peel and chop up the walnuts. Warm the honey in a small saucepan and dissolve the sugar slowly in it over gentle heat.

Remove from the flame and add all the other ingredients, stirring carefully. When the mixture is well blended, take a spoonful and place on a slightly floured baking tray. Repeat the operation until you have used up all the mixture and bake in a medium oven for about twenty minutes.

Cavallucci should be kept in a glass jar with a tightly-fitting lid. As they tend to harden, in the Siena district (where they originally came from) they are dipped in a sweet, liqueur-like wine, such as *vinsanto*, *aleatico* (from Elba), a raisin wine, malmsey and so on, before eating.

Charlotte all'arancia

ORANGE CHARLOTTE

- 4 ORANGES
- 3 SHEETS OF LEAF GELATINE OR 1 1/2 TSP / 1/2 PACKET POWDERED GELATINE
- 200G / 7OZ / 1 CUP GRANULATED SUGAR
- VANILLA POD (BEAN)
- 5 EGG YOLKS
- 1 LIQUEUR GLASS OF ORANGE BRANDY
- 500G / 1PT / 2 CUPS WHIPPING CREAM
- 200G / 7OZ SPONGE CAKE

PREPARATION TIME: 3 HOURS

TO MAKE THE SPONGE base, you will need 4 eggs, 150g (5oz / 3/4 cup) granulated sugar, 150g (5oz / 1 cup) white flour, the grated peel of one lemon, a pinch of salt and a knob of butter (in actual fact, as only 200g (7oz) of cake is needed in this recipe, doses will have to be reduced by a third). Whisk the eggs with the sugar for about fifteen minutes, until light and fluffy and can "write", i.e. a thread of the egg falling back into the bowl from the whisk will float on the surface for a moment, unless the eggs have not been whisked properly). Add the flour, grated lemon rind and salt. Blend, and pour into a buttered cake tin and bake for half-an-hour in a hot oven. It is important to allow the cake to cool before cutting it, or the sponge will crumble.

SOFTEN THE GELATINE in cold water. Squeeze the oranges and, keeping a little aside, pour most of the juice into a saucepan. Add the sugar, 1/4l (1/2pt / 1 cup) water and the vanilla. Heat the pan, removing it just before the water comes to the boil. Whisk the egg yolks, diluting with the orange brandy, and add to the other ingredients in the saucepan. Return to the heat, bring to the boil, then remove immediately and dissolve in it the softened gelatine (squeezed if in sheets). Whip the cream and fold it in. Line a charlotte mould with slices of sponge cake which have been moistened with the orange juice set aside (or with orange brandy or maraschino), pour the cream over and chill for 2 hours or more.

Dessert di yogurt alla frutta

FRUIT YOGHURT DESSERT

- 2 VASES YOGHURT OR 1 SCARCE CUP
- $^1/_4$L / $^1/_2$PT / 1 CUP MILK
- 3 ORANGES, SQUEEZED
- 50G / 2OZ / $^1/_4$ CUP GRANULATED SUGAR
- 6 SHEETS GELATINE OR 1TBSP (1 PACKET) POWDERED GELATINE
- 2 PEARS AND 2 MANDARINS
- 12 PRUNES IN SYRUP
- 1 LIQUEUR GLASS OF GRAND MARNIER

PREPARATION TIME: $2^1/_2$ HOURS

MIX TOGETHER THE YOGHURT, milk, sugar and orange juice. Steep the gelatine in water, then, if in sheet form, squeeze it and transfer to 6 tablespoons warm water or, if in the powdered form, heat carefully over hot water to dissolve. Allow to cool and fold into the yoghurt cream. Divide the mixture into 4 individual bowls and chill for 2 hours to set. Peel the pears and cut into pieces. Peel the mandarins. Drain and stone the prunes, keeping their syrup. Put the fruit in a bowl, sprinkle over 40g ($1^1/_2$oz / 3 tbsp) sugar, the Grand Marnier and the prune syrup. Stir and leave to rest for half-an-hour. Take the individual bowls out of the refrigerator and turn the dessert out, masking with the fruit and the syrup.

Frittelle di riso

RICE FRITTERS

- 200G / 7OZ / 1 CUP PLUS $1^1/_2$ TBSP RICE
- 100G / 4OZ / $^2/_3$ CUP WHITE FLOUR
- 250ML/8 FL OZ / 1 CUP MILK
- HANDFUL MUSCATEL RAISINS
- RIND OF HALF A LEMON
- 150G / 5OZ / $^3/_4$ CUP GRANULATED SUGAR
- 1 EGG
- 1 SHERRY GLASS OF MARSALA
- 1 TSP GROUND CINNAMON
- 10G / $^1/_2$ OZ BREWER'S YEAST OR 2 TSP ACTIVE DRY YEAST
- OIL FOR FRYING

PREPARATION TIME: 50 MINUTES (PLUS LEAVENING)

DISSOLVE THE YEAST in a little warm water and stir into the flour with a pinch salt. Beat with a wooden spoon, adding a little water. Leave aside for about an hour to rest.

Boil the rice in a saucepan with the milk and an equal amount of water for 20 minutes. Drain and stir in the grated lemon zest, half of the sugar, the beaten egg, the cinnamon, the muscatel raisins and the Marsala (or some other liqueur which is not too sweet). Allow to cool until just warm and mix with the risen dough, which must be very soft. Leave it all to rest for another hour. Heat a good quantity of oil in a frying pan and deep fry spoonfuls of the mixture over a high flame. The fritters must float on top, otherwise they will soak up too much oil.

Drain well and roll in the remaining sugar. Serve them nice and hot.

Gianduia

HAZELNUT AND CHOCOLATE CAKE

- 4 WHOLE EGGS AND 2 EGG YOLKS
- 220G / 8OZ / 1 CUP PLUS 2 TBSP GRANULATED SUGAR
- 70G / 3OZ / 1/2 CUP WHITE FLOUR
- 50G / 2OZ / 1/3 CUP CORNFLOUR (CORNSTARCH)
- 120G / 5OZ / 2/3 CUP LARD OR BUTTER
- 50G / 2OZ / 1/2 CUP COCOA POWDER
- PINCH VANILLA POWDER / FEW DROPS VANILLA EXTRACT
- 10 HAZELNUTS, SHELLED, SKINNED AND TOASTED

THE FILLING:

- 70G / 3OZ PLAIN (SEMI-SWEET) CHOCOLATE
- 2-3TBSP POURING (HEAVY) CREAM
- 1 LIQUEUR GLASS OF MARASCHINO

THE COATING:

- 200G / 7OZ / 1 CUP GRANULATED SUGAR
- 20G / 1OZ / 3 TBSP COCOA POWDER
- 2-3 TBSP APRICOT JAM

PREPARATION TIME: ABOUT 1 1/2 HOURS

WHISK THE WHOLE eggs and yolks with the sugar (barely 2 tablespoons) in a flame-proof casserole. Heat without boiling, continuing to whisk even off the flame until the mixture is light and frothy. Chop the nuts, turn into 2 tablespoons of sugar previously dissolved gently in a saucepan and reduce to a smooth paste in a food processor. Melt the butter (leaving aside a knob) over gentle heat, add the cocoa powder and the nut paste, stirring. Mix the cornflour and the flour, sprinkle onto the whisked eggs, add the vanilla and the chocolate-and-nut cream, blending everything in well. Butter a round pie dish, spoon in the mixture and bake in a medium oven for three quarters-of-an-hour. Now the filling: melt the chocolate in a small saucepan and whisk in the cream, keeping the mixture warm so that it does not solidify. Then make the coating: melt 150g (5oz / 3/4 cup) sugar in a small saucepan, diluting with a little water. Leave it to thicken without allowing to caramelise. Add the cocoa powder, stirring with a wooden spoon until you get a spreading cream which you will keep warm. In another small saucepan, melt the apricot jam with the sugar, diluting it if necessary to a pouring consistency. Slice the base in half horizontally, moisten with maraschino and spread the filling over. Cover the bottom half with the top one and mask with the apricot sauce. Spread the cocoa cream evenly over the top with a spatula. As the cake cools, it will form a semi-solid crust.

Gubana

GRAPPA-FLAVOURED PASTRY RING

- 250G / 9OZ /1 2/3 CUPS WHITE FLOUR
- 180G / 6OZ / 3/4 CUP PLUS 2 TBSP BUTTER
- HANDFUL EACH OF PINE-NUTS, WALNUT KERNELS, SULTANAS AND MUSCATEL RAISINS
- 4 DRIED FIGS AND 4 PRUNES
- 50G / 2OZ / 1/4 CUP ASSORTED CANDIED PEEL
- 50G / 2OZ PLAIN (SEMI-SWEET) CHOCOLATE
- RUM AND GRAPPA
- RIND OF 1 ORANGE
- 2 EGGS

PREPARATION TIME: 2 HOURS

SOAK THE SULTANAS and muscatel raisins in the rum. Beat the softened butter briskly with the flour, half a glass of water, half a glass of grappa and the salt. Then leave to rest for an hour. To make the filling, squeeze the water out of the sultanas and the raisins and mix with the orange rind, the finely-chopped nuts and the beaten egg. Roll out the dough to form a thin, rectangular sheet and spread the filling evenly over the surface. Then roll up the pastry diagonally, starting by turning over one corner. Join up the two ends of the "cigar" to form a circle and place on a buttered baking tray. Brush with beaten egg. Bake for half-an-hour in a hot oven, removing the *gubana* when nice and golden. *Grappa*, the distilled grape spirit, indicates that this is a speciality from Friuli.

Mousse di marroni

CHESTNUT MOUSSE

- 600G / $1^1/_4$LB CHESTNUTS
- 100G / 4OZ / $^1/_2$ CUP GRANULATED SUGAR
- 2 EGG WHITES
- 200G / 7OZ / $^2/_3$ CUP WHIPPED CREAM
- $^1/_2$L / 1PT / 2 CUPS MILK
- PINCH OF VANILLA POWDER OR A FEW DROPS OF VANILLA ESSENCE
- 15ML / 1 TBSP GRAPPA

PREPARATION TIME: $2^3/_4$ HOURS

MAKE A SLIT in the hard chestnut skins and boil for a quarter-hour. Peel, remove the second skin and place in a saucepan with the sugar, milk and vanilla flavouring, leaving to cook until the liquid is completely absorbed.

Remove from the heat and blend in a food processor, flavouring with the grappa. Allow to cool.

Whip the egg whites until stiff and, together with the cream, fold into the mixture in circular movements from the bottom upwards, using a wooden spoon.

Turn the mousse into individual dessert bowls. Leave to chill in the refrigerator for a couple of hours before serving.

VANILLA POWDER is a flavouring obtained from the vanilla pod. A few drops of vanilla essence may be used, if preferred.

On account of high production costs, an artificial surrogate is obtained from cloves.

Pandoro

VERONESE COFFEE CAKE

- 270G / 10OZ / 1 3/4 CUPS PLUS 2 TBSP WHITE FLOUR
- 7.5G / 1 TSP YEAST
- FEW DROPS VANILLA ESSENCE OR A PINCH OF VANILLA POWDER
- 80G / 3OZ / 1/4 CUP PLUS 2 TBSP GRANULATED SUGAR
- 2 WHOLE EGGS AND 2 EGG YOLKS
- 170G / 7OZ / 3/4 CUP PLUS 2 TBSP BUTTER
- PINCH OF SALT
- ICING (CONFECTIONERS') SUGAR

PREPARATION TIME: 1 HOUR 20 MINUTES (PLUS AN OVER 5-HOUR LEAVENING PERIOD)

GIVEN THE TIME required to make *pandoro* (rather a complicated procedure) and the repeated leavening periods, you will need to have the whole afternoon free. Besides, the main, absolutely inescapable merit of this extremely refined Veronese cake, that is to say, its extraordinarily light texture, is mainly due to the complex technique of kneading (intended to develop the volume to the maximum with the minimum amount of raising agent), as well as, of course, the conspicuous quantity of butter. Agreed… it is quite an undertaking. But every now and then treat yourself to tasting a *pandoro* as it should be. By the way, it should be baked in the special octagonal-star cake tin, but if you can only get hold of a round one, not to worry; the important thing is that it be spacious.

DISSOLVE THE YEAST and 25g (1 oz / 2 tbsp) flour in a cup with a few drops of warm water. Mix and leave aside for about a quarter-hour.

Meanwhile, mix 60g (2 oz / 1/3 cup) flour, 25g (1 oz / 2 tbsp) granulated sugar, an egg and a knob of melted butter together in a bowl. Add the prepared yeast from the cup, knead well, cover with a tea cloth and allow to stand for an hour or so.

In the meantime… start all over again from the beginning! That is to say, mix 120g (4 oz / 2/3 cup) flour, 40g (2 oz / 4 tbsp) granulated sugar, a knob of melted butter, an egg, two egg yolks and the salt together in another bowl. Add the leavened dough and knead forcefully for a quarter-hour, adding 50g (2 oz / 1/3 cup) flour a little at a time. At the end, the dough should be elastic, but not sticky.

Shape into a ball, cover and leave for at least three hours to rise. You may now dedicate yourself to your various hobbies or to your family - let it not be said that cooking takes up too much of your time!

After that, roll the dough out on a floured board with a rolling pin. Dot the surface with 120g (5 oz / 1/2 cup plus 2 tbsp) soft butter. Incorporate it by rolling the dough up on itself several times, each time flattening it out again with the rolling pin.

Leave aside for a quarter-hour. Then repeat the flattening and rolling up process several times. Allow to rest for another 20 minutes. Place in the buttered and sugared cake tin and leave to rise finally for about a quarter-hour, until the dough has reached the edges of the tin.

Bake in a medium-to-slow oven for half-an-hour. Remove from the oven, allow to rest for a few minutes, then turn out the *pandoro*. Allow to cool and dust liberally with icing (confectioners') sugar.

Panettone

SPICED BRIOCHE

- 800G / $1^3/4$LB / $5^1/3$ CUPS WHITE FLOUR
- 15G / $^1/2$OZ YEAST
- 150G/ 5OZ/ $^3/4$ CUP BUTTER
- 2 WHOLE EGGS AND 4 EGG YOLKS
- 400G / 14OZ / 2 CUPS GRANULATED SUGAR
- 80G / 3OZ / $^1/4$ CUP PLUS 2 TBSP ASSORTED CANDIED FRUIT
- 15G /$^1/2$ OZ/ 1 TSP ANISEED
- 50G / 2OZ / 8 TBSP PINE-NUTS
- 40G / $1^1/2$OZ / 4 TBSP SULTANAS (WHITE RAISINS)
- 25G / 1OZ / 2 TBSP VANILLA SUGAR
- PINCH OF SALT
- 60ML/2 FL OZ/ 4 TBSP MILK

PREPARATION TIME: ABOUT $1^3/4$ HOURS (PLUS LEAVENING)

YOU NEED TO START a day ahead to make this cake and on baking day there is no letting up; you start in the morning and continue working the whole day long. Just as with the previous recipe for *pandoro*, it is not that there is a lack of "quick" recipes (at times rather "patched up"). But if you follow this one, which is a little more complex and elaborate, the outcome will be a very tasty and refined cake. If you have to go to so much trouble, you might as well make a *panettone* to be remembered. After all, Christmas comes but once a year.

The day before the "big event", mix the yeast with a quarter of the flour in a bowl, diluting with the warm milk. Shape into a ball, cover with a tea cloth and leave overnight to rise in a dry place.

The following morning, soak the sultanas and dice the candied fruit. Take the ball of leavened dough, work in 100g (4 oz / $^2/_3$ cup) flour and a few drops of warm water. Knead gently at length. Form into a ball again, cover and leave 2 hours to rise.

Repeat the previous operation with the dough, adding another 100g (4 oz / $^2/_3$ cup) flour and warm water. Cover and leave to prove another 3 hours.

Then add the remaining flour to the risen dough. Knead at length, making sure that lumps do not form. In the meantime, put two small saucepans over the heat. Melt the butter in the first, leaving aside a nut to grease the baking tin. In the other, dissolve the sugar in a little water, gently blending in the whole eggs and yolks.

First add the butter to the dough, a little at a time. Then add the sugar and egg mixture. Finally toss in the sultanas squeezed of their soaking water, the candied fruit and the salt.

Continue kneading until the dough is even, springy and firm. Shape into a round loaf, cover with a tea cloth and leave to rise for 3 hours.

Now transfer the dough into a buttered and lightly-sugared cake tin (there are special large, deep *panettone* tins available on the market). Bake in a medium oven for three quarters-of-an-hour.

The brioche is ready when the top has become nice and brown and has split. Remove from the oven, allow to rest in the tin for five minutes, then, tapping it lightly on the table, take the cake out of the tin, supporting the "head" of the brioche in your hand.

Cut it when it has quite cooled down, otherwise it tends to crumble. Now go ahead and taste the difference between this and the commercial variety.

Panforte

SIENA HONEYCAKE

- 150G / 5 OZ BITTER (SEMI-SWEET) CHOCOLATE
- 150G / 5 OZ / 3/4 CUP GRANULATED SUGAR
- 400G / 14 OZ SWEET ALMONDS
- 300G / 11OZ /1 1/2 CUPS HONEY
- 350G / 12OZ CANDIED LIME AND MELON
- 1 TBSP CANDIED ORANGE PEEL
- 200G / 7OZ / 1 1/3 CUPS WHITE FLOUR
- 40G / 1 1/2 OZ BITTER ALMONDS
- 2 CLOVES
- GROUND CINNAMON
- PINCH OF GRATED NUTMEG
- PINCH OF PEPPER
- SCANT HANDFUL OF PINE-NUTS
- ICING (CONFECTIONERS') SUGAR

PREPARATION TIME: 50 MINUTES

PEEL THE ALMONDS and crush all the bitter ones and half of the sweet ones (mix the other half with the pine-nuts). Heat the honey in a saucepan until it becomes transparent, remove from the flame and add the other ingredients, mixing gently for quite some time. When everything is perfectly blended, transfer the mixture to a low, wide, round, lightly-floured cake tin. Bake in a medium oven for half-an-hour. This *panforte* (or *panpepato*, i.e. peppered bread) must be dark and firm, no thicker than a finger. Allow to cool and serve dredged with icing sugar.

Panna cotta

COOKED DAIRY CREAM

- 500ML / 1PT / 2 CUPS SINGLE (HEAVY) CREAM
- 3 EGG WHITES
- PINCH OF VANILLA POWDER OR A FEW DROPS OF ESSENCE
- ZEST OF 1 LEMON
- PINCH OF GROUND CINNAMON
- KNOB OF BUTTER
- 100G / 4 OZ/ 1/2 CUP GRANULATED SUGAR
- PINCH OF SALT

PREPARATION TIME: 1 HOUR

WHISK THE EGG WHITES in a bowl. Stirring constantly, add the cream, vanilla flavouring, cinnamon, grated lemon rind and the salt. Blend well and transfer the mixture into well-buttered individual oven moulds. Cook in a *bain marie* in the oven at 180°C (350°F / Gas Mark 4) for forty minutes. Allow to cool before turning out of the moulds and serving. If you wish, you may garnish with a very bland caramel sauce, made by diluting two tablespoons of sugar with one of water. Allow to colour over intense heat, strengthening with a couple of teaspoons of ground coffee. As an alternative to cream, milk may be used, provided that it is fresh and whole-fat… however, the result is not the same.

Pastiera napoletana

NEAPOLITAN EASTER TART

TO SERVE 6 PEOPLE

FOR THE FILLING:
- 150G / 5OZ CRACKED HARD WHEAT GRAINS
- 250G / 9OZ RICOTTA CHEESE
- 1/4L / 1/2PT / 1 CUP MILK
- 180G / 7OZ / 3/4 CUP PLUS 2 TBSP CASTER (SUPERFINE GRANULATED) SUGAR
- 1 LEMON
- GRANULATED SUGAR
- GROUND CINNAMON
- ORANGE FLOWER WATER
- 3 EGG YOLKS AND 2 EGG WHITES
- 100G / 4OZ / 2/3 CUP CANDIED LIME AND PUMPKIN
- 40G / 1 1/2 OZ / 4TBSP BUTTER
- ICING SUGAR

FOR THE SHORT PASTRY:
- 150G / 5OZ / 1 CUP WHITE FLOUR
- 80G / 3OZ / 6 TBSP GRANULATED SUGAR
- 70G / 3OZ / 6 TBSP VERY FINE SUET (OR BUTTER)
- 1 EGG YOLK

PREPARATION TIME: 1 HOUR 40 MINUTES (PLUS THE TIME FOR SOAKING THE WHEAT)

IT IS NOT UNUSUAL to come across "fake" versions, where cracked wheat is replaced by ordinary flour or pearl barley or other "impostors". Compromising is not allowed. The delicious *pastiera napoletana* should be made properly (otherwise what kind of Easter would it be?) with its scent of spring, sun, happiness and flowers. By the way, orange flower water, sold in Italy in little bottles in delicatessens and the better pastry shops, is the distilled essence of the macerated flowers of the variety of citrus which produces "bitter" oranges.

THIS ANCIENT RECIPE, traditionally associated with Easter, requires much time and care. It is a rather special tart to celebrate the return of the fine season. Pick over the cracked wheat and soak for two or three days before making up the tart. On the day, prepare the pastry by kneading the ingredients briefly but firmly with your knuckles. Leave to rest in a cool place for half-an-hour. Drain the wheat and cook for twenty minutes in a small saucepan full of water. Drain off the liquor and substitute with the warm milk, which you will have heated in the meantime. Add half the lemon zest in strips (devoid of the white pith) and a teaspoon of sugar. Cover the pan and cook very slowly until the wheat has absorbed the milk completely and is soft and thick. Remove the zest and leave the wheat on a plate to cool. Beat the ricotta in a bowl with a wooden spoon to soften it and add the caster (superfine) sugar, the egg yolks (one at a time), a pinch of cinnamon, the grated rind of the other lemon half, a tablespoon of orange-flower water, the diced candied fruit and the wheat last of all. Fold in the stiffly-whisked egg whites. Butter a deep metal pie dish, preferably with a detachable base. Roll out the pastry (leaving aside a fist-sized portion) and line the bottom and the sides of the dish without overlapping the edges. Spoon in the filling. Make inch-wide strips with the remaining pastry and arrange over the top in a criss-cross pattern. Bake the *pastiera* in a medium oven for three quarters-of-an-hour, until the surface is nicely golden. Remove from the oven and dredge with icing (confectioner's) sugar, if you wish. It must be eaten when cold or, at the most when just warm.

Pere cardinale

CARDINAL PEARS

- 4 WILLIAMS PEARS
- 250ML/8 FL OZ/1 CUP WATER
- 100G / 4OZ CREAM
- 100G/4OZ/1/2 CUP SUGAR
- 200G / 7OZ BLACK CHERRIES (OR RASPBERRIES, IF PREFERRED) IN SYRUP
- JUICE OF 1 LEMON
- 125 ML / 4 FL OZ / 1/2 CUP WHITE WINE

PREPARATION TIME: 1 HOUR

DISSOLVE THE SUGAR in the water in a saucepan and boil for 5 minutes, together with the lemon juice and wine. Remove from the heat and allow to cool slightly. Peel and core the pears and halve them. Place in the syrup in the saucepan and simmer for 10 minutes. Remove from the heat once more and leave the pears to cool in their liquor. For the fruit sauce, drain the cherries and sieve 50g (2oz). Return them to their syrup (if using raspberries, follow the same procedure, but slightly increase the quantity to be sieved, leaving aside a few as a garnishing). Arrange the pears on the serving dish, place a few whole cherries in the hollows and cover with the sauce. Trickle a little single cream over to finish off.

Ricciarelli

ALMOND BISCUITS (COOKIES)

QUANTITIES FOR 6 PEOPLE

- 350G / 3/4LB / 1 3/4 CUPS GRANULATED SUGAR
- 600G / 1 1/4LB / 6 CUPS ALMONDS
- 100G / 4OZ / 2/3 CUP WHITE FLOUR
- GRATED RIND OF 1/2 ORANGE
- 1 EGG WHITE
- 1 TBSP VANILLA SUGAR
- ICING SUGAR

PREPARATION TIME: 50 MINUTES (PLUS 2 HOURS RESTING TIME FOR THE ALMOND PASTE)

PEEL, SKIN AND CRUSH the almonds (or grind in a food mill) into a paste. Mix with the sugar, 80g (3oz / 1/2 cup) of the flour and the orange rind.

Blend well and leave aside two hours at least. Add the vanilla sugar and the egg white to the paste, cut out little diamond-shaped biscuits 4in long and 1/4in thick. If you cannot get hold of the special biscuit cutters, your imagination will help you to come up with an alternative.

Line the biscuits up on a lightly-floured baking tray and bake in a medium oven for about twenty minutes.

Allow to cool and dust with icing sugar mixed with the remaining flour. Delicious! Like the *panforte*, these biscuits belong to the great tradition of Sienese pastries, too.

Struffoli

FRIED PASTRY PYRAMID

QUANTITIES FOR 6 PEOPLE

- 300G / 11OZ / 2 CUPS WHITE FLOUR
- 4 WHOLE EGGS AND 1 EGG YOLK
- 40G / 11/OZ / 3TBSP BUTTER
- 1 TSP GRANULATED SUGAR
- PINCH OF SALT
- GRATED RIND OF HALF A LEMON
- GRATED RIND OF 2 ORANGES
- 150G / 5OZ / 1/2 CUP HONEY
- 100G / 4OZ / 1/2 CUP ASSORTED CANDIED FRUIT
- HANDFUL OF COMFITS AND OTHER SWEET DECORATIONS
- OIL FOR FRYING

PREPARATION TIME: 3/4 HOUR (PLUS 2 HOURS RESTING TIME FOR THE DOUGH)

HEAP THE FLOUR into a mound and break the eggs into a hollow at the top. Add the yolk, the softened butter, sugar, salt and lemon zest. Work it all in together, shape into a ball and leave aside for half-an-hour. Take a pellet of the dough, rub it between your palms and give it the shape of a bread stick. Repeat the operation with all the flour. Cut the "bread sticks" into chunks the size of a phalanx of your little finger and deep fry. Scoop them out when they are nice and crisp and drain off the oil. Put the honey in a wide pan and liquefy over a low flame. Toss a few fried pastry fingers at a time into the pan, stirring carefully with a wooden spoon and adding the orange zest and the candied fruit. Turn the pastries out, shaping them up into a dome, with a squeezed lemon half in your hand. Sprinkle sweet decorations over. Allow to cool.

THEY ARE CALLED *STRUFFOLI* in Naples, where they are traditionally prepared for Christmas. They are found in other Italian regions from Emilia Romagna to Sicily under different names. At Ferrara they are *lupini*; in Lazio they become *castagnole*; they make up the typical *cicerchiata* of Abruzzo and Molise; the *pignolata* in Messina; and so on… .

Torrone

NOUGAT

QUANTITIES FOR 6 PEOPLE

- 200G /7OZ / 2/3 CUP HONEY
- 200G / 7OZ / 1 CUP GRANULATED SUGAR
- 600G / 1 1/4LB ALMONDS, TOASTED AND CHOPPED
- 400G / 14OZ HAZEL NUTS
- 2 EGG WHITES
- ZEST OF HALF A LEMON
- 50G / 2OZ / 1/4 CUP ASSORTED CANDIED FRUIT (ORANGE, CITRON, MELON, ETC.)
- 2 WAFERS

PREPARATION TIME: 2 1/2 HOURS

SHELL AND SKIN the hazel nuts and almonds and toast in the oven. Chop up coarsely. The candied fruit is chopped more finely and the zest grated. Heat the honey in a *bain marie* on top of the stove, stirring continually with a wooden spoon (it should stay clear and liquid). Whisk the egg whites until stiff. After an hour, pick up a little honey on a wooden spoon and allow it to set under cold water; drop it and it should splinter like glass. Clarify the honey by gradually adding the whisked egg white, stirring all the time. Caramelise the sugar in a little hot water, bringing to the boil for a few minutes. When the caramel is thick, add it to the honey. The mixture will become increasingly stiff and sticky as cooking progresses. After half-an-hour, add the almonds, hazel nuts, candied fruit and lemon rind and blend.

Pour the nougat onto a surface where you will have placed the wafer, shaping it into a parallelepiped with a wide knife blade. Cover with the other wafer. Press the sweet under a weight, allow to cool a little and cut into sticks as evenly-sized as possible.

TO PREVENT THE NOUGAT from sticking, cooking in a water bath is essential: woe betide you if there is even a faint smell of burning!

The sweets keep well in a glass jar with a lid.

Torta della nonna

CUSTARD PIE

FOR THE SHORT PASTRY:

- 100G / 4OZ / 3/4 CUP ICING (CONFECTIONERS') SUGAR
- 125G / 5 OZ / 1/2 CUP PLUS 2 TBSP BUTTER
- 250G / 9OZ / 1 2/3 CUPS FLOUR
- 1 WHOLE EGG AND 1 EGG YOLK

FOR THE CONFECTIONERS' CUSTARD:

- 100G / 4OZ / 3/4 CUP ICING SUGAR
- 1/2L / 1PT / 2 CUPS MILK
- 3 EGG YOLKS
- 1 GENEROUS TBSP WHITE FLOUR
- STRIP OF LEMON ZEST, GRATED
- 1/4 TSP VANILLA EXTRACT

FOR THE FILLING:

- 200G / 7OZ RICOTTA CHEESE
- 1 LIQUEUR GLASS OF RUM
- 1 TBSP ALMONDS, SKINNED AND TOASTED
- 1 TBSP PINE-NUTS

PREPARATION TIME: 1 HOUR 10 MINUTES

PREPARE THE SHORT PASTRY by mixing the icing sugar (the classical Italian cook, Pellegrino Artusi, preferred it to caster sugar) with the flour.

Mix in the eggs with your fingers. Blend in the softened butter. Knead the pastry briefly and firmly. Then roll it out with a rolling pin, being careful that there are no lumps.

The confectioners' custard is made by taking a wooden spoon and mixing the sugar and the yolks into the flour and the grated lemon rind in a saucepan (off the heat).

Bring the milk to the boil and then pour a little at a time into the saucepan, constantly stirring so that lumps do not form.

Place the saucepan over a low heat and allow the custard to thicken, stirring the whole time without stopping. Boil for 5 minutes. Transfer into a bowl to cool.

Roll out a thin circle of short pastry and line a round pie dish with it. Bake in a hot oven for a quarter-hour.

Meanwhile, prepare a well-blended mixture of ricotta, confectioners' custard, rum, pine-nuts and almonds.

Heap the filling up in the centre of the blind-baked flan and cover with another circle of short pastry. Sprinkle with pine-nuts and chopped almonds.

Bake in the oven at 180°C (350°F, Gas Mark 4) for about twenty minutes. Just before serving, dust liberally with icing sugar.

Torta di cioccolato e nocciole

Chocolate and Hazelnut Cake

For the sponge cake:
- 150g / 5oz / 1 cup flour
- 100g / 4oz / $^1/_2$ cup granulated sugar
- 80g / 3oz / $^3/_4$ cup bitter cocoa
- 6 eggs
- 10g / $^1/_2$oz / 1 tbsp butter

For the coating:
- 100g / 4oz bitter chocolate
- 100g / 4oz / $^1/_2$ cup granulated sugar
- 200g / 7oz / $^2/_3$ cup fresh whipping cream
- 2 egg whites

Preparation time: 1 hour

Whisk the eggs with the sugar until frothy and very gently fold in the sieved flour and the cocoa, being careful that the mixture does not collapse. Butter and flour a cake tin, turn in the mixture and bake in the oven at 180°C (350°F, Gas Mark 4) for twenty minutes.

Now prepare the coating and filling. Dissolve the bitter chocolate in half of the cream in a water bath over very low heat. Whip the remaining cream (by hand or electrically) and, in another bowl, whisk the sugar and the egg whites until stiff.

Divide the melted chocolate equally between two containers and, when almost cold, add the whipped cream and the stiffly-whisked egg whites to one half.

This chocolate cream will be used to fill the cake: cut it across horizontally and sandwich discs of the sponge together. The remaining chocolate will be used to ice (frost) the top, with a final sprinkling of chopped hazelnuts.

Torta di mele

ITALIAN APPLE PIE

WORK THE FLOUR, BUTTER, milk, sugar and salt together to make an even, springy, firm dough.

Roll it out to a thickness of 1/4in. Peel, core and halve the apples. Slice crosswise evenly, but not too thinly.

Butter a baking tin or dish, line it with the pastry and fill up with the apples. Sprinkle the chopped walnuts over. Bake in a medium oven for 30 minutes.

FOR 6 PEOPLE
- 100G / 4OZ / 1/2 CUP BUTTER
- 100G / 4OZ / 1/2 CUP GRANULATED SUGAR
- 250G / 9OZ / 1 2/3 CUPS WHITE FLOUR
- 500G / 1LB 2OZ / APPLES (RENETTA OR GOLDEN DELICIOUS)
- 60ML / 2 FL OZ / 1/4 CUP MILK
- HANDFUL OF WALNUT KERNELS
- PINCH OF SALT

PREPARATION TIME: 50 MINUTES

Torta di noci

WALNUT CAKE

- 4 EGGS
- 280G / 11OZ / 1 1/4 CUPS PLUS 2 TBSP GRANULATED SUGAR
- 70G / 3OZ / 6 TBSP BUTTER
- 125ML/ 4 FL OZ / 1/2 CUP MILK
- 200G / 7OZ / 1 1/3 CUPS FLOUR
- 250G / 9OZ WALNUTS, SHELLED AND CHOPPED
- 20G / 1 OZ / 2 TBSP HONEY
- 7.5G / 1 TSP BAKING POWDER
- 1 LIQUEUR GLASS OF RUM
- 1 LEMON, GRATED
- 0.5G / 1/4 TSP VANILLA POWDER OR 1/2 TSP EXTRACT
- 12 WALNUT KERNELS, ICING SUGAR

PREPARATION TIME: 1 HOUR

WHISK THE EGGS and 180 g (7oz / over 3/4 cup) of sugar in an oven dish until quite frothy. Blend in the melted butter and the milk. Stirring constantly, add the flour, vanilla, baking powder, walnuts, honey, rum and the lemon zest. Blend well and bake in the oven for about 45 minutes at 180°C (350°F, Gas Mark 4). Serve the cake garnished with caramelised walnut kernels (dissolve the remaining sugar in a small saucepan, throw in the walnuts when it turns golden and coat) which are dredged with icing sugar. It may be filled with butter cream.

Torta paradiso

PARADISE SPONGE CAKE

- 2 WHOLE EGGS AND 3 YOLKS
- 150G / 5OZ / 1 CUP FLOUR
- 170G / 6OZ / 1 1/4 CUPS CORNFLOUR (CORNSTARCH)
- 250G/ 9OZ/1 1/4 CUPS BUTTER
- 250G / 9OZ / 1 1/4 CUPS GRANULATED SUGAR
- ZEST OF 1 LEMON
- ICING SUGAR

PREPARATION TIME: 1 1/2 HOURS

POUND THE SUGAR as finely as you can. Beat the butter with a wooden spoon until soft and creamy. Continue beating and add the sugar and the eggs, one at a time, just as you will gradually add the beaten egg yolks. Sprinkle in the flour and cornflour with the grated zest. Blend the mixture well and transfer to a round pie dish, previously dusted with cornflour. Bake in a medium oven for an hour. Remove from the oven and allow to cool. Dredge it with icing sugar.

This cake, delicious just as it is (try it with your coffee break in the morning) becomes divine if you fill it with whipped cream or confectioners' custard (it is a good idea to keep it in the refrigerator before serving) or else fruit jam.

Tronchetto agli amaretti

Macaroon and Chocolate Custard

- 300ml / 10fl oz / $1^1/4$ cups milk
- 4 egg yolks
- 100g / 4oz / $^1/2$ cup sugar
- 50g / 2 oz plain chocolate
- 70g/3oz/$^3/4$ cup hazelnuts
- 80g / $3^1/2$oz macaroons
- 50g / 2oz / $^1/4$ cup candied fruit
- $^1/2$l / 1pt / 2 cups whipping cream
- 125ml/ 4 fl oz / $^1/2$ cup rum
- 3 sheets of gelatine or $^1/2$ packet powdered gelatine

Preparation time: $^1/2$ hour (plus 2 hours' chilling)

Mix the milk, sugar and egg yolks in a saucepan. Allow the mixture to thicken in a *bain marie*. Add the plain chocolate in flakes and take the pan off the heat immediately.

Leave the custard to cool a little, stirring from time to time. Crumble in the macaroons and the shelled and toasted hazel nuts. Add the candied fruit. Dissolve the sheets of gelatine previously softened in the warm rum and pour into the mixture.

Whip the cream and carefully fold into the chocolate custard. Pour it all into a rectangular mould (or individual ones) and chill in the refrigerator for a couple of hours.

Turn out the *tronchetto*, slice thickly and serve garnished with macaroons (little biscuits made of almond paste) and sugared almonds.

Zuccotto

ZUCCOTTO CREAM GATEAU

- SPONGE CAKE (SEE PAGE 208)
- ZEST OF HALF A LEMON
- PINCH OF SALT
- 50G / 2OZ / 4 TBSP BUTTER
- 1/2L / 1PT / 2 CUPS CREAM
- 50G / 2OZ / 1/4 CUP PLUS 2 TBSP ICING (CONFECTIONERS') SUGAR
- 30G / 1OZ / 4 TBSP POWDERED COCOA
- 100G / 4OZ / 1/2 CUP MIXED CANDIED FRUIT
- 100G / 4OZ PLAIN (SEMI-SWEET) CHOCOLATE
- SWEET LIQUEUR-LIKE WINE

PREPARATION TIME: 2 HOURS (PLUS 4-5 HOURS FINAL CHILLING)

TO GIVE THE CAKE the typical shape of a cardinal's zucchetto, a special dome-shaped mould is needed. Make the sponge base by following the instructions on page 208, but reduce the quantities to 4 eggs, 150g (5oz / 3/4 cup) sugar and 150g (5oz / 1 cup) flour, eliminating the cocoa and adding the grated lemon zest and salt. Turn the light, fluffy mixture into a buttered cake tin and bake for half-an-hour in a hot oven.

Then allow to cool. Whip the cream with the icing sugar and chill in the refrigerator. Melt the remaining butter in a small saucepan, add a tablespoon of sugar and 4 tablespoons of water and simmer gently for 5 minutes, carefully stirring with a wooden spoon even after turning off the heat. When the chocolate sauce has cooled down, add the whipped cream to a third of it and place in the refrigerator. Mix the diced candied fruit and the roughly-grated chocolate with the rest of the whipped cream and put this, too, to chill in the refrigerator. Slice the sponge cake and line the mould with it. Brush the slices with the wine (it really ought to be *vinsanto* , but this can be substituted with another good sweetish, liqueur-like wine, though it must not be too sweet). Pour the chocolate cream into the mould and fill up with the cream containing the candied fruit. Cover with a disc of sponge cake, also steeped in wine, pressing it down so that it sticks. Keep the gateau in the refrigerator for at least 4-5 hours. Remember that the *zuccotto* must be cold, but not icy.